"My parents belonged to that section of society known as the 'idle rich,' and although, in that golden age, many people were richer, there can have been few that were idler."

Thus begins Kenneth Clark's engaging account of life among the upper crust—of a family who devoted their lives to the twin rituals of overeating and shooting everything that moved . . . of a schooling marked by "hunger, chilblains and a perpetually sore bottom" . . . of a courtship in which, because he's "by nature exceptionally mean," the only gift he gave his wife-to-be was a paper bag of peppermint bullseyes . . . and of a career he says was saved "from the poison of success . . . [by] an unabated and insatiable joy in the contemplation of works of art."

"One of the most delightful books of the season."
—*Providence Journal*

"Passage after passage made me . . . roll on the ground with laughter. Self-important people . . . appear here tied and trussed, like capons for roasting. . . . And he is as funny about himself as he is about everyone else."

—*New York Times Book Review*

ANOTHER PART OF THE WOOD

A Self-Portrait

Kenneth Clark

BALLANTINE BOOKS • NEW YORK

Library of Congress Catalog Card Number: 74-15816

ISBN 0-345-24919-4-225

This edition published by arrangement with Harper & Row,
Publishers, Inc.

Manufactured in the United States of America

First Ballantine Books Edition: July, 1976

To Alan, Colin and Colette

Contents

	Preface	ix
I	An Edwardian Childhood	1
II	The Making of an Aesthete	43
III	Further Education	87
IV	Italy	125
V	Growing Up	168
VI	Innocents in Clover	213
VII	Rain on the Lawn	264
	Index	283

Preface

MY APPROACH to 'the difficult art of autobiography' has been to follow the easiest course. I have recorded the events in my life that have remained most vividly in my mind or that still make me laugh when I recall them. I never kept a diary and have resisted the temptation to look at old letters which are so often printed more for self-gratification than for their intrinsic interest. In consequence my narrative may contain mistakes of chronology and other inaccuracies. But one thing I can guarantee— the complete accuracy with which I have recorded the spoken word. Some of the sentences I quote may seem improbable, but I could still reproduce the tone of voice in which they were said. I relish what used to be called 'characters,' and this book can be read as a series of miniature portraits. But I have introduced these characters only when they have had a formative influence on me. For better or worse, the author of an autobiography must be the chief character in his book, and when it is finished he may well ask what crazy impulse has pressed him on to make an exhibition of himself. I am afraid there is only one answer.

I

An Edwardian Childhood

I WAS BORN on July 13th, 1903, at 32 Grosvenor Square, a space now occupied by the American Embassy. My parents belonged to a section of society known as 'the idle rich', and although, in that golden age, many people were richer, there can have been few who were idler. They took no part in public affairs, did not read the newspapers, and were almost entirely without the old upper-class feeling of responsibility for their tenants. My father gave so little time to his business interests that in the end he lost more than half his fortune. His father had been a successful thread-manufacturer in Paisley (my great, great, grandfather invented the cotton spool) and was, I suppose, fairly conscientious by the not very exacting standards of the time. My father had been put into the family firm and, at the age of twenty-two, was made a director. He used to tell me with deep emotion that for two years he worked. The experience made an indelible impression on him. An historian of the family firm found no evidence of this. On the contrary, he discovered that after two years young Kenneth Mackenzie Clark was told by the Board that he must choose between sport and business. He chose sport. My family were big frogs in the small pool of Clyde yacht racing and my father was determined to be the biggest frog. He realised his ambition and immediately abandoned it.

The upbringing of a large middle-class family in commercial Scotland of the late nineteenth century was haphazard. Gone were the days when Robert Burns's father could see to it that his plough-boy son learned French and Latin. My father was sent to Johnny Graham's school in Greenock but, when one of his older brothers was shipped off to Australia (for what reason I have never discovered—he must have been making a nuisance of himself), my father, aged fourteen, was taken away from school to accompany him. I never heard what happened to the brother: no doubt the whisky bottle claimed him, as it did every other member of the family but one, boys and girls. Yet my father enjoyed himself hugely, loved the Blue Mountains, subsequently called three of his yachts Katoomba, and managed to make his way to New Zealand. There he went to live in a Maori village. The leading citizen owned a billiard table (then a mark of distinction greater than a piano, although less considerable than an organ), and my father was an excellent billiard player. The Maori thought that his skill would bring credit to the village, and offered him his daughter in marriage; 'a verra nice girrl, too,' said my father. But he declined. He always said that a large green jadestone *mere,* which I still possess, was part of the *dot.* My father was not above embellishing an anecdote, and the *mere* appears to me to be a nineteenth-century forgery, made for the tourist.

He did not marry until he was thirty-five. To judge from photographs he was a 'broth of a boy', but when he finally came to choose his bride he decided on a cousin who had been living quietly at Haslemere with her Quaker mother, her unmarried sisters, and a small, half-crazy bachelor brother. Two more different people than my father and mother can hardly be imagined. He was convivial, natural, totally unself-conscious; she was shy, inhibited, and prone to self-deception. They were united by two qualities, intelligence and a total absence of snobbery. My father had a remarkably good mind, and with either education or self-discipline might have become a distinguished mathematician. I was reminded of my father when I met Lord Rutherford. My mother had one gift which she bequeathed to me; she loved words. By the time I knew her she had become too indolent to read anything but the most vapid novels which arrived, preselected, from Day's Library, every fortnight; but she retained a feeling for vivid phrases, overheard or read when she was young. She also had a keen and humorous eye for character and, when she could conquer her inhibitions, talked amusingly. She once told me that, when she had double pneumonia and a high fever, she wrote a play in the manner of Bernard Shaw; I never heard her refer to Bernard Shaw again. Whatever their differences of character and upbringing my father and mother adored one another. He put up good-humouredly with her bouts of self-pity, and she devoted her whole life to an unsuccessful attempt to stop him drinking.

For my mother the transition from the quiet, frugal atmosphere of her home to the rich, sporting world of her husband must have been a disturbing experience. She suddenly found herself encumbered by a small house in London, a large house in Perthshire, a very large house in Suffolk, and two yachts, to say nothing of a rout of boon companions. How my father had acquired the money to pay for all these properties I have never understood. Since all but one of his brothers and sisters had died at an early age he must have inherited a good deal of the family fortune, but this would not have been enough for such a prodigal expansion. I suppose his wealth was due to a number of lucky speculations. Up to about 1920 he had prodigious luck in everything he undertook, and from 1900 to 1914 it was possible to make money without much effort—if one had the capital.

I cannot remember the house in Perthshire. It was called Kinaird. We rented it again in 1912, and I had the disagreeable experience of seeing a ghost in an upper gallery at about 3.30 in the afternoon. I ran out of the house, much shaken, and stood in the middle of a hard tennis court. Twenty years later, reading Carlyle's letters, I came on a passage in which he says that he has been employed as a tutor in Kinaird House, Perthshire, and adds 'it is a fine old place, but terribly haunted.' So perhaps my ghost was not altogether a delusion.

To me my home was Sudbourne Hall, about a mile from Orford in Suffolk. It had belonged to the Marquis of Hertford—Thackeray's Lord Steyne—who bequeathed it to his son, Sir Richard Wallace. I should not have supposed that so great an exponent of self-indulgences as Sir Richard could have found much to attract him in this featureless house, set in the cold East-Anglian countryside; but he seems to have liked it. He gave shooting parties, after which the guests were presented with souvenir game-books, recording the week's bag. I still have one of them, found in a drawer at Sudbourne. It is exquisitely bound in green morocco, with gold pheasants and partridges tooled on back and front; but the number of birds shot is relatively small. By the time my father came to Sudbourne—he bought it from an intervening proprietor named Wood—the bags had increased enormously, and this, of course, was his reason for buying it. Shooting had replaced yachting as his chief occupation; he was an excellent shot and was determined that his guests should have the opportunity of shooting more pheasants than anywhere else in Suffolk.

He certainly did not buy Sudbourne Hall for its architectural qualities. It was one of Wyatt's typical East Anglian jobs, a large, square brick box, with a frigid, neo-classical interior. I say 'large'; of course it was not large compared to Boughton or Wentworth Woodhouse, but it was a considerable size. My parents wished to make it more comfortable and were advised to employ an architect named Fryer. They then went abroad. When they returned they were surprised to find the main hall, galleries and staircases transformed into a pseudo-Jacobean style. Richly carved walnut covered every inch of the walls. There

4

were pheasants, partridges, woodcocks, squirrels and spaniels, all in high relief. It was in very bad taste, but may well have been warmer and friendlier than Wyatt's neo-classicism. The chief room of the house was called the library, and did in fact contain books left behind by the previous owner. I have a number of them still and observe that in all of them a Clark bookplate is pasted over the name of Wood. I doubt if my parents ever bought a book, except to give it to me, which they did most generously. The library at Sudbourne has nothing but happy memories for me. It must have been a large room, as it contained seven full-sized sofas, but I remember it as warm and cozy, and the physical presence of so many books was a wonderful source of pleasure. It would be unfair to say that I prefer the back of a book to its contents, but it is true that the sight of a lot of books gives me the hope that I may some day read them, which sometimes develops into the belief that I have read them.

Next to the library my favourite room at Sudbourne was the billiard room. It was in even worse taste than the hall, being panelled in dark fumed oak; and at one end was the indispensable organ, fortunately for me a pianola organ, on which I could pedal away at Rossini's *Stabat Mater* and Mendelssohn's *Elijah*. My father played billiards or snooker every night of his life, and never lost his early skill. Before I could reach up to the table I was placed on a stool and given a miniature cue. I was immediately enchanted. The swift geometrical movement of the ivory balls gave me the same satisfaction that I was to feel again when I first read the works of Euclid. Chess is purely intellectual: there is no physical pleasure in moving a chessman, except insofar as the movement noisily emphasises a moment of triumph. Bridge leads to acrimony. But billiards provides a perfect balance of mental and physical powers. The planning of a break involves a calculation of cause and effect; the control of the cue ball requires precise and delicate judgement. Nothing else absorbs and concentrates my faculties to the same extent. The day my father died I spent the afternoon practising billiards.

My nursery was behind a green baize door on the edge of the servants' wing. It was a large room with a linoleum floor, which suited me, as my favourite nursery occupations demanded a smooth surface. They were building with bricks and arranging circus performances with jointed figures of clowns and acrobats. In those days of plenty, toys were far better made, more various and more inventive than they are today. My bricks were made of a non-shiny, stone-like substance and included pediments, arches, columns, bases, trabeations and an endless variety of blocks. It was possible to make quite large and elaborate buildings and learn a good deal about the laws of construction. I took my buildings very seriously, preserved them for weeks on end, and demanded criticism from the unfortunate guests who were press-ganged into visiting my nursery.

I must have learned to read rather late, as I remember the pains of doing so. I learned from a book called *Reading Without Tears,* which was based on the belief that the shapes of letters could be remembered by means of some human or animal analogy. A is like a house with a thatch; B is like an old woman with a bundle on her back; and so forth. Having no gift of abstraction I could—and still can—remember the pictures, but not the letters they were intended to suggest. Like Charlemagne, I thought I would never succeed in mastering this difficult art, but in the end I succeeded, and what joys were available to me. The chief of these was a series of illustrated books, by Florence and Bertha Upton, published in America, but reprinted in England, which recount and illustrate* the adventures of a golliwogg and five Dutch dolls. I do not think it an exaggeration to say that they

* Many of the original illustrations belonged to Lady Lee of Fareham, and now hang in the spare bedrooms at Chequers where they must come as a surprise to serious-minded delegates spending a night with the Prime Minister.

influenced my character more fundamentally than anything I have read since. I should explain that in this series Golliwogg lives on terms of perfect happiness with five girls, wooden dolls, one of whom is a midget. In the first volume the girls feel the need for some sort of covering, and cut up the American flag to provide it. Peg, the Juno or Fricka of this little Parnassus, took the stripes and Sarah Jane, the most dashing of the party, wore the stars. The twins, Weg and Med, remained in a state of nature, although in the later adventures they always fitted themselves out with charming pink bonnets. As with Don Quixote and Mr Pooter, the personality of Golliwogg grew far beyond his creator's original expectations. He became a euphoric character, eternally hopeful at the beginning of each adventure—boastful, even, in his excitement —raising his arms in the air, while the admiring girls thought of the costumes that would be appropriate for a voyage to the moon or to the seaside. Then would follow a series of reverses, after each of which Golly would sit in a dejected heap, until consoled by the indomitable Sarah Jane. She and the midget were the life and soul of the party, but they always looked on Golliwogg as their hero and he, in return, was always courteous to the tiresome, accident-prone Peg. He was for me an example of chivalry, far more persuasive than the unconvincing Knights of the Arthurian legend. I identified myself with him completely, and have never quite ceased to do so.

Next to the Golliwogg books I enjoyed the staple fare of Edwardian children—Beatrix Potter. Her enchanting series must be one of the few works that have been loved continuously, without pretence, ever since they were written. They have become part of a *lingua franca* between old and young, between human beings and animals. How irritating it must be for a Marxist to find the bourgeois virtues made so acceptable by being embodied in the person of Mrs Tiggy Winkle. But much as I loved Beatrix Potter's drawings, she did not influence me in the way that the Golliwogg books had done, simply because her best characters—Peter Rabbit, Squirrel Nutkin and even Hunka-Munka—were *naughty,* and some of them, like Mr Tod, were positively criminal. They represent the spirit of enterprise and rebellion, which is no doubt one of the things that have endeared them to normal children. Being myself abnormally passive and conformist, I could not identify myself with such a high-spirited rebel as Squirrel Nutkin. Beatrix Potter also wrote one of the most beautiful of fairy tales, *The Tailor of Gloucester;* and it was almost the only fairy tale I liked, because the two most famous collections—those of Hans Andersen and the Brothers Grimm —contain so much that is painful and terrifying. Perhaps the born story-teller (like Dickens) feels impelled to hold his hearer's attention by frightening him, and the teller of children's tales, knowing that his audience is fickle and fidgety, lays on the horrors more abundantly. Or do the majority of people really like being frightened?

Perhaps there are some less alarming stories in Grimm, but I did not dare to open them on account of Arthur Rackham's illustrations. This quiet, gentle man of genius certainly had a vein of *schadenfreude* (what is now misleadingly described as sadism) and took an intense delight in scraggy fingers. I sometimes caught sight of his drawings, before I was on my guard, and they stamped on my imagination images of terror that troubled me for years. Many people have told me that they had the same experience as children. I wonder if anyone ever told Rackham. Like most children I was afraid of the dark, and some strange convention of the time made nannies and parents refuse to put night lights in children's rooms. My night nursery, with its brass bedstead and wallpaper of Kensington Palace roses, was reassuring enough; but the other bedrooms at Sudbourne were dismal and alarming, and when I graduated to one of them I suffered terribly from night fears and from retinal images so strong as to amount almost to hallucination. Fortunately these retinal images disappear with

8

puberty and do not reappear unless one has D.T.'s, or happens to be the poet Blake.

Early in the morning I was glad to leave the house and make my way to the stables. As so often in the early nineteenth century, they were better designed and constructed than the house, and their walls were covered by the biggest magnolias I have ever seen. Half of the large courtyard was occupied by motor cars, half was reserved for practically non-existent horses. In my childhood the cars consisted of a Rolls-Royce, two Delaunay-Bellevilles, a Panhard and a quiet, insinuating electric car which had been intended for use in London, but had so small a range that it could not make the journey from Sudbourne. How it ever got down there is a mystery. Although not mechanically minded, I loved the sight of these shining contraptions and visited them every day. On my fifth birthday my father organised a motor race in the park, and I used to think that this was my earliest memory. But what is a memory? I remember remembering this episode, but it has become static in my mind, like an old photograph; in this book I use the words 'I remember' only about episodes which I can still recall in movement, or which seem to cause a slight vibration in my mind. In this sense, all I can remember about the motor race is my disappointment that the cars did not all set off together, but were timed over a measured two miles (the length of two drives); and that it was won by a neighbour's Mercedes.

Opposite the collection of polished machinery were the stables proper which were intended for at least a dozen horses, but contained only one old, fat cob named Tommy who drew my father's governess cart, and a succession of ponies on which I was supposed to ride. Neither of my parents were riders; I have never seen even a photograph of my father astride a horse, and only one of my mother on a donkey. But it was considered correct for a young gentleman to ride, and for once my parents were influenced by convention. I admire horses but they don't admire me, and as soon as I mount one it either bolts or rears. Needless to say, my ponies were chosen for their docility and had probably never bolted in their lives until I sat on them and they felt the incubus of an alien body. Finally a pony was discovered so aged and apathetic that it was guaranteed incapable of high spirits. I mounted it without enthusiasm; it advanced a few paces, and then lay down. After this my parents gave up the attempt to make me into a chevalier, and I was allowed to roam the park on my own feet.

Making all allowance for the magnifying glass of memory the park must have been fairly large. Four avenues, each a mile long, converged from different angles on the area in front of the house. One was lined with chestnuts, one with elms, and two with beeches. There had been a fifth, planted with elms by Lord Hertford, which attacked the house frontally, but it was overgrown and grandly mysterious. I spent much time in speculating whether this direct approach would have been more effective, and so was familiar from my earliest childhood with the problem that puzzled Bernini in St. Peter's Square.

In between two of the avenues was a nine-hole golf course, complete with a professional, who must have had an easy life, because nobody ever played on it but me. My father was an unskilful and impatient golfer, and after two or three bad shots would thrown down his club and walk home. But one by-product of the game gave him pleasure, which was to bet his friends that they could not hit a ball over the house. This must have been quite a difficult shot (perhaps a No. 2 iron from a low tee) and the extraordinary thing is that my father never failed to do it, whereas far better golfers hit the house, and often smashed the windows. This delighted my father; but my timid and niggardly nature was pained. Waste on a far bigger scale was going on all round me, but it was part of the air I breathed. A broken window (or rather a succession of broken windows), was something I could isolate and understand.

In the other half of the park were two circles of

beech trees which enclosed the stables of our Suffolk Punches. The reader should, I suppose, be told that these were a special breed of cart horse, which must originally have been useful, but which by my time were bred almost entirely for their beauty.* They were solid and heavy, but as perfect in proportion as the horses of the Sforzas or the Gonzagas. For ten years the Sudbourne Stud was the most famous in the world and won the first prizes at every show. We all loved them, and visited their stables several times in a week; but the great moment was on Sunday mornings, when they would have coloured ribbons put in their manes and be trotted round to stand for our admiration on the lawn in front of the house. My father would then give them minute peppermints of a brand known as 'Curiously Strong', which made them sneeze, but seemed to give them pleasure. After the ceremony they would trot home to their stables in the beech trees as complacent as Morris dancers. I have often thought that the memory of these dear animals, which I recapture every time I open a 'conker', is the basis of my sense of form. They are, indeed, very clearly connected in my mind with trees, and searching in my mind for the first moments in which I seemed to be lifted out of my immediate childish preoccupations, the first emotions that could be described as religious, they seem to have been inspired by the trunks and roots of trees. Of conventional religious instruction I received nothing at all. My father's mother had been in the habit of saying about church-going "if it doesn't do you any good, it can't do you any harm", and on the strength of this somewhat negative judgment I was sent to Sudbourne Church on Sunday. My mother felt that it was her duty to go once or twice, but she hated church with real animosity, her natural laziness and Quaker background being for once in agreement. Later in life she would not even go out of the house

* They are now bred for work, are 17½ hands instead of 15, and have lost the perfect proportions that so much delighted me.

on Sunday in case she met people who had been to church. My father went once out of bravado. Sudbourne Church is small, my father was large and conspicuous and, as he entered the nave, it seemed as if the ship of Christ would founder. The organist dropped his music, the choir-boys stopped singing, and the parson fumbled with his words. After a few minutes my father stalked out, bored and disgusted, and trotted off home with Tommy in the governess cart. My own church going was gradually reduced and was replaced by the inspection of the Suffolk Punches which I have just described.

The reader will have recognised that I was an only child. I was a Caesarian birth, which in those days made it impossible to have more children. An old friend of the family once said to me how astonished she was that my mother had had a child at all, the indignity of child-bearing and the subsequent, conventional display of sentiment being both so abhorrent to her. As a matter of fact I do not remember her displaying sentiment at any time until a few minutes before her death. But the reader need waste no sympathy on my solitary state. My toys, my teddy bears and my guinea pigs were all the company I required. I dreaded the efforts that were made to find me companions of my own age. These were always stronger and better fitted for life than I was; they had their own groups of friends and naturally thought my interests ridiculous. When they left the house I returned with relief to my bears, my bricks, or, at a later date, my billiard table. The only trouble came when I was left entirely alone with the servants. Had I been in this situation in Russia or Italy, I would have been almost smothered by affection and indulgence, but the inhuman treatment of servants in England had created a hostility, or, rather, a kind of formalised estrangement, that made any natural act of kindness impossible. The servants felt, in a confused way, that by taking it out on me they were getting back at their employers. They gave me uneatable food, although they themselves lived off the fat of the land. I remember a cheese so full of weevils that small pieces jumped about the plate; I remember branches of bitter rhubarb, sour milk, rancid butter—and, of course, nothing but obstinate silence. It was an unconscious programme of revenge.

In spite of these inconveniences I enjoyed my solitude, but I doubt if it was a good preparation for life. It made me absolutely incapable of any collective activity. I cannot belong to a group. Although I have been elected to nine clubs and have paid the entrance fees, I have resigned from all but one simply because I have been too embarrassed to speak to any of the members.* This is a ridiculous shortcoming, the more so as I am very fond of talking; but I am still unable to conquer it. I may add that my only recent effort to be clubable confirmed my fears. A dinner was given in the St James's Club for Oliver Chandos, who had been its chairman for many years and had just been made a Knight of the Garter. As he was an old friend of mine I thought I ought to attend. I found myself among a group of members none of whom I remembered having seen, who naturally did not address a word to me. After about ten minutes a man who looked like a Naval Officer, wearing a claret-coloured bow-tie, advanced towards me and said "You're Sir Kenneth Clark." I agreed. "The Bart, of course", he said. "No," I said, "I am not a baronet." "But you must be," he said, "the other Sir Kenneth Clark is a fearful shit; everybody says so." "Well, I'm afraid I'm the only one"; and as he left me I wondered if he had meant to insult me or was simply misinformed.

Between the years of six and seven a happy change came over my condition. It arose as the result of a rare and unexpected visit by my mother to the nursery. She found me weeping, while a German governess,

* As one reader of this script thinks I am romancing I give their names: the Royal Thames Yacht Club, the Athenaeum (twice), Bucks, the Garrick (twice), the United Universities, The Travellers, The St James, the Beefsteak and the M.C.C.

with the interesting name of Frankish, yelled at me "You horrid boy, you wicked boy." The accusation was certainly unjust, as I was a docile, well-behaved child. Perhaps she was enraged by my self-sufficiency. My mother stood for a moment by the door, then silently withdrew and Miss Frankish left next morning.

She was replaced in due course by a young lady named Miss Lamont. Lam, as we all came to call her, was the daughter of a minister in Skye, and the transition from a highland manse to the rich, godless, bibulous atmosphere of my home must have been strange to her. But she took it, as she was to take everything in her subsequent life, with dignity, humour and calm. The arrival of Lam was the first of several pieces of human good fortune which have befallen me in my life. At last I had someone whom I could love and depend on, and who seemed to share my own interests, even in trees and guinea-pigs. She was entirely unsentimental, but there was no doubt about her affection. She had a strong sense of duty, tempered by commonsense and Highland laziness. I felt so sure of her goodness that, when my own children were of an age to require a governess, I invited her back, and she appeared to be unchanged. When they went to school she was appointed lady curator of Chequers (of which I was then a trustee), and became a calming influence on Mr Churchill, in whom she correctly saw a resemblance to my father. In the Churchill family she was known as Monty, which led to confusion with the Field-Marshal. She appears in his memoirs, gallantly described as 'a highland lady in her prime', receiving and rebuking Mr Molotoff in Gaelic when he visited Chequers. She lived to stay with us at Saltwood, almost fifty years after she first came to Sudbourne.

I must now try to describe those great events in our lives at Sudbourne, which were in effect the only point in our living there at all—the shooting houseparties. They began soon after October 1st (when the pheasant shooting begins) and lasted for about three months. The Delaunay-Bellevilles would collect the guests from Wickham Market Station on Monday or Tuesday evening, and I would peer over the Jacobean banisters, sniffing the odour of petrol fumes (then an exciting rarity), furs and cigars, to see if any of my favourites had arrived. By favourites I meant, first of all, those whom I could victimise into coming to my nursery and admiring my architecture, and secondly those who did conjuring tricks or feats of acrobatic skill; because, in those days of competitive house-party going, the guest was expected not only to be a good shot but to have some special accomplishment. The age of singing, thank heaven, was over, or my father would have joined in all too heartily; but eggs were taken out of mouths, flower-pots on walking-sticks were balanced on foreheads and marvellous *tours de force* performed on billiard tables.

Not all my favourites were conjurors or acrobats. At least one of them was a wit. He was referred to as Tommy Dewar and was supposed to be the best after-dinner speaker of his day. His face was grey with late nights and long drinks; he had a limp, and said terrible things out of the corner of his mouth. Perhaps fortunately I could understand no more than a quarter of what he said, but I recognised that it had a quality lacking in the hearty utterances of our other visitors; it was perhaps my earliest intimation of what Flaubert meant by 'style'. Why this corrupt old bachelor should have made friends with a small boy of seven I cannot imagine, but at that age he presented me with a copy of a book he had written entitled *A Ramble Round the Globe,* inscribed 'To Master K. Clark (The Modern Chesterfield) With the Author's Compliments. Thomas R. Dewar'.* This is the first evidence I have (for neither my parents nor their friends were letter writers) of what I seemed like to an outside observer. At a later date he used to bring his friend, Harry Lauder, to stay with us. My parents did not welcome

---

* I must confess that the book, which I still possess, is not at all like Flaubert, but painfully like the anecdotes that raise a laugh in after-dinner speeches.

these visits, because, whether from generosity or exuberance or force of habit, Harry Lauder never stopped performing. He would sing at the drop of a hat and leap from the luncheon table to do a few steps. My father was bored, my mother painfully embarrassed. He can seldom have had a stickier audience; but the little man (for, like most famous comics, he was almost a dwarf) was undeterred. He was very kind to me. He took me seriously, read me the poems of Burns, which I have loved ever since, and tried out Scottish folk songs on me. "I'm great on melody", he said, "and I've a wee fellie who puts in the harmony afterwards".

But I must return to the shooting party. After a festive evening, the guests, both men and women, came down to breakfast at nine. They began with porridge, which it was considered smart for the men to eat standing up, scrambled eggs and bacon, kidneys, kippers. When all these had been eaten and the guest was about to settle down to scones and marmalade, old Scott, the butler, would mutter commandingly in a lady's ear "I've got—ah—cold ham, cold tongue, cold turkey, bath chap, and boar's head, m'lady". Overcome by this litany, the wretched breakfaster would accept yet another course. It is an example of the elasticity of the human body that women who ate these breakfasts, with presumably the same digestive organs, now say, with a hypocritical grimace, "Only a little black coffee, please".

After breakfast the guns left for the district where the beats were to take place, in the Delaunay-Bellevilles. My father trotted after them in the governess-cart with Tommy, and occasionally Lord Dewar. I ought perhaps to explain that the birds were driven over the guns by an army of beaters who, at Sudbourne, wore specially designed smocks with red lapels. They crashed through the wintry woods, shouting "Hi, hi, hi", and beating the trees with their sticks. They were accompanied by keepers, who wore bowler hats and carried guns to deal with any defaulters. Each district had about five beats and the six or seven guns were so aligned that the birds flew out of a wood high over their heads. Naturally the guns in the middle had the best chance, and in order to secure their positions they used to draw lots—little silver spillikins. If, by ill luck, some famous shot found himself at the end of the line, with some duffer in the centre, the day's troubles would begin. At lunch time they were joined by the ladies in enormous hats with veils, and the whole party would then repair to thatched pavilions in the woods which had been specially constructed, one in each district, to contain a lunch party of fourteen. Striped awnings were stretched round the walls and from brass-bound hay-boxes there appeared a magnificent meal. How they ate! Local oysters and liver pâté, steak and kidney pudding, cold turkey and ham, treacle tart, double Cottenham cheese and always, to fill in the corners (as was often said with satisfaction), a slice of plum cake. The guns also drank as much as they dared (which was a good deal), but they sometimes had to forgo that second glass of Kümmel, because on the afternoon beats the ladies would be at their sides and they would be more than ever anxious to show their skill. No one, of course, could have been invited who was not a good shot; but this was a highly competitive sport, and throughout England shots were graded, like seeded lawntennis players, with Lord Ripon and the Prince of Wales (George V) at the summit. It sometimes happened that a famous performer had an off day. Then his chagrin knew no bounds. The lady at his side would withdraw and he would return silently to the house, not to be seen again till dinner. Indeed, if things had gone really badly, he would refuse to come down to dinner and a tray would be taken up to his room.

The last stand took place when it was already growing dark, and a flash could be seen from the barrels of the guns. Then the whole party would return and, I suppose, queue up for baths because although there were twenty-five bedrooms at Sudbourne I remember only about four bathrooms. The ladies changed into tea gowns and the gentlemen into smoking suits. I presume that the ladies drank tea, but I do not remember it, because my attention was always occupied by the gentlemen in the billiard room. I watched critically their performances on the billiard table, listened to the angry recriminations which seemed to follow every hand at bridge, and to the splash and crash of soda syphons ceaselessly diluting enormous tumblers of whisky. However, before the game was over I was sent upstairs to eat my prunes and junket. Then, safely in bed, came my favourite moment of the day. The ladies had changed again into dresses of splendour and elaboration, and by some means I had persuaded them that they must parade in my bedroom, in order that I might give a prize to the one I thought most beautiful. I now see that it was kind of them to humour me in this way; but at the time I thought I was conferring a favour on them. Three of the prize-winners, all over ninety, were still alive when I wrote these lines, and described to me the pains I took in arriving at my judgements.

All this must have happened before I went to school, for after that time I would have thought the dress parades unmanly; and at the age of ten or so, I was given a gun, and allowed to join in the afternoon battues. I cannot say I enjoyed this privilege. The number of pheasants that thumped down beside us was sickening. I remember that on one afternoon in 1915 three guns, beside myself, shot over a thousand. Before the war the bags were almost twice as big. I was a thin, weedy child, and suffered terribly from the East-Anglian cold. I was naturally placed at the end of the line, and was expected to deal with those birds who were mean enough to swerve away from the centre. I am afraid a good many of these deviationists escaped. My most dreaded moment was when the cry of 'woodcock' went up from the beaters. For some reason a few woodcock were supposed to give tone to the day's bag, and it was a point of honour to secure them. They are extremely hard to hit, especially late in the afternoon, when the light is failing; and they had a habit of flitting in and out of the trees, down the line to where I stood, shivering and numb. I would then blaze away into the brown shadow. To my astonishment on one occasion a woodcock fell and I was warmly congratulated. I suppose it was shot by a keeper.

I had an escape from the extravagant, and sometimes rather alarming, life at Sudbourne—my grandmother Macarthur, who lived a mile away in Orford. My father, who adored her, had built a house for her, and her three unmarried children, overlooking Orford Castle. The Castle House, which still stands, is not an inspiring piece of architecture, but it was to me a haven of peace, order and predictability. My grandmother, the only English member of my family, had been called Flintoff, and originally came from Easingwold, near York. Her forbears were quiet gentlefolk with few possessions—Crown Derby, silhouettes, Tassie's gems and some unpretentious Sheraton furniture. The curious thing is that, whereas all the proliferation of possessions in my parents' houses seems to have vanished, the furniture and objects that belonged to my grandmother are still with us and have supplied our children's houses, as well as our own. My grandmother had been widowed early, and her sons had been a disappointment. The eldest had been hurriedly shipped off to Australia, the second was a minor civil servant. The youngest was thought to be the genius of the family. His mother and three sisters scraped and saved to send him to Balliol, then at the height of its intellectual glory. I don't think he took a degree, but he at least achieved the manner and appearance of a don; small body, high forehead, short staccato utterance, followed by a knowing chuckle, and a pipe smoked with an air of portentous wisdom. He was the most completely futile human being I have ever met; he could not ride a bicycle or dig in the garden, and never seemed to read a book. His only visible occupation was to repaint used golf balls, which he picked up on the course. My aunts were committed to a belief in his early promise, but my mother loathed him and would address him only in the third person. He gave her an underlying prejudice against academics in general, and dons in particular. Queen Victoria herself had no greater detestation of Oxford.

My grandmother and her eldest daughter were sweet, sensible human beings, whose opinions differed very little from those of the inhabitants of Cranford. After a heavy, bibulous house party, in order to avoid a scolding, my father would trot out to the Castle House in very poor shape, and they would receive him calmly, as if nothing were amiss. He was infinitely grateful to them.

Shortly before Christmas the last shooting party left the house. My father went to bed for three days, and my mother sat about with a pale face. Christmas itself passed almost unnoticed. My mother hated ceremonies, my father was indifferent to them. Turkeys were sent to the tenants—the only recognition of their existence that I can remember—and we ate one for Christmas lunch, but this was as far as my parents were prepared to go. Unfortunately one of the Golliwogg books is concerned with Christmas and contains a 'double spread' of a glorious tree; I therefore asked if I could have a Christmas tree. My mother pulled a long face (I can see it now), but a tree was ordered and set up in a back room. None of us knew what to do with it, so after a time it was cleared away by old Sam, the odd man, as none of the other servants considered it their duty. I may add that old Sam was also the man who ironed the newspapers. This is sometimes referred to as the most ridiculous of Edwardian customs. It has a reasonable origin, because in the nineteenth century the ink on newspapers was still tacky when they were delivered; but long before my time the ink was dry, and the ironing was purely a ritual.

After the new year shooting started again, but the heart had gone out of it. There were fewer guns and less jovial visitors. One reason was that the pheasants had grown wily, and would not rise, even if prodded by a beater. I suppose it is possible that my father, who was a humane man, had got sick of slaughter; but this did not prevent him shooting hares in the marshes, which is the most pitiful form of sport, as the hares scream in anguish when wounded. I had been sickened by the slaughter of pheasants, but my real detestation of blood-sports dates from the one and only time that I was taken to shoot hares at Gedgrave.

At some time towards the end of January my parents moved to the French Riviera. My father loved gambling and wanted to be within easy reach of Monte Carlo. At first he achieved this by living on one of his yachts, which was sent out from the Clyde and moored in Monaco harbour. I greatly enjoyed this mode of existence, as I could visit the other splendid yachts that surrounded us. I remember one that belonged to an American who was very tall and blind. All the fitments were high above my reach, and it was entirely lined with cork, as he could not bear sound of any kind. I also paid a call on Mr Pierpont Morgan on his yacht the *Corsair.* He was seated on deck fighting a losing battle with a game of solitaire, and he glared at me over his famous nose, as if I had been a defaulting creditor. But my mother found the social life of Monaco too exciting, and we moved to the less competitive atmosphere of Mentone, where our yacht was moored for several seasons. We were even allowed to paint a coat of arms, or rather an *impresa,* on the wall opposite our berth, and there it remained until defaced by the Germans in 1941, when they also threw the statue of Queen Victoria into the sea. It seemed to me a pleasant existence, but my father found the accommodation too restricted, and decided to build a much bigger yacht, the third *Katoomba.* It was completed in a few months, and furnished down to the last detail. My parents and their guests came out to join it at Mentone, and everyone agreed that it was perfection. On the third day my parents gave a luncheon party for some local residents. Amongst them was Madame Herriot, proprietress of a store named the Louvre, then the most prosperous in Paris. "It is delightful", she said to my father, "I would give *anything* for a yacht like this". "Anything?" "Yes, anything". My father named an enormous sum. "But it must include everything". "Yes, everything". "Even the notepaper". "Yes, the notepaper". "And I must have it *tomorrow*". "Yes, to-morrow". Accommodation was found in neighbouring hotels, we all packed hastily, and Madame Herriot came on board next morning with her cheque. I much disliked this episode, and so I suppose did my parents' guests. But my father enjoyed it hugely, and immediately commissioned his dear friend, G. L. Watson (one of the two greatest yacht architects of the time) to build him another *Katoomba*. Unfortunately he changed his mind and decided to build a house instead. He bought a large slice of land in the middle of Cap Martin, which then belonged to only two or three proprietors. He employed a small and villainous-looking local architect named Tersling, but insisted that the actual construction be done by Scottish builders. As a result it was exceptionally solid for a house on the Riviera, and when the daughter of a subsequent proprietor tried to pull it down it proved almost impossible to do so.

Before about 1922 it was considered suicide to stay on the Riviera after the end of April. Most people left about the 16th. I asked our Scottish gardener what the natives did during the months between May and December. He said it was terrible, and that he had made it a condition that he could return to Pitlochry during at least three months. Bathing pools had not been thought of, and ladies did all they could, by means of parasols and enormous hats, to avoid exposure to the sun. Considering that we spent less than three months there it seems extravagant to have built and equipped so large and solid a residence; but we all enjoyed it. My mother had her garden, my father had his gambling and I had two unfailing delights: donkey rides in the hills and the variety shows in the Casino at Mentone. The donkey rides were organised

by a group of amiable ruffians with cherries in their
hats, who spoke the local patois and gave me my first
experience of the warmth and geniality of the Italian
people. The reader must be reminded that before
1914 Mentone was practically an English *dependence*.
At the centre of the town were the English church
and the English tea-rooms; in the main back street
was the Presbyterian church. There were also a number of Germans who, from 1912 onwards, became extremely arrogant and pushed one off the pavement;
but most of the hotels contained only English people.
I remember that, in one of them where I was staying,
a Frenchman took a room. He was looked at with astonishment, and referred to as 'the Frenchman'. After
half an hour on a donkey with my jolly sunburnt
companions shouting Italian songs to encourage the
tripping steps of their charges, one entered a different world. On one of these occasions an astonishing
thought crossed my mind. There had been people
here before the English. They had cultivated olives
on a complex series of terraces, had lived in these
steep streets of stone houses, perched high out of
reach of pirates, and had thought nothing about sani-
tation. Needless to say my parents were not at all
interested in these banal observations, but they mark
a stage in my consciousness.

My other treat was of an exactly opposite kind.
Every evening between five and seven the Casino of
Mentone put on a programme of conjurors, jugglers,
acrobats, comedians and stunt men. The programmes
changed twice a week. They did not draw large audi-
ences. Lam and I were usually alone on the gallery,
and I don't suppose the standard was very high, but
before the age of crooners performers had to show a
certain amount of talent. I love conjuring tricks, and
I already had a strong urge to be an actor, so these
weekly entertainments were a delight to me. They
were not so much a delight to my mother and her
guests when I returned home and insisted on their
forming an audience to listen to my own performances.
I had found a room in the villa which seemed to

me to provide a proper stage. I wrote elaborate scripts; my fellow performers were my gollywog and teddy bears. It must have been a ghastly bore.

My father was spared this ordeal, as he rose late and spent the rest of the day in the Casino at Monte Carlo. He was an amazingly lucky gambler and broke the bank (which is not as unusual or as rewarding as the song implies) a number of times. What is almost incredible, but I can vouch for its truth, was that he got a *maximum en plein* at roulette twice running. After a successful evening he would buy enormous hats for all his lady friends, including Lam, who bore those monstrous additions to her wardrobe with her usual calm. To placate my mother he would order quantities of linen from the Grand Maison du Blanc, and I am glad to say that we have it still, because it has hitherto been considered too good to be used. In those days gambling was done with Louis d'or, and when I went in to say good-morning to my parents at breakfast time, the dip in my father's bed would often be deep in golden coins. When, after the first war, gambling was done with counters, my father lost interest in it.

At this point the reader may be prepared for a description of my father's appearance. He was tall and stout, with a reddish moustache which in the days of his maximum prosperity was waxed. He had a dimpled chin and a cheerful complexion. With his hat on, he could have been mistaken for Champagne Charlie, the Great Macdermot, or any of the other *lions comiques* of the Edwardian music halls, but under his hat was a magnificent head, large and finely modelled. He had beautiful hands, an artist's hands, and shapely legs, of which he was rather proud, so that he liked, if possible, to wear knee-breeches. He normally wore a butterfly collar, and a white silk knitted tie with a large pearl tiepin just under the knot. This seemed to combine rather incongruously with the knee-breeches, but I remember the Duke of Bedford wearing the same combination in about 1932, so it may simply have been old-fashioned. His broad-brimmed, flat felt hat was also a relic of the last century, for one sees it in Whistler's etched self-portraits; Lord Carnarvon was the only other man I have seen wearing it. Finally my father always wore white yachting shoes, which, for some mysterious reason, gave great offence in the Monte Carlo Sporting Club. The total impression was unconventional; but it was appropriate because in every way my father was an eccentric of the first order. He was, said my mother ruefully, a law unto himself; but although boastful and self-confident, he was the least arrogant of men. He talked to everyone in the same natural, friendly, straightforward manner; he hated humbug and if some pretentious public figure began to air his views, he would simply walk away without explanation. He drank a bottle of champagne every evening, and heaven knows how many whiskies, but remained courteous and benevolent. Later, when he suffered from cirrhosis of the liver, and must have felt like death, he used to warn people by saying, 'Go away, I'm irritable!"

I had no friends on the Riviera, or rather no friends of my own age and species; but I formed a curious attachment to a neighbour, the Empress Eugenie. Our friendship began badly, because when we first met she invited me to kiss her. I doubt if I had ever kissed anyone and did not feel like beginning with this ancient face. I fled in horror. However, she forgave me, and invited me to accompany her on her morning walks in the olive grove to the west of Cap Martin. I was charmed by her courtesy and greatly enjoyed my mornings, but our conversation was far from brilliant. If only I had been ten years older, seventeen instead of seven, I would have known enough history to ask her questions, although I am not sure that she would have welcomed them. As things were we talked about local events, the Carnival and the Battle of Flowers. The latter was my favourite event of the year. It consisted in a number of floats being drawn through strands specially erected on the Promenade des Anglais. The floats were decorated with flowers, and the spectators pelted them with little bunches of flowers, usually stocks, which smelt deliciously at first, but must have stunk next morning. Hideous silk banners, elaborately painted with views of Mentone, were presented to the most pretentious floats. Between 1910 and 1914 I won a banner every year. Our *chef d'oeuvre* was an almond tree in flower cut down and mounted on wheels, on which was constructed a nest made of flowers. I was dressed as a bird. On this occasion it was thought appropriate to invite a little girl to accompany me. Of course I see now that I should have given her the silk banner that was inevitably awarded to us. Golliwogg would certainly have done so. But I could not bear to break my series. Many years after I met her again, married to a pro-consular general, and found that she still bore me a well-deserved grudge.

I have said that I had no friends of my own species, but there were two creatures at Cap Martin who meant more to me than most human beings. One was a grey parrot, the other a blue frog named Jacqueline. My father had bought the parrot in Monte Carlo, where she had lived in a house overlooking the Parade ground of the Monegasque army. Her chief occupation was therefore to drill, marching up and down our terrace, with words of command in French. When put back in her cage she was reminded of an earlier existence in England, and would emit only market cries "Pork and rabbit, buy, buy, buy", and "Mind your own bloody business"—it might have been worse. She was a most affectionate bird, and would sit on my shoulder as I walked about the garden. One day, to my consternation, she flew away. I wept bitterly, not only at the loss of a friend, but at a breach of confidence. But I could have spared my tears, because a few days later my polly returned, and settled on my shoulder. After a decent interval she laid an egg. Although I knew nothing about biology, I had an intimation that she had been answering some call of nature, and loved her more than ever. I brought her back to England witth me in 1914, but she was not happy in the cold air of Suffolk, and died.

After April 20th my parents went for a cure to Marienbad, Carlsbad, or, later, Vichy. They liked Carlsbad best. These annual cures, when the rich ate and drank only twice as much as we do normally today, must have saved them from apoplexy. I never went to Carlsbad, but one year I was taken to Vichy, which I thought the fullest place I had ever been to. As a rule I was sent back to Sudbourne to face the resentful servants. My parents returned about the middle of May, and after a few weeks prepared to move to Scotland for the early salmon and the first run of the sea trout. This involved a short stay in London and, as the house in Grosvenor Square had been sold, they took a flat in 25 Berkeley Square, one of the first blocks to be erected in that district. At that date only what were known as tradesmen would have lived in a flat. My father, like a north-country industrialist, was proud of his status, and would have gone out of his way to avoid the *moeurs* of the upper class. He often said that no one with a title ever wrote to him, except to ask for money. I remember at Sudbourne coming into my father's study when he was being interviewed by two men in black coats and striped trousers. I paused to look at these unusual apparitions, and one of them, who turned out to have been the notorious Mr Maundy Gregory,* said to my father, "Wouldn't you like this little chap to succeed you?" "Go to hell", said my father, and they drove off.

We never stayed in London for long, because my mother thought, and rightly, that my father would get into trouble; but I enjoyed our brief visits, because it meant going to the theatre. I saw all the famous Edwardian actors: Sir Squire Bancroft and Sir George Alexander, both of whom I thought worthless boobies, Gerald du Maurier, who enchanted me in the plays of J. M. Barrie, and above all Charles Hawtrey, whom I am quite sure was the most ex-

* Maundy Gregory was Lloyd George's chief agent in the sale of honours.

quisite master of comedy of his time. Every intonation, every gesture, every hesitation, was as precise as the playing of a great pianist, and yet the whole effect was so natural that one could not believe he was acting at all. I also saw all the great comics (except Dan Leno), either in musical comedy, pantomime or the music hall. Oh, for the pen of Hazlitt or Charles Lamb to describe the rolling eyes of George Robey, the twirling moustache of Harry Tate, the terrible moment when Little Tich rose on the toes of his long boots, or when Wilkie Bard, the supreme Widow Twanky, leant down from her step-ladder to hang her washing on a clothes-line far beneath her! When my father was in London he used to take a box in both the Empire and the Alhambra and walk from one to the other across Leicester Square. It may seem odd that my mother allowed me to accompany him, but I suppose she thought I would keep him out of mischief. To tell the truth, I found these expeditions rather alarming, as my father was so unpredictable, and I was happier when Lam and I could settle down to a matinée of a musical comedy like *The Girl From Utah*. Ina Claire was the first actress I fell in love with. Alas, I have never met her; perhaps someone who knows her will give her my love.*

During one of these visits to London I was taken to Sir John Lavery's studio to have my portrait painted. It seemed to me the most beautiful place I had ever seen, painted dark blue, with gold stars on the ceiling; and as I sat entranced awaiting my turn, there was wafted into this fairy-tale room a vision of grace which no one who has seen it can forget—Pavlova. Again and again she fluttered across the parquet floor and then sank into it, down, down, as if she would languorously disappear beneath it. What luck for me! I was much less happy when she pranced around the studio as a Bacchante. It seemed profane and (to tell the truth) slightly vulgar. My father bought the sketch for the Bacchante, but we never liked it and gave it

* He has.

28

away to a cousin in Oregon. If only he could have bought the sketch for the dying swan.

My portrait, in the manner of Velasquez—by no means bad—was sent to the Paris Salon, as Lavery was out of favour with the London Royal Academy. We stopped off at Paris on the way back from Cap Martin in order to look at it, but it proved difficult to find. The Grand Palais, which contained the Salon, is divided up into sections and we seemed always to find ourselves on the wrong side of the division. Finally my father discovered a bar, which was common to both sections. My portrait was remotely visible on the other side, and he thought that the simplest thing would be to walk through. This caused a terrible uproar. An enormous barmaid stood with arms akimbo to block his passage; but he was not a man to be thwarted. Finally the barmaid sent for two gendarmes, and I suppose my father admitted defeat, but I don't remember because the sight of the gendarmes and the enormous woman (*l'Intransigeante*) had aroused in my mind confused memories of the French Revolution. I pictured my father going to the Bastille, let out the loudest scream of which I was capable, and was hurried away from the scene.

From London we made our way to our house in Ross-shire, pausing uneasily at the North British Hotel in Edinburgh. I say uneasily because my father always made this, or any other visit to an hotel, the occasion of getting more than usually drunk. Not wishing to see my mother's pale, reproachful face (and nobody could look more pained than my mother), he would stretch himself out at full length on the most prominent sofa in the hotel drawing-room, to the righteous indignation of the guests and the embarrassment of the hotel staff. There would be complaints; and my mother would send me down to retrieve him. I was, of course, too small to move him, but I could shake him awake, and after a few minutes' persuasion he would usually come upstairs, supported by one of the porters, muttering, as he staggered into the lift, "An old dog for a hard road". It was the kind of incident often drawn by Phil May, but the on-lookers in his East End pubs and alleys were more sympathetic than the guests in the North British, and I must confess that these errands caused me much distress. Indeed, I am inclined to think that they had a lasting effect on my character, making me prematurely self-controlled and defensive.

After an interminable journey, changing at Inverness, then going west to Achnasheen through a formless, sodden landscape, the shapes of the hills muffled by a purplish fuzz of heather, we motored along the banks of Loch Maree, and finally arrived at Poolewe, where the river Ewe, flowing from Loch Maree, enters a tidal loch. Pool House, which we rented furnished, was panelled with shiny pitch pine; the walls were hung with engravings of Highland cattle after Peter Graham, the chairs were covered with hideous cretonnes and the threadbare carpet was full of holes. The only book in the house was Queen Victoria's *Leaves from Our Journal in the Highlands*. This kind of dilapidated simplicity is said by sensitive people to have great charm, but it had none for me. My heart sank. It had none for my parents either, and they immediately decided to live on their yacht, the *Zoraide,* which was anchored half-a-mile out in Loch Ewe. Lam and I were left alone in the house. There was a lawn too short for the smallest cricket pitch and the usual luxuriant Highland kitchen garden, crammed with fruit. Otherwise nothing to fill a small boy's day. As a result those Scottish visits left no traces on my conscious or unconscious memory. They never come back to me in dreams, as Sudbourne does, even now, almost once a week. Many of my ancestors were said to have come from this part of the world; most of our neighbours were called Mackenzie, and two were actually called Kenneth Mackenzie. If I had been an imaginative child I might have consoled myself with the fantasy of being in my native land. 'Breathes there a man with soul so dead?' Well, I am sorry to say there does. I am, and have always been, completely devoid of genealogical piety.

The sight of a family tree is as distasteful to me as a VAT form. Endless bogs, not an acre of cultivated land, persistent rain, followed by swarms of midges—it did not need the villainous landlords of leftist mythology to drive people away from this melancholy, unproductive coast line.

We went to this dreary house and dead-beat village (now, I believe, deserted) in order that my father should fish on the river Ewe. Here again, I showed a disappointing lack of enthusiasm. I did not positively hate fishing, as I did shooting. Standing on a stone, with the river swirling round one, and casting a good line, is a pleasant experience for an hour or two. But except in late June, when the sea trout are running, the rewards are infrequent. As for salmon, one may thrash a river for weeks without a bite. A small boy who could spend his days like that must have inner resources that I lack. Besides, I have, from my earliest years, been obsessed by the passage of time. I am the original White Rabbit of Alice in Wonderland, "Oh dear, oh dear, I shall be too late". Several of my lady friends have told me that they have never known anyone who looked so often at his watch: not the right temperament for a fisherman, or for a ladies' man, one would have supposed. But I must admit that the rare occasions when one does hook a salmon are worth waiting for. The whirling reel, the splendid curve of the fish leaping out of the water as it makes for a waterfall, the terrible moment when one's line begins to run out and one has to run up and down the bank, sploshing into the stream—all this arouses a state of mindless exhilaration which I suppose men used to feel in a cavalry charge. From the humanitarian point of view it must be indefensible, but it does seem to be connected with a deep and necessary human instinct. There are few more harmless ways of experiencing the sense of glory than by playing and landing a twenty-pound salmon, and it is an interesting example of folk-philology that the ugly, short stick with a lump of lead at the end of it with which this magnificent specimen of the will to live is finally killed is known colloquially as 'a priest'.

When the fishing in the river Ewe became too monotonously unsuccessful and the midges unbearable, we went for expeditions in the yacht—to Skye, to Stornaway (which stank of herring from five miles out), to Iona and Loch Coruisk, which seemed respectively to provide for me the images of heaven and hell. (Indeed I screamed with terror when I first saw Coruisk, and had to be taken back to Scavaig.) Aesthetically there was much to be said for the old-fashioned Edwardian yacht. It was made up of wood and brass, both of which needed continual attention. One was wakened by the rhythmical sound of the wooden decks being scrubbed, one rose to find men scrubbing the teak bulwarks while other men with tins of polish were at work on brass cleats, capstans and door-handles. By ten-thirty, when the laziest guest had put away his last kipper, the decks were a symphony of contrasting materials. Socially however, yachts are a menace, and I have seldom heard of a yachting party that did not end with at least one broken friendship. This idea would have had no meaning for my father, who was not a social man. He simply loved the sea, and would have been much happier alone with his dear Captain, Archie Hogarth, and perhaps one old crony to drink with. He was at his best on the bridge. His last yacht, the *Zoraide,* was a tough old packet, and he would take her out in any weather. Rounding R'hu Rae or Ardnamurchan in a gale, he was really magnificent, and when we had turned into calmer water in the Sound of Mull, and he came down with his cheeks and moustache dripping with spray, he looked like Flaubert, the last of the Vikings. Fortunately I am never sea-sick and am too unimaginative to be disturbed by physical danger; I greatly enjoyed these buffetings, and remember with pleasure the sound of all the pots and pans in the galley being thrown on the floor, and the sight of a huge wave that had almost engulfed us smashing itself into a tower of spray against the cliffs of Ardnamurchan. On these grounds, at least, I may be better qualified to understand Turner than some of my fellow critics.

I also remember afternoons of unbelievable calm, when we could heave to and row the dinghy over to a sandy cove unapproachable from the land, and thus still inhabited by hundreds of innocent flounders. The water was so clear that one couldn't imagine how the boat remained suspended. One could watch the bait fathoms down, dangling above the sand. Then, after a few seconds the sand would undulate and out would come a small greedy mouth to dart at the mussel-covered hook. A jerk, and up she comes, poor flounder. At first I was proud of my skill, but after three or four such triumphs I began to take the flounders' part and made an excuse to land on the beach and look for lobsters. It was then, perhaps, that I might have been glad of someone of my own size to slither with me into the crevasses of rocks and jump from one tuft of lichen and sea-pinks to another.

In my description of life on the Riviera and the West Coast of Scotland I have telescoped my memories of at least four years. At some point during these years, that is to say between the ages of seven and nine, I was sent to a boarding school, of the type known as a 'preparatory school'. Lam came back to look after me in the holidays. This curious, and, to my mind, objectionable feature of English education, was maintained solely in order that parents could get their children out of the house. A few of these preparatory schools may have been interested in educating their pupils, but Wixenford, the school to which I was sent, had no such pretensions. The three partners who owned it realistically accepted the fact that it was the parents and not the children who mattered. They tried to look as little like schoolmasters as possible (which wasn't difficult, as they had the sketchiest academic background), and received the parents with well-judged bonhomie. They poured out strong whiskies and soda for the fathers—those tea-time whiskies so much appreciated in Edwardian England; and to the mothers they could show a charming garden, leading to an avenue of pleached limes, under which, it was alleged, school meals were served in the summer term. This arcadian prospect was not clouded by any reference to lessons. They also alluded, in scarcely audible asides, to the number of titled people whose children were in the school and who came down to see them at week-ends. This, in fact, was true, and the rich social climbers who sent their children to Wixenford got their money's worth. So, indeed, did the boys, because at that date it was usual for members of the upper classes to marry stage favourites, and these charming creatures, gloriously overdressed, used to move among us like birds of paradise. Of course this particular argument had no influence on my father, but both he and my mother liked the unacademic character of Wixenford. He often complained that when he went down to see my prospective housemaster at Winchester no one offered him a drink. And, sure enough, neither of my parents ever set foot in the place again, even when I had pneumonia.

The odd mixture of upper class children and the children of American or South African millionaires suited me. I was happy at Wixenford. But the almost total lack of instruction was a drawback that has troubled me all my life. Certain subjects a child can learn on his own, but Latin is not one of them. It must be ground into him at a time when his mind is malleable. Although I learned Latin at Winchester, I never acquired that innate familiarity with it which any reputable scholar must possess. But then, Wixenford was not intended for future scholars. Every boy in the school went automatically to Eton. I was the only one who ever went to Winchester. All that I can remember of the school curriculum is the gender rhymes and Euclid. As Latin is no longer taught in schools, I should explain that the old Latin primers contained a rhyming *aide memoire* to the genders of Latin nouns. That things or qualities should have genders at all was sufficiently odd, and this was made even more mysterious by the verses in which this irrational and very complex situation was supposed to be made memorable. I say 'supposed' but in fact it *was* made memorable and any English school boy of my generation will have no difficulty in completing such a quotation as this:

> To nouns that cannot be declined
> The Neuter gender is assigned
> Examples Fas and Nefas give
> And the Verb Noun Infinitive
> Est summum nefas fallere
> Deceit is gross impiety.

The gender rhymes also contain lists of words that no one with a feeling for the magic of language can resist. James Joyce would have loved them: but then he had the Latin Missal.

> Masculine are fons and mons
> Chalybs, hydrops, gryps and pons
> Rudens, torrens, clems, cliens
> Fractions of the 'as', as triens.

The gender of a gryphon (gryps) may seem to be a curious feature of a child's education. But I fancy that the secondary or accidental value of the gender rhymes as a form of sacred incantation, was considerable, especially in a protestant country. The very words they contained—opifex and artifex—were suggestive of arcane practices. All over the world children learn magic rhymes which they are told to take seriously and like the Latin Mass they should be largely incomprehensible. Finally, the gender rhymes contained one distych which any writer should take to heart:

> Masculine will always be
> Things that you can touch and see.

Perhaps these lines were the foundation of my distaste for the stellar nebulae of literature—Shelley, and St John Perse.

My taste for Euclid I have mentioned already. I am a born visualiser, cannot really understand anything that I do not see, and am as perplexed by metaphysics as a Trobriand islander. So my joy in seeing abstractions made visible by what appeared to be (wrongly, as it now turns out) a logical process, was complete. I looked forward to my lessons in geometry as keenly as to my lessons in drawing, which may perhaps be allowed as a qualification for writing a book on Piero della Francesca. I remember nothing about my history lessons, which I would normally have enjoyed; the teachers must have been exceptionally bad. But then, before 1914, teachers in private boarding schools were exactly as described in Evelyn Waugh's *Decline and Fall,* and during the 1914–18 war they were worse. The small boys were conscious that their masters were lazy and incompetent, but nobody could explain to us that these poor freaks had been driven into their profession by necessity, cryptohomosexuality or some other misfortune, and so we treated them without mercy.

Dredging in this particular pool of memory, almost the only nuggets I can bring up are the theatrical performances that I used to organise and the school dance. With my passion for musicals, or what were then called revues, I could not resist writing libretti which would incorporate my favourite music-hall songs; I then devised the scenery and had the fun of casting. Most small boys like showing off, and I had no difficulty in forming my company. I remember a particularly charming leading lady named Mark Ogilvie Grant. In my *hubris* I invited the masters to attend these performances, and this turned out to be my undoing, because at one point I introduced the hymn 'All things bright and beautiful', because of its jolly tune and ridiculous words, and the school chaplain, who had hitherto been almost invisible, felt bound to protest. I gave up theatrical production, and took to journalism. My paper was called 'Milk and

Biscuits' in reference to the mother-soothing item which appeared most often in our curriculum. Small boys are not so easily taken in.

The school dance was the first time I had met girls, and I was enchanted beyond words, not by anything tangible, but by the aura of femininity. *Incipit vita nova.* People sometimes wonder how Dante at the age of eleven could have had his life changed by love. I can only say that if a 'little girl of perfect beauty, wearing a dress of most noble hue, a subdued and modest crimson', had cast her eyes in my direction at a Wixenford dance, I should have pursued her to the end of my days. I saw no Beatrice, but large laughing girls, a good deal older than myself, who were kind-hearted enough not to make me feel a fool. It was the beginning of the great happiness I have had all my life in the company of women. 'Green grow the rushes, O.'

At the end of my last term at Wixenford, my head-master's report consisted of three words—'A jolly boy' —and it was in a cheerful frame of mind that I entered the school train to Winchester. I am naturally talkative, and I addressed a few words to a handsome boy, who appeared to be only a year or two older than myself. To my surprise, he did not reply, so I moved off to address another group of boys who looked less awe-inspiring. This was not much more successful, and I began to realise that I had entered an entirely differ-ent society, the children of generals, judges, bishops and higher civil-servants, with a small admixture of old-fashioned country gentlemen, whose hierarchical values I had never encountered, and to this day do not entirely understand. I arrived at my 'house'* crestfallen, and my spirits were not raised when I was

---

* In case this book is read by someone unfamiliar with the traditional English system of education for upper-middle class children, I should explain that a 'public' school, known, more accurately, in America, as a private school, was divided into houses where the boarders lived, about thirty to a house. This was the effective social unit, and in my time one was strongly discouraged from even speaking to a boy in another 'house'.

told to go and see the head of the house in the library. He turned out to be the handsome youth whom I had so incontinently addressed on the train. "Sport an arse", he said (which in Wykehamist language means 'bend over'); and he gave me three or four very painful strokes with a stick, known as a ground ash. "That will teach you to speak to your seniors", he said. It did. In the twinkling of an eye the jolly boy from Wixenford became a silent, solitary, inward-turning but still imperfect Wykehamist.

I will not describe my schooldays. The subject has been done to death by intellectuals who seem to regard bullying and injustice as a personal attack on themselves, instead of the invariable condition of growing up in any society. Compared to the initiation rites of the Australian Aboriginal we got off lightly. And there were compensations. I made friends; I learnt useful skills, like polishing shoes; I learnt history from a great teacher. Above all, Winchester helped to open for me what Blake called the doors of perception; that was its most important role in my life, and I shall try to describe it in the next chapter. But on the whole I cannot say that life was agreeable, especially during the 1914—18 war. Hunger, chilblains and a perpetually sore bottom. I remember one midday meal that consisted solely of the *skins* of boiled potatoes, and on such sordid nourishment we were expected not only to work (early school) and play games, but go for two long runs each week, one of them three and a half miles round St Catharine's Hill. Our performances were timed by the prefects, and we were beaten if we took too long. The Athenian cunning, traditional at Eton, would have found some way round these hardships; but Wykehamists are as virtuous as Tamino.

My own personal misfortune was an exceptionally stupid housemaster, named Herbert Aris, who might have made a good officer in the Boer War, but was not qualified to look after growing boys. He took a great dislike to me because I was not a gentleman, and encouraged his prefects to beat me more, even, than they felt inclined to do. I heard him telling them that I should be put in the middle of the front row of the football scrum, saying "I want to see that big head knocked about". He arranged for me to learn boxing, and after a few weeks asked me how I was getting on. "I'm enjoying it, sir." He was furious. "I don't want you to enjoy it, I want you to get hurt." This sounds like what is loosely described as sadism, but I am sure that he was moved only by a sincere desire to 'make a man' of me. Unfortunately he never succeeded. He should have been squatting on the ground with a leopard skin draped over his head and shoulders. Having no knowledge of anthropology, I could not see it in this light, and felt resentful at his repeated attacks. Finally, he took the bold step of saying that I must be 'sent down' (i.e. expelled) on account of my stupidity. My headmaster would, I think, have tried to save me from this, although it would have been difficult for him to reverse a house-master's decision. Fortunately he did not need to, as the father of Mrs Aris (who was charming) died and left his daughter an island covered with bird manure called guano, which the executors sold for close on a million pounds. Mr Aris retired, bought an estate in the New Forest, and lived out his life as an acceptable country gentleman.

His place was taken by a fiery little bachelor known as 'the Jacker' who, outside the academic world, might have been considered peculiar. He knew that I belonged to a different species, and I remember once when he was sitting between myself and Tony Keswick* he looked at us balefully and said, "Never, never again will I have the son of a businessman in my house". In fairness I must add that the Jacker had inherited from his father, who was Professor of

---

* Tony Keswick's father was director of the great Far Eastern trading house, Jardine Matheson. Tony himself was to become Chairman of the Hudson Bay Company, and is the Senior Governor of the Bank of England. Also in his house was Sir Denys Lowson, so perhaps some prophetic instinct inspired the Jacker's remark.

Latin in Cambridge, a belief in perfection, which he expressed by collecting the etchings of Meryon and D. Y. Cameron, scrutinising the states as his father would have scrutinised a doubtful reading. Considering that I lacked all the accomplishments that he valued—knowledge of Greek, skill at football and martial spirit—he treated me very fairly.

On my eleventh birthday, July 13th, 1914, my father thought of a surprising celebration, which shows that he understood my tastes better than some of the foregoing pages might imply. A row of mortars were dug into the grass in front of the house at Pool Ewe and into them were placed large but light cannon balls. The general effect comes back to me vividly when I look at a Leonardo drawing at Windsor (12275). The mortars were then discharged, the cannon balls shot up into the pale blue sky, and when they burst there emerged huge paper effigies, which floated down like leisurely parachutes into the surrounding hills. Elephants, geishas (for of course these wonderful toys came from Japan), tigers, buffaloes, slowly descending on to the distant heather, the local children (few enough even then) dashing after them with screams of delight. Bang, bang, bang, and out came a ship in full sail, a snowman and what I now realise was a Zen Buddhist monk. Bang, bang, bang; and less than three weeks to go before the fourth of August.

That ominous date found us still anchored in Loch Ewe and in a state of despondency; not, of course, for political reasons, but because the sea-trout had vanished and the salmon had grown sluggish and disinterested. None of us read the three days old newspapers, although I think that the news that the Archduke Francis Ferdinand had been assassinated somehow reached us, because I remember the name Sarajevo having a sinister sound for me. We had no idea of the possible consequences. One of the neighbouring houses, called, I think, Inverewe, had been rented by Lord Cunliffe, Governor of the Bank of England. One would have supposed that at such a crisis he would have returned to London, but that would have been unthinkable in August, and on the second (I see the date in one of my father's old diaries) he lunched with us on the yacht. I had fallen in love with his daughter, who had red hair and wore a monocle, and so was glad to be present. "There's talk of a war", said Lord Cunliffe, "but it will never happen; the Germans haven't got the credits". I was much impressed. In September 1939 I was dining in the Beefsteak Club and three or four directors of famous banking houses—Bensons, Hambros, Lazards —happened to be present. They discussed the possibility of war with Germany. "It's not on, old chap", said the most respected of them, "the Germans haven't got the credits". They all agreed. This time I was not so much impressed: indeed I was very frightened to think that our finances were in the hands of people suffering so seriously from professional deformation.

The news of the declaration of war on August 4th was well received by our friends and neighbours. They had long hated the Germans and were glad to 'have a go' at them. My father, although uninformed about public affairs, had more sense. He said that it would be a long and desperate war, leading to financial ruin and the collapse of society. Naturally people prefered Lord Cunliff's point of view and thought of my father as an ignorant outsider. He entirely disassociated himself from the whole affair, refused to make recruiting speeches and pushed away the newspapers that accumulated on his bed. "All lies", he said, quite correctly. From this time dates my own aversion to newspapers, which I have never been able to conquer, even when I was at the Ministry of Information.

I suppose the war touched us much less nearly than most. I had no relations to be called up and killed, except for one unknown cousin, who survived, and became a general. The slaughter that decimated the upper classes did not touch us. Bombs, jettisoned by returning zeppelins, fell in the park at Sudbourne and made small hazards on the golf course. My parents continued their way of life. Sudbourne was sold to a speculator who only visited it once, and we continued to live there for another two years. We even went out to the Villa at Cap Martin. Lam and I crossed the Channel from Folkestone to Boulogne, looking uneasily for mines, and got into a train which took us straight to Mentone. My father had turned a hotel called the Imperial, of which he was effectively the proprietor, into a hospital for French soldiers, and I used to go there to carry round cups of coffee and cigarettes to the wounded. I felt no disgust, no compassion—nothing; and might have forgotten the whole incident had not someone digging in the garden of a house in Gloucestershire, where we had once stayed, discovered a bronze medal presented to me in 1918 by the Dames de France. My parents spent their time playing bridge with Sir Phillip Watts, the designer of the *Dreadnought,* and his stout Belgian wife. He asked me what I wanted to study. I said "History", he replied "It rots the mind". His wife always arrived with an enormous handbag into which, after tea, she would stuff all the uneaten ginger cakes and foie-gras sandwiches. "Oh, so good. It would be a sin to leave them". The servants must have hated her.

It might have seemed as if nothing had happened. But for some reason it entered my formless consciousness that my father had been right. The vulgar, disgraceful, over-fed, godless social order that we call Edwardian was finished. I was brought up in this world at its most questionable; and I enjoyed it. I suppose that a serious-minded sociologist could describe me as the worthless product of a decadent system. Well, not quite; because I had one gift which has played so great a part in my life that it must be the subject of a separate chapter.

II

The Making of an Aesthete

IN THE year 1910 the Japanese Government, anxious to cement the alliance of 1901, sent to London a great manifestation of progress and goodwill. It was displayed in an exhibition ground at Shepherd's Bush called the White City. This was the most enchanting fun-fair imaginable, with lakes and cascades of water and little boats made to look like swans. The buildings were all painted white. They were in a degraded style, which might be described as poor man's Garnier, but they were much more festive than the dreary concrete of Wembley and most subsequent exhibitions. A small fragment of one of them, no longer white, was visible until quite recently. Lam and I had spent a deliriously happy day there at the Franco-British exhibition a year before, and we took the first opportunity to visit the Japanese exhibition. We were, I remember, somewhat disheartened by the number of gigantic bronze cranes (birds, not machines) that were arranged around the lake, and we decided to explore the interior. We found ourselves in a long gallery of lifesize dioramas representing the more agreeable aspects of Japanese life—a tea garden, evening on the Sumida river, and of course a number of cherry blossom festivals. They were pleasant enough, but unconvincing. At the end of the gallery was a small flight of steps. We ascended rather wearily, entered another gallery and immediately I was transported. On either side were screens with paintings of flowers of such ravishing beauty that I was not only struck dumb with delight, I felt that I had entered a new world. In the relationship of the shapes and colours a new order had beeen revealed to me, a new certainty established.

I had never seen Japanese painting before. I suppose that the words 'work of art' had never been spoken in my presence and would have been completely meaningless to me. The realistic dioramas in the adjoining gallery were far more appropriate to my childish tastes. But I felt immediately that they were contemptible, and refused to go back that way, thus involving Lam in a very long walk through corridors of commercial art. I remember that she complained of her legs. I was walking on air.

This seems to me, 'far as frailty would allow', a test tube specimen of our poor old friend the 'pure aesthetic sensation'. That concept, once received in the highest intellectual society, would now dare scarcely to show its head in a provincial discussion group. And yet without some such hypothesis the whole experience is very hard to explain. I am not so vain as to compare it to an infant musician's immediate understanding of a fugue, or to a youthful mathematician's joy when he first encounters Euclid's proof of the Infinity of Prime Numbers. Their gifts are, of course, incomparably more impressive. Nevertheless I think it must be reckoned a freak aptitude of the same kind, and in case any psychologist is rash enough to investigate this mysterious branch of the human psyche, I will record the sequel. Fifty-five years later I was visiting a temple near Kyoto, called the Chisha-kuji, one of the less well-known temples and mercifully free from tourists. It contains a sequence of rooms, one side open to a lake, the other three decorated with sixteenth-century screen paintings of flowers, even finer, to my mind, than those in the Kufukoji. As I sat on the floor I experienced the clearest recollection of having seen these paintings before, and said so to my companion, the official guide from the Foreign Office. "Nooh, nooh, not possible", hiss, squeak, giggle. "Perhaps they were reproduced in the Kokka then?" (repeat three times). "Nooh, nooh, Kokka." "In the Shimbi Taikwan then?" (repeat three times). "Noon, nooh, Shimba Taikwan." I was still unconvinced, and on returning to Tokyo told the story to my dear friend Yukio Yashiro. "Yes", he said, "they were once exhibited, and in London. You see, when the government sent over a sort of trade fair to London in 1910 they were asked to include a few fine paintings and told that they would be shown in the National Gallery. Actually they were exhibited in the fun fair with a lot of horrible Madama Butterfly (Yuki's favourite term of abuse) and nobody noticed them". Somebody had.

A strong, catholic response to works of art is like a comfortable account in a Swiss bank. One can never become emotionally bankrupt. Given tolerable health (for a response to works of art is partly physical), there is always plenty to live for, because one will never come to the end of the things one wants to see, or read all the poetry one wants to read; and if one did, one could go back again to the beginning, go back to the Arena Chapel after ten years, go back to the Velasquez Room at the Prado, re-read 'Lycidas' or *Antony and Cleopatra*. But I must confess that from the first my freak aptitude took me a little further than self-indulgence. I wanted to impart my feelings to other people, to analyse and describe them and even (for I am by nature an activist) to do something in the same line; not, heaven knows, because I thought I could produce a work of art, but because through copying and imitation I could perform a kind of ritual homage that would bring me nearer to understanding. I never doubted the infallibility of my judgements. At the age of nine or ten I said with perfect confidence "This is a good picture, that is a bad one". When I was moved by a work of art it never occurred to me that someone else, with more mature judgement, might feel differently. This almost insane self-confidence lasted till a few years ago, and the odd thing is how many people have accepted my judgements. My whole life might be described as one long, harmless confidence trick.

I had at first little enough material on which to base my certainties. Sudbourne, it is true, was stuffed with pictures. My father was a genuine lover of painting, and given a push in the right direction would have formed a good collection. But on his rare visits to London he went only to one or two dealers, who naturally tried to unload their rubbish on him. He also went to Christies and bought some good minor examples of the Barbizon school, then at the height of its reputation. It was his great ambition to own works by Theodore Rousseau and J. F. Millet—"Buy one if ever you can", he said to me, and I am glad to say that I have been able to do so. He had known personally the Scottish painter, Sir W. Q. Orchardson (what a talent!, as Degas said, if only *he* had had a push in the right direction), and had bought his haunting, unfinished picture, *The Last Dance*. He also bought a number of less admirable painters of the same generation—Sam Bough, John Pettie, Erskine Nichol and even B. W. Leader. Coarse diet for a growing aesthete. Yes: but love of art is an appetite, and the real lover of any art is not as fastidious as the man of taste. Desmond MacCarthy, the best dramatic critic of his day, used to say that his heart beat faster every time the curtain went up. I distrust the connoisseur of wine who can drink only a few rarefied vintages. And so it was probably better for me to be surrounded by this hodge-podge of bourgeois painting, than by some exquisite works by Burne-Jones, or perhaps even Simeon Solomon, as would have been my lot in more aesthetic circles.

My father's canvases, in their huge, gilt plaster frames, did not irradiate me with the same pure joy as the Japanese screens had done, but they accustomed me to looking at a picture for what it can give. And it is surprising how often a mediocre painter, or one corrupted by success, still has something to offer. I would go so far as to say that every painter who has achieved celebrity has at least once in his life experienced a true aesthetic sensation and done something from that part of his being that led him to become a painter in the first place. This theory (if I may be allowed a digression) was put to its severest test in the studio of a very prosperous portrait painter named Frank O. Salisbury. He lived in Hampstead in a sham Jacobean house which he had built for himself, and everything in the house was sham, including things that might just as easily have been genuine. It had a marvellous consistency. Frank O. Salisbury, dressed like a Harley Street gout specialist, with purple stock and a cameo tie pin, took me into his painting room. On the easel was a portrait of Sir John Simon, in his robes as High Steward of the University of Oxford. And there, standing on the cross-piece of the easel, beside the horrifying portrait, was a small painting, done on the lid of a cigar box, of a quiet and touching beauty. My host saw that I had noticed it and had, so to say, changed gear: he was quite fly enough for that. "It's a memory sketch I did", he said, "of Leighton's *Iphigenia,* which was exhibited in the R.A. my first year as a student. I always keep it there—I don't know why"—but he knew damn well.

My chief amusement outside my nursery was rehanging the pictures, old Sam being once more the only status-less person who could be asked to help me. I could not change the larger items—Millais' *Murthley Moss* or Fred Walker's *Bathers,* but the rest (and there must have been at least a hundred) were rearranged every few months. Sometimes, when re-hanging a room in the National Gallery, people have been surprised at my sudden air of authority and have asked me "How long have you been hanging pictures?" The answer is "Since the age of seven, and I know no more about it now than I did then". I think this familiarity with the crude raw material of one's trade is best absorbed at an early age. Just as actors and even dramatists gain something from sleeping in coils of rope at the back of the stage and first appearing in panto, so I fancy that I have a slight advantage over the average student in the Courtauld or the Fogg.

The visual material in the library at Sudbourne was confined to illustrated editions of Dickens and Thackeray, which I hated, and a complete set of the back numbers of *Punch*. But at the age of seven I received a present which may truly be said to have started me off in my line of business, a large volume on the Louvre with a text by a tout named P. G. Konody and a renegade art-historian named Brockwell. Even I, with my hunger for information already developed, could not derive much nourishment from their hackwork: but it also contained fifty colour plates, very poor by modern standards, but enough to give me some notion of classic European painting. I found the book still in my library, and on opening it saw an inscription in my father's hand 'Kenneth M. Clark from Granny, Xmas 1910'. Before turning the pages, I tried to remember which pictures had meant most to me during the year or two that this book was my most treasured possession. I give them in the order in which they come back to me. Correggio's *Marriage of St Catherine,* Giorgione's *Concert Champêtre,* one of Botticelli's frescoes from the Villa Lemmi, Titian's *Entombment,* Rubens' *Helena Fourment,* Watteau's *Cythera,* Rembrandt's *Hendricke Stoffels,* Frans Hals' *Gipsy Girl.* Go on, try again, close your eyes, think harder. Yes, of course, Holbein's *Erasmus,* Vermeer's *Lacemaker,* an old grey lady by Memlinc and Corot's *Le Vallon.* That is all I can do. Reading through the list I am interested to see how many of these pictures are of girls, which confirms my belief in the close connection between art and sex. But not so close, because on opening the book I find that it contains Ingres' *La Source,* which evidently made no impression on me, and Greuze's *Cruche Casée,* which I remember actively disliking. And I also find that one of the plates is missing, Antonello da Messina's portrait of a man known as Condottière, and I now remember that it impressed me so much that I cut it out and pasted it on to a piece of cardboard to copy it. I naturally showed my book to my dear grandmother, and by way of expressing my gratitude offered to expound my favourite pictures. Unfortunately I began with Giorgione's *Concert Champêtre*. We were sitting on a sofa near the window and I turned to the page in triumph. "Oh dear, it's very nude," said my grandmother, and rose from the sofa in confusion. Of course I had never thought of the two ladies in this way; their ample forms did not stir my infant sexual feelings. They were simply part of a pre-ordained harmony.

The bound volumes of *Punch* influenced me at a different level. I was too young to see the fun of Leech—his drawings simply looked to me incompetent; and I was bored by the fussy elaboration of du Maurier, to say nothing of his incomprehensibly snobbish jokes. But I found one artist after my own heart, Charles Keene. I could have echoed Pissarro's words to his son Lucien, when he went to live in the artistic desert of England. "Well, at least there is Charles Keene." My first instinct was not to make patterns, but to record what I saw, and Keene gave me a style in which to do so, delicate, unobtrusive and responsive to the most fleeting movement. One could not learn from Phil May. His marvellous economy of means was a personal gift. The understatement of George Belcher was too dismal for a young man. The rest were nowhere.

From the age of eight to thirteen Keene remained my model; then his place was taken by the far less salubrious influence of Aubrey Beardsley. However, this corrupting presence (I mean artistically corrupting, because morally I think he did me good by providing a focus for my developing sexuality) was to some extent mitigated by a fortunate accident. On my twelfth birthday my father gave me a large album full of original Japanese drawings which he had discovered in a sale in Bath. I suppose I had told him earlier about my experience at the White City a few years earlier. This album turns out to be a scrap book put together in about 1830 by some Japanese collector who was evidently in touch with Hokusai and his pupils. It contains a few drawings by Hokusai himself, and a large number by Hokkei, Gatukei and other *Surimono* artists. Also a few prints including some excruciating Kunisadas. The collector must have been quite humble, for these are chiefly studio sweepings; but what a marvellous treasure for a small boy! I immediately set about trying to draw in the Japanese style, and the drawings I did then are probably the only ones I could look at today without shame. When Beardsley assumed his fatal sway I already had an antidote in Hokusai.

The reader will have recognised that from the age of eight or nine I had decided to be an artist. This decision greatly pleased my father. He enjoyed the convivial company of artists, was a member of the Arts Club, and was invited to the annual banquet of the Royal Academy, although he seldom bought pictures from the Exhibition. I have no doubt that he played his part at a far away table, where elderly R.A.'s traditionally interrupted the speeches of Ministers of the Crown, and ended up sliding off their chairs on to the floor. Edwardian society was a good deal more pompous and conventional than we can imagine, and only among artists could my father escape from what he called 'humbug'. Artists came to the house. I played cricket with David Murray, and painted sheep (not in the snow) with Joseph Farquharson. But he gave himself airs as a Highland chieftain, and in any case my father had nothing but contempt for his monotonous potboilers. In the Academy of 1910 my father took a fancy to a picture by Charles Sims called *Mischief*. It had been sold, but Sims undertook to paint a second version, which, strangely enough, was much better than the first. My father also commissioned him to paint my portrait.

Thus began a friendship which lasted until a few months before his death. Technically Sims was a gifted artist and he was also an intelligent man; but, alas, he had no real centre. He made his name by painting girls (he seems to have been very fond of girls) in fountains; then he did two years of dryads. By the time he came to paint my portrait he was just emerging from a Whistler–Wilson Steer phase, and he had the good idea of painting me paddling in a sandy cove near Iken, looking across the river Alde to Aldeburgh. He worked on the spot, but the final result lacks freshness or immediacy. He made the initial mistake of putting me into an artificial pose and never recovered from it. But I shall never forget the joy of our picnics in that little cove (unchanged today) and the excitement of watching a genuine artist at work.

As I may not have another opportunity to write about Sims, I will record now that he was the first person whom I ever heard mention the name of Cézanne. Here, almost verbatim, is one of his pieces of advice, given a few years later: "When you are a boy you must imitate someone. You're all right, you imitate Charles Keene. Go on to imitate Degas" (I did). "It must be someone who doesn't make art look easy. The worst person to imitate is Gauguin" (which was exactly what I was about to do). "He's a great artist but a lethal influence. You can't paint like Van Gogh without being like Van Gogh, which", and he looked out of the window on to the terraces of Cap Martin, "doesn't seem likely. But stick to Cézanne; you'll never come to the end of Cézanne. I should like to stop painting for a year and then begin again as the humblest pupil of Cézanne. But it's too late." Strange words to hear from the man who had just painted the 'Picture of the Year', his portrait of Lady Rocksavage. When he was Keeper of the Royal Academy I used often to visit him, and one day found him confronting, without much appetite, an enormous and rather stupid canvas depicting an eighteenth-century French painter in his studio. It was painted in a sort of tempera, and in order that I might try the medium, which is agreeably difficult, Sims allowed me to work on it. It was afterwards bought by Lady Cunard. "I painted a bit of that picture," I said to her.

"Oh, Kenneth, how can you tell such disgraceful lies." In 1924 my old friend passed through a classic sequence of triumph and disaster. He was chosen to paint an official portrait of George V, and it was dutifully put on the cover of the *Royal Academy Illustrated*. It was a brilliant work; but unfortunately Sims had been fascinated by the King's very elegant legs and turned-out toes, and had given them undue prominence. King George thought he had been made to look like a ballet dancer and ordered the canvas to be destroyed. It was brought back from America and burned on the Academy's premises. Sims, whose opinion of the establishment had never been high, decided to have no more to do with it. He did a series of pictures which were described as 'mystic', and were an uneasy mixture of Blake and Kandinsky; but from behind the semiabstract clouds there appeared the same sexy girls. How I longed to admire them! But I couldn't do it. Eleventh hour repentances may be theologically acceptable, but they do not work in art. Sims had not found his true self because by that time there was no true self to find. When, a year later, he committed suicide, I was very sad, but not at all surprised. *Mischief,* which is still in the family,*

* *Mischief* became the subject of an Inland Revenue story, so fantastic and, in a way, so touching, that I cannot resist telling it. My father ultimately succeeded in buying the *Mischief* exhibited at the R.A., so that on his death in 1931, he owned two versions of the picture. For some reason, one of them, the second version, was exempted from Estate Duty. In course of time I sold the first for (I think) £11. About fifteen years later I received a letter from the Estate Duty Office charging me with having sold an exempted picture without informing them. I explained the circumstances, and invited the official concerned to visit me in Hampstead, where he would find the exempted *Mischief* still hanging on the walls. As he was stationed in Lytham St Annes, he never came. I could not help sympathising with the chagrin of this exemplary official who had spent almost twenty years tracking down a sale which would have brought into the national finances about £6 10s. 0d., only to find himself foiled by this bizarre coincidence.

remains one of his best pictures, and is perhaps as good as any English picture of its time except a Sickert.

My mother did not altogether share my father's enthusiasm for my vocation although she liked works of art. There were many reasons why she mistrusted artists. *La vie de Bohème* was not for her. And beyond a generalised picture of boozy evenings, there was a personal reason. Her greatest friend, called Mrs Buckley-Jones, had a son by an earlier husband named Heseltine, brother of the great collector of drawings. She was my favourite playmate and a great uninhibitor, who could make even my mother laugh. Her son, Philip, was a musician of considerable talent. Some of his songs, published over the title of Peter Warlock, are about as good as anything in the English music of their time. As a boy he had been gentle and withdrawn; I always remember him on our yacht suffering tortures of sea-sickness, but soldiering on through a score of Purcell. It seemed admirable to me, though ridiculous to the rest of the party. But when he broke loose on the world he developed a strain of combative amorality which made him legendary in the life of the early 'twenties. He was the original of Coleman in Aldous Huxley's *Antic Hay*. His mother was not at all strait-laced, but Phil went too far for anyone brought up in nineteenth-century England, and she used to send my mother long, despairing letters relating all her son's misdoings. My mother would read them at breakfast with ill-disguised relish and when I came in to see her would roll her eyes to heaven, and say in a tragic voice, "Phil's broken out in a new place". Naturally I was not shown the letters, so cannot imagine what the 'new' places were—I should have thought that there couldn't have been more than three. From about 1915 onwards Phil was held up as an awful example of what could happen to me if I became an artist, and I was never allowed to see him; but we kept in touch. With the last sweepings of the Heseltine fortune he had purchased a dying periodical called *The Sackbut, a Magazine for Organists,* and transformed it into a stock-pot for all the tastiest morsels in war-time Bloomsbury—a sort of house-magazine of the Eiffel Tower restaurant. There were stories by Ronald Firbank, erotic drawings by Augustus John, 'very nude' nudes by Gaudier Breszka, and pages of musical score by Bartok, Van Dieren and Kai Koshru Sorabji. It also contained violent attacks by Phil and Gray on the accepted editing of English madrigals, done by a pillar of the musical establishment called Canon Fellowes, with as many concessions to Edwardian taste as Tristram's copies of English mediaeval paintings. I like to imagine the feelings of the old readership of organists, when this spicy dish arrived on their tables. Phil very kindly sent me the *Sackbut,* and I had for the first (and almost the last) time in my life the agreeable feeling of being in the forefront of a movement. Alas, the outrageous jokes of Aldous Huxley's Coleman evidently concealed a profound melancholy, and on Christmas Eve, 1930, having put out the cat, Phil Heseltine put his head into a gas oven.

When I went to Wixenford I already fancied myself as a budding artist, and I was fortunate in that among the pathetic misfits and boozy cynics that comprised the staff, there was a sincere and charming art-master. His name was G. L. Thompson, and he looked like a ship's captain, bronzed, grizzled and round as a barrel. He had been trained in Paris, but had made his livelihood by illustrating children's books of humanised animals. He brought considerable ability to this humble task, far more technical skill than a successful practitioner like Cecil Aldin; but his drawings were without the least personal flavour and were not even funny, so I suppose his publisher dropped him. He was a godsend to me because he taught me the methods of Paris art schools of the 1850's, or for that matter the Florentine art schools of the 1450's. "It's all based on the cube, sonny" he used to say, "the cube, the cone and the cylinder." He would then arrange cubes, cylinders and the occasional cone, in such a way as to suggest a group of houses. This

we would draw with strict attention to perspective*
and the sense of volume. He would then allow us to
make them into a landscape, as pretty and fanciful as
we pleased. When we showed him the result he
would repeat, "All based on models, sonny. The cube,
the cone and the cylinder." Of course he had never
heard of Cézanne. He also encouraged me to copy
and even to do tracings of drawings that I liked, Ingres'
favorite method of teaching, which is far more
difficult and more instructive than one would
suppose. When I left Wixenford I said goodbye to
Thompy with as much emotion as a young person can
feel. I must have asked him what he was going to do,
meaning, I suppose, what book he was going to illustrate. His jolly, smiling face suddenly clouded over.
"One day, sonny, I'll just swim out to sea, and not
come back." I thought no more about it, but this in
fact is what he did, exactly as Sims had done, except
that Sims couldn't swim, and deliberately walked out
into the Firth of Forth, with his pockets full of stones.

If I had been too pleased with my graphic skill
when I arrived at Wixenford, I must have been insuf-
ferably cocky when I arrived at Winchester, because
on my second night one of the prefects, who was
himself an amateur artist, said "Bloody little new man.
Think you know all about art. Sport an arse." Fortunately he was short-sighted and clumsy, as was apparent from his water colours, and his blows were much
less painful than those of the night before. I was not
at all discouraged by this incident. Where life was
concerned I was resigned to the drudgery and discomfort of Winchester College and obediently rose
half-an-hour before anyone else to clean eighteen pairs
of prefects' boots, and six pairs of brown shoes. But
where art was concerned I was irrepressible.

I had recently discovered Whistler's *Gentle Art of
Making Enemies* and his cheeky replies inwardly sus-
tained my Wixenford impudence. I knew long passages out of the *Ten O'Clock Lecture* by heart. So the

* Empirical perspective, not *costruzione legitima,* which I
have never mastered.

day after the artist-prefect had taken his premature revenge on the budding critic I trotted down Kingsgate Street to call on the art master. He lived in a small, irregular seventeenth-century house and as I entered his sitting-room I saw on his walls two of the finest prints of Utamaro, *The Water Carriers* and the Awabi *Pearl Fishers*. His name was Macdonald, and he was the son of Alexander Macdonald, whom Ruskin had appointed as the first master of the art school that he founded, at his own expense, when he was Slade Professor at Oxford. Ruskin's first master was still alive, and used to visit his son. I frequently went out drawing with him, so that I have a living link with the greatest member of my profession. The son was a kindly, agreeable person, but the laziest man I have ever known. In his youth he had a certain talent as a pastellist and a few sensitive drawings hung in his studio. But he had long ago 'packed it in', and spent his life sitting by the window dozing, with a volume of Pepys' Diary upside down on his knee. Art was a voluntary subject and his pupils had dwindled to about three, so he seldom found the energy to visit the drawing school. He must have been dismayed by the appearance of an eager pupil. However, my unbounded delight in his two Utamaros won his heart. "Come next Sunday", he said, "I have some more in those drawers". He pointed to a Sheraton bureau. He had, in fact, one of the choicest collection of Japanese prints I have ever seen. Sunday after Sunday a new drawer would be opened. At first it was a series of Utamaros, in mint condition, the ones on the wall being hung there precisely because they were slightly faded; then we moved on to a drawer full of Harunobo; then Kyonaga and Yeishi, Shunsho, Shigemasa and Koriusai, then the landscapists, noble Hokusai and some remarkable prints by the rare, uneven Kunyoshi. And finally, as a *bonne bouche,* a fabulous collection of *Surimonos.* These Sunday afternoons with Mr Macdonald's Japanese prints were amongst the happiest and most formative in my life. They confirmed my belief that nothing could destroy me as long as I could enjoy works of art, and for 'enjoy' read 'enjoy': not codify or classify, or purge my spirit or arouse my social consciousness, just enjoy. From this hedonist, or at best epicurean, position I have never departed. It is true that I have tried to communicate my pleasure to other people, but that is not because I feel it my duty to do so, but simply because I cannot contain myself.

The drawing school at Winchester was a small, ill-proportioned room in the only ugly building in 'Meads', known as the Museum. It contained a shelf full of casts, most of which were from the hand of the great Italian forger of *quattrocento* portraits, Bastianini. On account of their academic naturalism, these nineteenth-century imitations were more to the taste of art teachers than genuine works by Donatello, Desiderio da Settignano or Rossellino, all of which would have had too strong an imprint of style. There was also Houdon's *Voltaire,* and a somewhat sickly head of a girl, said to be from a death mask in the Morgue, but obviously worked up to commercial standards by some sentimental academician. In the museum proper were casts of more reputable pieces, including Donatello's *David*, panels from Luca della Robbia's *Cantoria* and *The Dancing Faun*. Mr Macdonald's only instruction was to tell me to draw these unappetising objects with an HB pencil. I drew them all dozens of times from every angle. The Bastianinis were the easiest, *The Dancing Faun* the most difficult. I won the school drawing prize every year I was at Winchester College, but as I was almost the only pupil this is not an indication of merit. Some drawings of casts that I recently discovered in a battered folder are careful, timid and commonplace—real prize winners. A ridiculous system, I suppose. But in so far as I was to become an art-historian, and not an artist, this was probably the best course of instruction I could have had. I was doing prescisely what young Florentines are shown doing in the famous engravings of Bandinelli's academy. Coming after Thompy's *corpi regolari,* I learnt the meaning of *disegno* in a way that

I should never have done if I had been given half-a-dozen pots of poster colours and asked to paint something I had dreamt about the night before.

※

One of my most intelligent friends believes that our appreciation of natural beauty is aroused only when it has been revealed to us by the work of a great painter: that nobody ever thought the rocky hills of Provence beautiful before Cézanne, or the flat fields of Holland even tolerable before Ruysdael. There is a grain of truth in this paradox, but I remember clearly that the examples of natural beauty that first moved me, and aroused in me very much the same emotions as the Japanese screens at the White City, in almost the same year, do not seem to have been related in any way to works of art I had seen. The long, irregular line of the street that winds down from Orford Church to the harbour gave me (and still gives me) inexplicable pleasure, although I can think of nothing like it in painting. The sight of the yachts on the Alde delighted me long before I had seen an impressionist picture. Equally with architecture, and I am reluctant to consider architecture independently of its setting, I fell in love with the Maltings at Snape at the age of seven, although no one had told me that there was anything remarkable about them; indeed no one seemed to have mentioned them till Benjamin Britten decided to build his concert hall there. Heaven knows what scraps of imagery feed the unconscious mind. I may have seen photographs of old buildings and cathedrals in the *Illustrated London News* or *Country Life,* and so have prepared my mind to think them beautiful. But, except for Orford Church, I had never seen them in reality. So when, on my first half-holiday, I walked through the close to Winchester Cathedral, I was bowled over. Nothing had prepared me for such a sequence of contrasting styles, each beautiful in itself, and yet palpably harmonious. Quick, my sketch-book; and I sat down to draw the ruined Romanesque arches beside the south transept. Down went the square and the cylinder, embellished with some picturesque trimmings which I must have got from reproductions of early Turners seen in a back number of *The Connoisseur*. Thenceforward drawing the architecture that surrounded me in the close, in College and in Saint Cross became my whole ambition, to the exclusion, as far as possible, of games and, to a certain extent, of work. And by a great stroke of luck two artists of real distinction had made a habit of visiting Winchester during those years. One of them was Albert Goodwin, the heir to Samuel Palmer, Ruskin and all the twilight poets of the English watercolour school. The other was Muirhead Bone, the greatest virtuoso of architectural drawing since Piranesi except, perhaps, for Meryon*. Painting with Albert Goodwin, the planes bending over the stream in the Warden's garden, trailing their leaves in its impetuous water, I experienced, in a diluted form, the emotions so beautifully described by Ruskin in *Praeterita*. The skill of Muirhead Bone I could not begin to imitate, but he helped me in another way—by his generous catholicity of taste. Mr Macdonald would not allow that even the early work of the impressionists was eligible for imitation (how do otherwise sensible men enclose themselves in such labyrinths of prejudice!), whereas Muirhead Bone was a close friend of Epstein, and when, twenty years later, I showed him drawings by Henry Moore and Graham Sutherland, he immediately recognised their quality. We remained close friends till his death in 1953, and I will always remember him as one of the most honest, warmhearted and unselfish men I have ever known.

Sensible people often say that schoolboys derive no benefit from fine architecture, and it is indeed true that most schoolmasters and Fellows of Oxford colleges seem to be blind to any form of art. I can only say that the beauty of the buildings at Win-

---

* I refer only to technical skill. As a critic of life Meryon was in a different class. Bone was eupeptic, Meryon tragic.

chester penetrated my spirit and had an influence that went beyond immediate pleasure. The gothic chantry and its surrounding cloisters were my favourites: there one could immerse oneself in the gothic spirit, as if one were peering into the backgrounds of the *Très Riches Heures*. But I loved almost equally the foursquare 'Wren' building, known as School, and even had the innocence, or freedom from prejudice, to admire Butterfield's Moberly Library. The only thing that disappointed me was the interior of the Chapel. Not only had the choir stalls been removed—sold as old junk—but the stained glass prophets who filled the side windows were green and purple monsters with beaky noses and staring eyes. After a good deal of trouble I learnt the explanation of this dateless ugliness. The Chapel was originally decorated with a set of windows made in about 1380 by a glazier called Thomas of Oxford. It must have been one of the most complete ensembles of fourteenth-century glass in the world. In 1821 a surveyor reported that the glass was deteriorating, and the Fellows had it taken out and sent to a firm called Betton and Evans, who undertook 'to restore the glass to its original brilliancy'. After a year or two they persuaded the Fellows to let them make a new set, which was described as a close imitation of ancient painted glass, in colouring, drawing and arrangement that has probably no rival'. The old glass from the Chapel was sold by Messrs. Betton and Evans. I suppose they thought that they were acting for the best: those were the days when whole west fronts of cathedrals were taken down and nineteenth-century sculpture put there instead. I discovered that a certain amount of the original glass was still in existence, scattered in private chapels and collections, ánd I used to think, while listening to a dull sermon, that nothing else in the world would give me so much happiness as to get back some of the glass for Chapel. Thirty years later a few pieces of the Jesse Window in a private chapel at Ettington were offered for sale at a price I could afford. I have never written a cheque with greater emotion.*

I presented the glass to College anonymously because I wished it to be associated with only one name —Montague John Rendall, who had been headmaster all the time that I was there. He was a personage so exceptional as to deserve a digression. He was a tall, handsome man with what can only be described as a magnificent presence, large romantic eyes and a flourishing moustache. His speech was a kind of stressed incantation, as of a poet reading his own works, and was punctuated by unpredictable snorts. All Wykehamists of that date tried to imitate him, but none could capture the chivalric quality of his intonation, which was the expression of a genuinely quixotic frame of mind. One felt that at any moment his speech might turn into old provençal. In every way he belonged to the nineteenth century and seemed to unite in himself two of its disparate movements, the muscular Christianity of Charles Kingsley and the aestheticism of the preRaphaelites—a union well expressed in the legend that he had bicycled up the hill of Assisi. There was an element of absurdity in him, but a far more considerable element of greatness, and it is much to the credit of the governing body that they recognised this and made him headmaster. The more commonplace members of the staff must have been outraged, and he did nothing to placate them. He loved the black sheep of the flock. When my housemaster forbade a friend of mine from playing at the school concert on account of his decadent appearance, Rendall said "You shall come and play alone to me". When Jelly d'Aranyi, young and beautiful, came to play to the school, as she often did, Rendall would escort her on to the platform with his

---

* The fragments have been most skilfully cleaned and installed in the window of an annexe to a chapel built by Butterfield, called Thorburn's Chantry. Other pieces are in America, and three of the original saints are in the Victoria and Albert Museum, not as ugly as their successors, although far from ingratiating.

arm round her waist, and say "Here's me little gypsy!"
He was shamelessly unconventional. On one occasion,
when he wanted to interview a new cook, he arranged to meet her on the platform of Reading station. He travelled on the school train which was taking
the boys back to London for the holidays. At Reading
we were astonished to see him get out and put a red
flower in his mouth. It was the agreed method of
identification, and in a few seconds a buxom middle-
aged lady, with a red flower in *her* mouth, advanced
towards him along the platform. As we did not know
that she was a prospective cook we were delighted
by the whole episode. Whether he engaged her or
not is unimportant, as the food in a headmaster's house
is always uneatable. I remember dining there with
two or three guests, including a young man with
glasses and a shock of red hair, who never stopped
talking for a second. Suddenly he picked up his plate
and said "This won't do—I'm going down to the
kitchen". We were glad of a few minutes respite, but
our red-haired guest soon returned, defeated, and began to talk as he entered the room. His name was
Brendan Bracken.

As a good Victorian, Rendall had a passion for Italy
and Italian art, and during the winter terms he gave
lantern lectures on his favourite artists. I can never
describe what these lectures meant to me. I had been
brought up on the realistic art of a godless bourgeoisie.
The very existence of religious art was virtually
unknown to me. I suppose that some of the other members of his small audience were in the same condition, so Rendall rightly began his series with a lecture
on Saint Francis of Assisi. It was for me like a religious
conversion, and if any reader of this page chanced to
watch the third programme in my *Civilisation* series,
he will have heard a not so distant echo of Monty
Rendall. This was followed by lectures on Fra Angelico, Pisanello, Botticelli and Bellini. This last was
based on a good little book by Roger Fry, and I suppose the Botticelli was derived from Herbert Horne's
archaic masterpiece. But the Pisanello lecture was

original and wholly enjoyable, because Rendall made
the portrait medals a pretext for talking about the
great teachers and schoolmasters of the Renaissance
—Vittorino de Feltre, Guarino da Verona. With what
persuasive eloquence did he describe that mixture
of learning, courtesy and fair play, which seemed to
him the ideal of a gentleman, either in Mantua, or
Winchester College. To supplement these lectures,
Rendall had installed in the 'museum' large wooden
cases of photographs—the admirable old prints of
Brogi, Alinari and Braun—mounted on board and
hinged. They were chiefly of Italians, and Rendall
himself had written notes to them in which the name
of Berenson sometimes appeared, and thus entered
my consciousness for the first time. These cases took
the place of my book on the Louvre as my chief
sources of education. Some years ago, on visiting Winchester College after a long absence I asked to see
them again. Nobody could recollect their existence.
Finally someone remembered that they had been
thrown away, not because they were worn out but
because 'they seemed to serve no useful purpose',
i.e. appealed only to an inconsiderable minority. It
was interesting to find that Winchester College, which
was once supposed to stand for an exaggerated attachment to tradition, had accepted so readily the
modern concept of education. But I suppose that
Rendall's belief in art (like Reith's belief in moral
values) was regarded as the caprice of a slightly un-
balanced individual, and could not long survive his
departure. Incidentally, Rendall composed the Latin
inscription in the entrance hall of Broadcasting House
—*Deo Omnipotenti*—*Templum hoc Artium et Mu-
sarum Anno Domini MCXXXI Rectore Iohanni Reith
. . .*—which Reith asked to have removed ('dyna-
mited' was his word to me) soon after his retirement
as Director General of the B.B.C. It is still there.

Rendall enriched my life in another way, through
the institution known to Wykehamists as Shrogus,
which stands for Shakespeare Reading and Orpheus
Glee Singing Society. I never heard the sound of an

orphic glee, but two or three times a term we met in
Rendall's dining-room to read a play by Shakespeare.
My own reading of Shakespeare had begun at Sudbourne when my mother had given me *King John*
and *Richard II* to read. At that date, when adultery
was spoken of as a fate worse than death, the histories
were considered suitable reading for the young and
the putting out of Arthur's eyes or the murder of
Richard II less shocking than the amorous or frolic-
some passages in the comedies. I enjoyed the language,
but how can a small boy understand the character of Richard II or sympathise with all that nonsense about the Divine Right of Kings. My first real
experience of Shakespeare was when I read *King Lear*.
It happened, most unsuitably, at Cap Martin, so the
date cannot have been later than 1916. I was awed,
crushed, elated and sleepless with excitement. The
storm scenes where, out of a counterpoint of feigned
madness, real madness and professional simple-
mindedness, there emerge miracles of wisdom and
poetic insight, gave me an entirely new notion of
the power of the human mind. I have always believed
that the brain is at its most active at the age of twelve
or thirteen (recent experiments seem to have confirmed this), and although I had no empirical knowledge with which to measure the truth of what I read,
my intuitive understanding was probably more vivid
than it would be today.

So as soon as I was eligible to attend the meetings
of Shrogus, I obtained the reluctant permission of my
housemaster (fortunately philistines have to swallow
Shakespeare owing to the Agincourt speech in *Henry
V*), and never missed a meeting. I must have listened
to and performed in about twenty plays of Shakespeare. The readings had their ridiculous side. Rendall
sat in the middle of a long table and read the principal male parts—Anthony, Macbeth, King Lear and
so forth; but there were often minor parts that he
could not resist, for example the fairies in *A Mid-
summer Night's Dream,* and these he would read in
a diminished sing-song, wagging an enormous finger.

When in *Anthony and Cleopatra,* we came to the drinking song 'Come thou monarch of the vine Plumpy Bacchus with pink eyen', Rendall was so delighted by the word 'plumpy' that he continued to intone it long after the song was over 'Plumpy, plumpy, plumpy'. On his right sat the most charming boy in College, who read with varying success the leading female roles. The rest of us applied for such parts as we fancied. A good Wykehamist does not like to make an exhibition of himself, so the secretary was glad to unload on me the kind of parts I preferred—Edgar, Shallow, the porter in Macbeth, Caliban. As I was a complete nonentity I had nothing to lose by making a fool of myself. The porter in *Macbeth* nearly brought about my downfall as I read it with a genuine Highland accent. No one present had ever heard a Highland accent and expected it to be played in Harry Lauder scots; they thought my accent was Welsh (which, historically, it is), and I was severely reprimanded. Caliban was my favourite part, and Rendall was at his best as Prospero. I may add that the soubrette parts were played by a little rolypoly boy named Richard Crossman.

Figures that have seemed gigantic in one's boyhood, often appear to be pathetically diminished when one meets them in later life. But not Rendall. I saw him several times, and visited him when he had retired to the Gate House of Butley Priory, with its splendid armorial of flint and stone. On the last occasion he must have been almost ninety, but he was erect and courteous as ever, and his aura of greatness had not faded. A few years after his death Jane and I went to place some flowers on his grave in the churchyard of Great Rollright, a north Oxfordshire parish where his father had been rector. Of course there was no one about, and no answer to the rectory bell. Finally, we discovered a sacristan; he had some recollection of burying a man named Rendall, but no idea of where his grave could be. We put out flowers on a fairly recent grave, and departed.

I was ill in bed several times during my first year

at Winchester, and these occasions must be counted as the only times at which I learnt anything of lasting value. The reason was that my housemaster's wife, who, as I have said, was as sweet and sympathetic as her husband was obdurate, used to bring me books. She had a complete set of the *Studio*. I began at the first volume; and there was Aubrey Beardsley; I got on to 1903 and there were the watercolours of Whistler. These were to become the dominant influences on my own feeble attempts for several years. She also lent me a book which had a far more lasting effect—*Turner's Golden Visions* by C. Lewis Hind. I have it still, and find that the reproductions of watercolours are fairly good, even by modern standards. Turner was derided by the critics whom I then admired, Roger Fry and Clive Bell, but the watercolours and seascapes were so ravishingly beautiful and so unassailably true, that for the first time I began to doubt my mentors. Turner was inimitable; whereas Whistler and Beardsley were imitable and I settled down to imitate them. I had read the Pennells' hero-worshipping Life, and wanted to admire Whistler as much as they did; but had been secretly disappointed by the etchings and most of the portraits. However, when I saw coloured reproductions of the sea-side watercolours and shop fronts in Limehouse and Amsterdam, I was enchanted. One of them, called *The Convalescent,* became almost my favourite work of art, and when today I see the original in the house of a friend, I can hardly look at it without blubbing. I suppose that the ingredients are rather too slight for the cooking, but I must confess that I prefer the light-weight artist who gets it right to the heavy-weight who thrashes around with a great display of emotion, but does not hit the target. It is a fault in my character. Beardsley is a different problem. I have never lost my early admiration for him, and a few years ago I could not resist giving a lecture about him in Aldeburgh. As I came in I heard people saying, "Who is this extraordinary man he's talking about—some sort of wishy-washy pre-Raphaelite, I believe". Within a year there was an hysterically successful Beardsley exhibition at the Victoria and Albert Museum (planned before my lecture), Beardsley decors began to appear in every Chelsea boutique, Beardsley dresses were advertised in *Vogue;* then the fashion ended, as suddenly and as mysteriously as it had begun.

Beardsley seems to be like some sort of short acting, but highly potent drug, strong enough to have intoxicated much greater artists like Münch and Paul Klee, to say nothing of a host of mediocrities. What gives this drug its power? Beardsley's art distilled an essence like one of those tiny phials of scent sold at the door of a mosque, which if you remove the stopper fills the whole courtyard with its godless, irresistible perfume. To drop the metaphor, he used his uncanny skill as a draughtsman and his mastery of simplified pattern to create hieroglyphs of evil, and in particular of sexual depravity, which catch us unprepared and so print themselves on our minds, when the obvious sexual stimuli on the covers of paperbacks merely sicken or repel. In the end Roger Fry was right when he called Beardsley the Fra Angelico of diabolism. The curious thing is that I should have felt all this at the age of thirteen; for it was not the curves of thighs and breasts that fascinated me, but the faces where, with exquisite economy, Beardsley concentrated the record of a thousand soul-destroying experiences and a mischievous will to corrupt. How could a sheltered little boy recognise the meaning of those sidelong glances, those depraved pouches and those dangerously short upper lips?

I was not ill for long enough. Turner and Whistler receded, and I was back to the grind of exercise, devised by schoolmasters in vain hope of tiring the boys out so that they should be less of a nuisance. Curiously enough, I became fond of running, partly because my emaciated body was so light that my legs could carry me without fatigue. There is a joy in this disembodied state that I remember, in my present gross condition, when I read about the rewards of asceticism. One day after my weekly run round Hills

I felt an uncomfortable pain in my chest, and later in the evening I fainted. I was found to have pneumonia and removed to the school hospital. After a reasonable interval my parents sent down their doctor, Bertrand Dawson, to look me over. He was a friend of the family and, whatever his qualifications in the higher branches of medical science, he was a wise and humane man. He saw that the rigours of wartime Winchester had been too much for me and advised my parents to let me spend a term at home.

I can imagine how much this proposal must have dismayed them, especially as Lam was no longer available, and by this time in the war (it must have been the spring of 1917) they could not escape abroad. They had moved to a small house in Bath near to Beckford's tower, and my father spent almost the whole day at the club playing bridge and billiards. How my mother spent her time I cannot imagine, for Bath in those days appeared to be inhabited solely by very old people, none of whom she knew. Indeed I cannot remember a single visitor or neighbour ever entering our house, except for the local doctor who seems, in retrospect, to have been like a character in the Commedia del'Arte. This suited me perfectly, for now at last I had the opportunity of educating myself. We had a large bookcase full of books which I had myself selected from the library at Sudbourne. I had felt it obligatory to bring a number of novels, as they were then almost the only books read by ordinary people, and I did my best to read some of them. I remember being genuinely moved by *The Return of the Native*, pleased with myself for having enjoyed *The Ordeal of Richard Feverel,* bored by *The Egoist* and haunted (as I am to this day) by Conrad's *Heart of Darkness*. But even at that age I was no novel reader. I suppose that most young people read novels as a short cut to growing up. By living other people's lives they achieve vicarious experience. I did not want experience of life. I wanted information. So what I valued most in the bookcase was the eleventh edition of the *Encyclopaedia Britannica*. It is

indeed a masterly piece of editing, for it retains the
best of the old articles—Macaulay's splendid eulogy of
Pitt and Swinburne's 'rave notice' of Victor Hugo;
Mark Pattison on Grotius and Erasmus, and contribu-
tions from the best critics of the nineties—Gosse,
Leslie Stephen, Morley and John Addington Symonds,
all doing their best, which subsequent contributors
to encyclopedias have not done. The articles on music
and musicians were by one of the greatest of all music
critics, Donald Tovey. In consequence, one leaps from
one subject to another, fascinated as much by the play
of mind and the idiosyncrasies of the authors as by the
facts and dates. It must be the last encyclopedia in the
tradition of Diderot which assumes that information
can be made memorable only when it is slightly coloured by prejudice. When T. S. Eliot wrote 'Soul
curled up on the window seat reading the Encyclopedia
Britannica' he was certainly thinking of the eleventh
edition, and he accurately describes my condition.

I read hundreds of entries, including many, like
Note or Number, of which I could hardly understand
a word. My mind was in a plastic condition, and for
the last time I was able to remember a good deal of
what I read. When today I bore or surprise a companion with a piece of useless information, it is probably something that I read in Bath during my term
away from school.

My other great source of happiness was my pianola.
I had been brought up without music. My father
sometimes started to sing a song that began with the
words 'Am I a man or am I a mouse', at which
point my mother would say "I hope he doesn't get
as far as the lodger". He never did, so the subject of
the song remains mysterious. My parents refused to
let me learn the piano, as they rightly thought that
the sound of my practising would annoy them, and
my mother really hated the sound of music, because
it affected her emotions. Only my grandmother would
let me play to her the pianola organ at Sudbourne,
and said that she would like to die with the sound
of Rossini's *Stabat Mater* in her ears. However, in

Bath I could play the pianola to my heart's content when my parents were out of the house. It was the old push-on variety that gave the executant much more control than the later one-piece model. I took my interpretations very seriously, but as I had never heard a live pianist, except in school concerts, they must have been very peculiar. There was a music shop in Milsom Street which had a lending library of pianola rolls and also of scores. The girl in the back of the music shop where the pianola rolls lived was my only friend in Bath. Fortunately she was very plain. Twice a week I trotted down the hill and came back with two new rolls and the appropriate score, which I propped up on the pianola in front of me. This will seem ridiculous to any serious musician, just as learning Latin from a crib seems despicable to a serious classical scholar. But in no other way could I have learnt even the rudiments of music, or been able to follow a score. The choice of rolls was limited, but there was a good selection of Chopin, Schubert and Schumann. I made my way conscientiously through Beethoven's sonatas, but was often a good deal bored. I recognised the transparent beauty of Mozart's sonatas but had the sense to see that they could not be played on the pianola, as it was impossible to achieve the kind of delicate phrasing upon which they depend. At the other end of the scale, in the joke department, were pieces that I pedalled through in a state of euphoria, Liszt's Hungarian Rhapsodies, and the pianola renditions of famous orchestral pieces, even operas. Many of these had been specially written for the Pianola Company by Busoni and had real pianistic quality. They must have been practically unplayable by the human hand, but made a glorious noise, and were reserved for times when my mother was out shopping. In the end it was Chopin who won my lifelong devotion—that fabulous craftsman, that Leopardi of music, who could apply the labour of the file to his deepest emotions, and bring them out fresh, sparkling and deceptively gay. When many years later I read Delacroix's description of his *Caro Chopinetto,* 'a bird of brilliant plumage hovering over the abyss', I recaptured exactly my feelings as I pedalled away at my pianola in Bath.

My walks into Bath had other joys for me. I loved the architecture, I swam in the warm water, I pottered round the antique shops and bought a hideous *netsuke* of which I was very proud. But my great discovery was the Victoria Art Gallery. This normally not very interesting collection had, owing to fear of war damage, been strengthened by a number of loans. Amongst them was the little Hugo van der Goes from Wilton, which was the first fifteenth-century picture I had ever seen in the original; and, even more of a revelation, a group of pictures by Manet, Monet and Cézanne which had been lent by the Misses Davies. These self-effacing ladies, under the advice of an eccentric collector-dealer named Hugh Blaker, had made one of the first collections of post-impressionist painting in Britain. Its quality may be judged by those who visit the Cardiff gallery today. The Manets meant nothing to me; and Monet's cathedrals left me as baffled then as they do now; but the Cézannes were a knock-out blow. One landscape, in particular, gave me the strongest aesthetic shock I had ever received from a picture. I could not keep away from it, and went down the hill to see it almost every day. There was an outbreak of mumps in the town and I was forbidden to go in. For once in my life I disobeyed instructions and confessed that I had done so. My mother made a dreadful scene—"If you are going to begin deceiving your parents etc."—the first I had ever experienced, and almost the last. In fact I caught the mumps, which was not as painful as the row.

The war ended on November 11th, 1918; the armistice was announced at eleven o'clock, and at that moment the train to Bath, in which my mother and I were seated, steamed out of Paddington Station. "How fortunate", said my mother, "we shall miss the worst of the celebrations", and, sure enough, by the time we arrived the rejoicings, less demonstrative perhaps in Bath than anywhere else in the country, had died

71

down. The end of the war made no difference to our life at home; but it did affect me personally in one life-giving way; it brought the Russian Ballet to London. Dozens of writers have tried to convey the excitement of the first Diaghilev season. In 1918 the ballet was less of a shock than it had been in 1912, and it lacked, of course, the electrifying personality of Nijinsky. But for me it had the great fascination that during Diaghilev's long exile from Russia he had made friends with the leaders of contemporary French painting. Daily conversations with Picasso, and I suppose Cocteau, had made the ballet no longer Russian but international. As a result the former Russian favourites like *Scheherazade* and *Prince Igor* had already begun to look old-fashioned, although Diaghilev was able to retain a Russian flavour through the disarming primitivism of Larionov and Gontcharova.

The first Russian ballet I saw, *Children's Tales,* was designed by Larionov, and in a moment I was transported. Poor old Mr Macdonald, with his weeping willows and mossy stones! I immediately attempted the bold flat colour of Diaghilev's decors, for which I had no talent at all. I remember showing one of my efforts to Mr Macdonald, who said kindly, "It's no good asking me to look at that sort of thing". But it was an intoxication, stronger even than Beardsley, which grew when I saw *Boutique Fantasque* and *Tricorne.* And here let me say that these early productions were incomparably more beautiful than later revivals. The reader will think that this merely reflects the enthusiasm of youth, but I have an unusually accurate visual memory and I could describe the changes of lighting or colour that were later to deprive ballets like *Boutique* of their unforgettable beauty. By a happy accident I was able to continue my visits to the ballet during term time. I had irregular front teeth and wore a plate, which had to be adjusted once a fortnight. It was painful and had no effect on my teeth which are still irregular and ugly. But it gave me an excuse for going to London. Normally my housemaster would have refused to let me go but, either because of the authority of Lord Dawson or because he had given me up as a bad job, he gave me leave. I went to the dentist in the lunch hour and to a matinée of the ballet immediately afterwards. The season took place in the old Alhambra music-hall, the most comfortable theatre in London, decorated extravagantly in the Moorish style—a perfect setting for *Scheherazade, Thamar* and *Firebird.* As an escape from the post-war rigours of Winchester College, the austere dormitories, the sordid corridors and the two lavatories that served for the whole house, this was a dream-world.

I had a friend in my 'house' with whom to share my enthusiasm for the Russian Ballet and modern art in general. He was a year or two older than me, half American and very much more precocious. He was a figure out of *The Yellow Book,* to which his aunt was one of the earliest contributors. One could imagine his face changing into Beardsley's *Tannhäuser* returning to the Venusberg. He was kind and gentle to me, but I always felt that he belonged to a different species. And here I must make a confession that psychologists and advanced educationalists will regard as shameful. I have never felt the faintest inclination to homosexuality. I realise that it is natural for young people to form emotional and sometimes physical attachments to members of their own sex, partly out of a fear of the unknown, partly from the structure of our educational system. For some reason I never did so. I was not one of those plump and pretty little boys who attract the attention of their elders, and I never fell in love with my contemporaries. I do not think this can be explained by emotional poverty or lack of vitality, but by the fact that my premature devotion to the girls was so strong as to fill my fantasy-world and leave no room for homosexual attachments. I was also exceedingly naïve. I had a vague notion that homosexual practices were going on around me, but I thought of them in the same kind of insubstantial way that one believes in ghosts. This abnormality of mine had the bad result of increasing my isolation. Most of the young men who shared my interests, both at school and at Oxford, were, temporarily at least, homosexuals, and I was to some extent cut off from them. Whether it turned out so badly in the end I cannot say. I must add that they always treated me with the greatest tact. Mature homosexuals sometimes complain of the lack of sympathy shown them by ordinary men. May I try to redress the balance by recording the remarkable sympathy and kindness that a confirmed heterosexual has always received from those of another persuasion.

What with the excitement of the Russian Ballet and the first onset of contemporary painting, I cannot say that my middle years at Winchester were unrewarding. But I never could reconcile myself to the bleakness and squalor of school conditions. I can put up with discomfort and austerity—I can put up with almost anything—but it is not my natural habitat. Even under the worst circumstances I continue to make myself fairly comfortable, and to surround myself with things I like, be it only a few postcards. I am at one with the wren and the bower bird; I like building a nest, and do not care for the de-personalised habits of those birds who lay their eggs on open ground. No doubt to be free from the pull of comfort and to be indifferent to one's surroundings is a source of strength, especially for men of action like T. E. Lawrence and saints like S Carlo Borromeo. I doubt if it is a desirable condition for an aesthete (although I believe that Mr Pater lived very simply) because he needs continuously to refresh and externalise his inner conviction of harmony through sensuous responses.

I was brought up surrounded by *objets de luxe.* My mother had what was known as 'good taste', and she was very fond of old Mr Mallett, known as Downey Mallett, as opposed to his admirable, but less seductive, son-in-law Snookey Mallett. My mother always said she hated sycophants, but if anyone flattered her in the right way it gave her more pleasure than almost anything else in her rather mournful existence. In consequence we paid many visits to Mallett's establishments both in London and Bath. My parents bought a lot of furniture in the eighteenth-century style, which was not always as old as it appeared to be, and a good collection of English porcelain. From an early age I played on the floor with gold anchor Chelsea figures, re-arranged the green Worcester (now at Luton Hoo) and loved the perfection of Kang Hsi porcelain. These became my toys; and to this day I arrange small *objets d'art* as if they were talking to each other.

Unfortunately for me Winchester is one of the few English boarding schools which does not allow the boys rooms of their own. We all sat in the same large enclosure, round the walls of which were small partitions (known as toyes), like uncomfortable polling booths, with just enough room for two shelves, one to serve as a seat and the other as a desk. For the first year one was not allowed any form of cushion, and as one's bottom was already sore from frequent beating it was extremely uncomfortable. Fortunately for me I had a luxury bolt hole within bicycling distance of Winchester, a pleasant eighteenth-century manor house at Sutton Scotney, belonging to some old friends of the family. When I entered their carpeted rooms and sat in a comfortable chair I purred with contentment. I suppose I went there far too often and only now that I am old do I realise what a nuisance I must have been to them. The young imagine that they are always welcome. I remember E. M. Forster telling me how, as a child, he went to call on some neighbours and misjudged the time. 'How pleased they'll be to see me so early', he thought. In this respect I am afraid I have never grown up, and always imagine that people will be pleased to see me, although I am by no means always pleased to see other people. My friends at Sutton Scotney showed no signs of impatience when I arrived, gave me china tea in porcelain cups and very thin cucumber sandwiches. It was a life-line to my Edwardian childhood.

There were practically no art books in the school library, except for the collected works of Ruskin in the great Cook & Wedderburn edition. I turned over the pages day after day, enjoyed the illustrations, and fell in love with an unfinished portrait by Sir Joshua Reynolds of a lady with a brooch. Ruskin characteristically included it as an illustration to a lecture on landscape painting. It belonged to him, and when his heirs, the Severns, sold his effects at Sotheby's in 1928 I was able to buy it. It is as beautiful as I thought. I did my best to read Ruskin's writings, but without someone to guide me they were incomprehensible. I expected them to be about art. Instead they were about glaciers and clouds, plants and crystals, political economy and morals—subjects which I cannot understand to this day. Even the prose style seemed to me then turgid and over-insistent. It was a relief to turn to the clear contemporary language of Roger Fry, whose skill in analysing the components of a design, be it a drawing by Daumier, a painting by Poussin or a Ch'ang bronze, was the finest education in art-criticism I ever received. I blush to say that for a short time I was even more influenced by Clive Bell, especially by a book called *Potboilers*. His jaunty, cock-sure style seemed just the thing with which to tease my masters in my own essays. But his book called *Art* seemed too exclusively 'Are you saved?': it didn't at all suit my own omnivorous appetite, and when I came to the historical passages that dismiss all painting between Giotto and Cézanne as an aberration, I suddenly thought 'This man is an impostor' (not that he was, dear Clive; he was a genuine lover of art and the gayest companion).

I also read the famous introductions to Berenson's small volumes of 'Authentic' pictures, *The Florentine Painters* and the *Central Italian Painters*. I was introduced to them by a cousin, an enormously fat man who had a taste for art and had formed a small collection of 'old masters'. He took an interest in me and allowed me to stay in his flat above Christies in King

Street, which I much enjoyed, as his corrupt valet produced black-market food. Berenson's essays, in spite of their unidiomatic English, made a deep impression on me. I saw that he was really trying to give an explanation for the sensations which Clive Bell had glossed over with the catchpenny phrase 'significant form'. His theories did not altogether satisfy me, but they gave me sleepless nights, always a sure sign that something revolutionary is happening to me. I followed this up by reading some of Berenson's other works and was, as so many other people were, impressed by their dogmatic tone. Indeed, I must have been very much impressed, because I remember that one day, when walking back from chapel, my companion, named Venables (later a Catholic priest), asked me what I would like to do when I left school, to which I replied, "Help Mr Berenson to produce a new edition of his book on the drawings of the Florentine painters". My housemaster (the second one), whom I had not observed walking just behind us, overheard the remark and said, "Bloody little prig". Quite right: it was a disgustingly self-satisfied remark for a boy of sixteen to make. But it had a curious sequel, which the reader will find on pp. 130-131.

In spite of this interest in connoisseurship I continued to think of myself as an artist. But I had got into a terrible muddle. At the Canadian War Artists' exhibition of 1917 I had seen two large pictures, Wyndham Lewis's *Howitzer* and William Roberts' *Gas Attack,** which had been an eye-opener to me,

---

* After the war these, and many other interesting pictures commissioned by the Canadian Government under the influence of Frank Rutter, and through the agency of Lord Beaverbrook, were sent back to Canada and put into a store in Ottawa, from which they had still not emerged when I visited Canada in the 1950's. As I was the guest of the Governor-General, Vincent Massey, it was possible to have the store located and, very reluctantly, unlocked. The dusty pictures were hauled out of their racks and I recognised that, whereas Roberts' *Gas Attack* was a very remarkable work, Wyndham Lewis's *Howitzer* was bogus and had 'conned' me by its effective simplifications.

and I immediately tried to imitate them. In fact vorticism would have suited my laborious style much more than the fanciful warmth of Larionov and I might have been a follower of Wyndham Lewis (although he would certainly have rejected me) had not a new ingredient been thrown into the macédoine— Matisse.

It must be hard for the modern reader to realise how cut off we were in England, even as late as 1920, from the contemporary movements on the continent. One could search through the bookshops of the Charing Cross Road without finding a single reproduction of a Matisse, a Picasso or a Braque. I remember on the night before the opening of the Matisse exhibition at the Leicester Galleries in 1919 I could hardly sleep for excitement and, when I did, I dreamed of what a Matisse would be like. In my dream it was a fuzzy, pointillist picture, something like a le Sidaner. My astonishment when I saw the originals was all the greater for this prelude, and for a few minutes I was put out by the asymmetry of the heads and the crudity of the actual painting. Then I began to see that the distortions 'denoted a foregone conclusion', and the simplicity of handling was due to a rigorous determination to combine intellectual economy with an apparent spontaneity. I went home determined to paint like Matisse. I must confess that part of their charm for me was that they looked rather easy to do, especially the landscapes. The results may be imagined.

Since I have mentioned the Leicester Galleries, this may be the place to say a word about that lovable institution, because future generations may easily forget the part it played in introducing people of my generation to modern art. In the 'twenties and early 'thirties two successive directors of the Tate Gallery, Charles Aitken and James Manson, had set their faces against all post-impressionist painting, and did their best to prevent such pictures entering the Gallery, even as gifts. During these same years the Leicester Galleries held the first 'one-man shows' in England of Cézanne, van Gogh, Gauguin, Pissarro, Picasso,

Matisse, almost every great artist down to (effectively)* Henry Moore. These staggering exhibitions were put on without the least pretension. The Leicester Galleries was more like a shop than a gallery and its three rooms were quite small and modest. There was no attempt at deliberate showmanship, no expensive catalogues, no outpouring of champagne; and in the front rooms there was always a mixed exhibition of young painters where one could hope to make a discovery. The presiding spirit, Oliver Brown, was as small and unpretentious as his gallery, and loved to help young artists and collectors. I made all my early purchases there, usually for sums under five pounds. When I was sixteen a friend (I think a godfather) gave me a hundred pounds with which to buy a picture. I went at once to the Leicester Galleries and as I entered a picture of a young peasant boy hanging over the turnstile at the entrance greatly took my fancy. It seemed ridiculous to buy the first picture I saw, but after a long search I could find nothing else I liked so well, so I timidly asked the price. It was sixty pounds and the painter's name was Modigliani. I said I would buy it, and went away much elated. But when I got back to Berkeley Square I foresaw great difficulties. My primitive-looking boy would not easily settle down with my parents' Barbizon pictures. To have him alone in my bedroom seemed too eccentric. My courage failed me, and after two days I asked the Leicester Galleries to take him back, which they very kindly did. In the end he found his way, through Hugh Blaker, to the Tate, so that everyone but me is better off.

After this failure of nerve, I thought I would spend my £100 on a sketch by Wilson Steer. He was then considered by all the art establishment as the best living English painter, and the successor to Constable and Turner. I obtained an introduction from Sims and made my way down to Steer's house in Cheyne Row. As I was expecting to meet an artist in his studio I

* 'effectively' because there was a small exhibition of his work in the Warren Gallery in 1928.

had put on rather a festive necktie; but as soon as I met Steer I realised that I had made a mistake. He was the son of a parson, and disliked all forms of display. He received me without enthusiasm and explained that he had no work for sale, except for a very unattractive nude, which did not appeal to me, and in any case cost much more than £100. I went away crestfallen. After his death it turned out that he had a back room full of sketches of exactly the kind that would have delighted me. I have often speculated on his motives for not producing one of these. I suppose he simply couldn't be bothered and wanted to get rid of me as soon as possible. He will reappear in a later chapter in a more amiable guise.

Partly because I was trying to assimilate too many contradictory influences and partly, I suppose, because I was beginning to lose the visualising faculty, my efforts at painting became worse and worse. I slogged away at drawing from nature, chiefly from myself in a mirror; but I had really lost confidence in my talent. I read a good deal more, and began to enjoy writing; and I remember reading in one of Arnold Bennett's articles in the *Evening Standard* that if an Englishman felt himself equally drawn to painting and writing he should not hesitate; he should write.

To be a writer one must read. What did I read? Chiefly poetry. At that date poetry meant lyric poetry of the *Golden Treasury–Oxford Book of English Verse* variety, and young people were supposed to prefer the nineteenth-century romantics. But I soon discovered that my favourite period of English poetry was the seventeenth century, not only Milton, but Donne, Marvell, Herbert, Vaughan, Crashaw and even dear old Herrick. Vaughan was my favourite, and I could never understand why my teachers preferred Herbert. I ploughed my way through the three volumes of Saintsbury's *Caroline Poets,* although I did not read the whole of Drayton's *Polyolbion*. These works were not to be found in the school bookshop (except, I suppose, Milton), but there was an excellent second-hand bookshop, Mr Gilbert's, in the

Cathedral Close. One passed through the front room,
with its banal current publications, down two steps
into a small dark recess full of second-hand books.
Like the back room of the Bath music shop, it became
a sort of potting shed for my mental growth. I usually
had Mr Gilbert's shop to myself, but one day I found
there a very small colleger (at Winchester boys in
College could be identified because they wore gowns)
with long hair over his eyes, like a Yorkshire terrier.
He must have been three or four years younger than
me but already knew infinitely more about
seventeenth-century literature, and told me that he
had just made a thrilling discovery—a copy of the first
edition of Donne's *Devotions,* then completely forgotten. His name was John Sparrow. One was not
supposed to make friends with a boy in another house,
still less a colleger, but John Sparrow and I had too
much in common to be kept apart, and by means of
Shrogus, Drawing School and other Oecumenical institutions, we managed to see a good deal of each
other (never enough), and have gone on doing so
till the present day. When I hear the Warden of All
Souls spoken of as if he were a sort of bogey-man
dedicated to teasing radicals I do not recognise the
gay and sympathetic friend who seems to have
changed so little.

Next to the English poets of the seventeenth century, my favourites were the Chinese of the ninth,
as rendered into English by Arthur Waley. And here
I would like to record my belief that of all the writers
of my youth Arthur Waley was the most valuable.
He combined a scholar's feeling for truth (and what a
scholar!) with a poet's feeling for language. One never
feels, as in so many 'translations' from the Chinese,
from Judith Gautier downwards, that one is being
'taken for a ride'. What a world he opened to us; an
appreciation of nature that we thought had been discovered by Rousseau and Wordsworth; a self-knowl-
edge that we thought had been discovered by Montaigne; a feeling for the delicacy of human relationships
within the complex structure of society that we thought

was the invention of Proust, until we read the Lady Murasaki; all revealed to us by that silent, self-effacing scholar-poet. I was introduced to the *170 Chinese Poems* by my drawing master, Mr Macdonald. With his love of Oriental art and his incurable laziness, Po Chu-i was his ideal man. 'I have got wine, but I am too lazy to drink it, so it's just the same as if my cup were empty. I have got a lute, but am too lazy to play it; so it's just as if it had no strings.' * How strange that he should have been the brother-in-law of my housemaster, Mr Aris, who used to send for me to say only two words "Go hard, go hard". I preferred Po Chu-i; and re-reading his work the other day, found that I loved him more than ever.

This section is called the making of an aesthete and it is true that up to the age of seventeen or so the aesthetic experience of painting, poetry and music occupied my mind almost to the exclusion of normal human life. But I must record the names of two or three writers who gave me some insight into intellectual and moral values and some notion of the *condition humaine*. The first of these was Ibsen. How I came to read his plays I cannot remember; perhaps because he is the subject of the first essay in Clive Bell's *Potboilers,* where he is, rather intelligently, compared with Cézanne. Ibsen was exactly what I needed to correct my sheltered up-bringing. He taught me how full of cruel surprises life can be, how mixed are all motives, how under each layer of deception lies a still deeper layer of self-deception. He taught me that moral rectitude could do more harm than lies, and that the life-force itself could be destructive. A lot for a young man to swallow; but it has remained a part of me to this day. Of this I had a curious demonstration only a few years ago. I was at a performance of *Ghosts* at the National Theatre feel-

---

* Po Chu-i: 'The Lazy Man's Song', from *170 Chinese Poems.*

ing perfectly well—sitting beside Dame Sybil Thorndike, which in itself is enough to make one feel well. In the middle of the second act I fainted. My wife supposed I had been taken ill and wanted to hurry me home, but I said that if I could go to the nearby pub and drink a large whisky, I could explain my curious behaviour; because I had suddenly remembered that on reading the play at Winchester, cold, hungry and horrified at human behaviour, I had fainted at precisely the same moment. The body had a better memory than the mind. Which leads me to the other influence on my youthful intelligence, a lesser man, no doubt, than the Norwegian giant, but I believe under-rated, Samuel Butler. I loved him because he was a sort of Diogenes, a type of the completely independent man. With his odd mixture of commonsense and mischief he could not resist attacking any established opinion. When he attacked the church (the 'musical banks' in *Erewhon* are a brilliant invention) the intellectuals were pleased; but when he attacked the dominant belief in Darwinian evolution they dismissed him as a mere crank, although many of his objections have gone unanswered.

Like all other young people I was enchanted by the genial dialectic of Bernard Shaw, and still enjoy his fair-mindedness and good humour. But he had no influence on me whatsoever; perhaps because he always remained an orator, and I instinctively resist orators; and partly because he was a moralist, and I was, at that date, a hedonist. The counter-influence to Shaw was the now discredited figure of Anatole France. I preferred the easy-going Catholic wisdom of Jerome Coignard to the self-contradictory arguments of John Tanner. Also I loved the irony which hides almost imperceptibly in the clear waters of Anatole France's style.

Another influence came to me by one of those curious chances that play so great a part in education. I was at the time a cricket enthusiast and would waste hours watching a performance that I now consider as boring as a *No* play; in consequence I had made friends with one of our masters, named H. S. Altham, who was an *afficionado* so devoted that he afterwards left Winchester and became Treasurer and later President of the M.C.C. One day, in the middle of a conversation about the new number of *Wisden's Almanack,* he said "Ever read Plato?" I said that I had not. "There's a second-hand copy of *The Republic* in Wells" (the School bookshop). "I suggest you buy it and read it at once." I did so, and found my mind acquiring a new faculty. At school education was, for the most part, an exercise of memory. Abstract concepts went unquestioned. In scripture lessons one learnt to repeat the discreditable episodes of the Old Testament, or drew a map of St Paul's journeys. Once, I remember, we were set to read one of the Epistles, and were asked for comments on it. We sent in blank papers. So, a long book devoted to analysing and discussing the meaning of truth, justice, wisdom and the good life was something completely outside our experience. But Plato's dramatic skill, the beauty of his setting and his style (in Jowett's inaccurate translation) led me on till I found myself absorbed in the argument. Plato's conclusions were entirely unsympathetic, and I still think them the most dangerous legacy that Western man has inherited from antiquity. But the character of Socrates seemed to me sublime, and for many years I re-read two or three of the Dialogues every year, although I have never got through the *Laws*. As for the *Timaeus,* Clive Bell used to say that when he thought he understood the *Timaeus* it was a sure sign that he was drunk. I agree.

Just before my last year at Winchester I went in for the school essay prize, the subject being the influence of the Puritans on England. I remember it fairly well and am certain that it was a pitiful performance—second hand, pretentious and full of moral judgements inspired by Carlyle—but it won the prize. What can the other entries have been like! This success gave my housemaster the idea that I might put in for a scholarship at Oxford; not that he expected me to get one, but he was afraid I might not pass the entrance examination and believed that those who had tried for a scholarship were treated more leniently. I realised that it was a farce, and went up to Oxford in a carefree spirit. I knew no history and was not likely to bluff experienced examiners.

I had put my name down for Trinity because my housemaster had been at Trinity College, Cambridge, and said, looking gloomily at the list of Oxford Colleges, "Well, anyway, it's a good name". I travelled to Oxford by train in the same compartment as a boy from another house named Roger Makins.* He was determined to succeed and so firmly set on his course that he hardly spoke, much less laughed that famous laugh with which he was to equal the great laughers of Washington. We arrived in Oxford as the light was failing, and I shall never forget my feelings as I stood in front of the Radcliffe Camera. This, I thought, mistakenly, shall be the centre of my world. Later that evening I dined in Hall, and found myself next to a handsome red-haired Etonian, called Bobby Longden, who became one of my dearest friends. Next day, in the Examination Hall, Bobby had introduced me to a friend of his in College at Eton named Cyril Connolly. He was obviously an extraordinary person, with a width of knowledge and a maturity of mind of an entirely different class to the rest of us. A kind-looking man with white hair and the pink complexion of a baby walked behind our chairs, and said towards the end of each session, "There is only twenty minutes left. You can't write much in twenty minutes, but you can cross out a great deal". Excellent advice, which has led me to cross out about a third of this chapter. Heaven knows what ignorant nonsense I wrote about history, but in the general paper there was one question which I felt qualified to answer—'Is a picture the better for being true to nature, or a poem for being true to fact'. I suppose

* Later Lord Sherfield, head of the Civil Service and Ambassador to the United States.

it was my answer to this question which won me a scholarship.

The news of this success was greeted at Winchester rather as the baptism of the penguins was accepted in heaven, in Anatole France's book. My housemaster was almost indignant, but consoled himself by thinking that Oxford was capable of anything. My dear history teacher, A. T. P. Williams, said "I won't deny that I am surprised". I was in a seventh heaven of joy; in fact only once in my subsequent life have I tasted such unadulterated happiness. But it was the end of my career as an artist, and my father, when he heard of it, was very sorry.

III

Further Education

BEFORE COMING to the friendships and travels that occupied the foreground of my next four years I must describe the background of my home life during the same period. My parents sold the house in Bath and bought another, rather larger and more comfortable, in Bournemouth, where they spent the winters. The Villa at Cap Martin was also sold to a marvellous and terrifying figure out of *Les Liaisons Dangereuses*. The advantages of Bournemouth were a mild climate (which I found depressing) and a club where my father could play bridge and billiards. Every morning he toddled down the hill past the Royal Bath Hotel to the club and played three or four games of snooker; then he returned for lunch in a taxi, described in detail the games of snooker, had a snooze, took another taxi back to the club and played bridge till about six-thirty. Then he would take a final taxi home, do the children's crossword puzzle in the *Daily Mirror,* and read aloud a strip cartoon called Pip, Squeak and Wilfred, including a penguin called Auntie who could not speak but said only 'Grrr', which greatly pleased my father. At eight he would dine, play a game of snooker and go to bed. For me Bournemouth was infinitely less agreeable than Bath; ugly buildings, dull shops, and the only compensation —a gigantic Conservatory known as the Winter Garden. Every Thursday there was a concert conducted by a good old trouper of the Henry Wood class called Sir Dan Godfrey. These concerts supplemented my pianistic education, and made me familiar, perhaps over-familiar, with the standard symphonies. We seldom went to London because if we did my father would have felt bound to attend to some business connected with an aluminium company. Already, before we left Sudbourne, it was evident that all was not well with this company. My father's prodigious luck had turned at last. But he was determined not to be defeated, and poured more and more money into it. Then one night in 1920, when my father was about to look for Pip, Squeak and Wilfred in the *Daily Mirror* he saw on the front page of the *Evening Standard,* "WELSH DAM DISASTER, Whole Village Washed Away'. I shall never forget his face, as he walked, carrying the paper, into the room, where my mother and I were sitting. I would hardly have recognised him.

The dam that had burst had fed the pipe line that powered the Aluminium Corporation's plant; the village of Dolgarrog, which had grown up around the works, had been almost totally destroyed. Inevitably there was an enquiry. It was found that the retaining wall of the dam, which should by contract have been sixteen feet deep, was six feet deep (I have forgotten the actual figures, but the relative proportions are more or less correct). It was a miracle that the dam had not collapsed years earlier. The contractor who did the job had gone out of business and died. The foreman and clerk of the works were both dead. The managing director, in whom my father had placed a somewhat uneasy confidence, had absconded with most of the funds and died. All he had left behind was a dubious Chinese Chippendale table. My father was the only responsible person still alive and, of course, had never set eyes on the dam, and visited Dolgarrog only once. He immediately recognised his responsibility and telegraphed to the North Wales authorities that he would compensate the workers for their losses and rebuild their homes. He then tried to do something to salvage the company. He got it into working order again, but it never paid, and after five or six years of further losses, during which time, to my great embarrassment, I was made a member of the board, he sold the company for a knock-down price. He told me that the whole affair had cost him over a million pounds, which in those days was quite a lot of money.

However, he seems to have had some left because, during the same years, he bought and maintained a large property in Scotland which consisted of the whole peninsula of Ardnamurchan from Loch Sheil to the point. It was said to be 75,000 acres, of which I should say that less than 20 acres were grass or arable land. All the rest was hill and bog. It had belonged to a man called Rudd, a creature of Cecil Rhodes, who had built on it two monstrous houses, one for stalking and one for fishing. We lived in the one for fishing, which was on the banks of the river Sheil. It was extremely ugly, without a single well-proportioned room, but, in a sense, it was well sited because it looked over a large pool formed by the river after it had passed through a narrow gulley. Over the gulley was a beautiful old bridge, which gave the house its name. In order to enjoy this view all the principal rooms looked north. No sun ever entered the house; but as the sun hardly ever shone during the months that we were there this was not a serious disadvantage. Behind the house stretched miles of bog, broken only by stacks of peat, but if one had the strength of mind to walk across it—one came to the Bay of Kentra (or Ceantragh—the end of the shore), a mile or two of silver sand, looking across to Eigg and Rhum. I had often noticed this white strip from the sea, and was not surprised to find that this was where the Vikings had beached their ships during their long occupation of Eigg. After a high tide and a westerly gale had disturbed the sand one could usually find relics of the Viking occupation—nails of boats, beads and the occasional brooch, the best of which are in a dismal museum at Fort

William. I have always loved walking, and the ten miles there and back to Kentra meant nothing to me. I shut out the dreariness of the bog by talking to myself. I have often been asked how I learnt the trick of talking to a television camera. I have no doubts at all that I did so on my long, solitary walks across the bog. People who are used to a companion require the stimulus of a listener. Actors are lost without an audience. But I formed the habit of soliloquy, and would even repeat out loud what I had learned on the preceding day, very much as I did in *Civilisation*.

The other house on the estate, a dotty red sandstone castle called Glen Borrodale, we let to a grim old Scottish financier named Fleming, who might have been the hero of *Hatter's Castle*. He had a very pretty daughter-in-law who had been painted by Augustus John, and was consequently an object of interest to me; but I could not approach her as she had four brilliantly equipped sons, three of whom, Peter, Ian and Michael, scared the wits out of me, and continued to do so when I met them in later life. The fishing at Sheilbridge was very bad. There was always a quantity of salmon in the pool and we could see them from the bridge rolling over lazily in the deep brown water. Presumably they could also see us, as nothing would induce them to swallow a fly. For years the only entry in my father's diaries is 'Fishing rotten!', and the only contents of his letters to me at Oxford were 'The brutes won't take'. But he flogged away by the hour, changing flies, and trying new tactics, to no effect. I don't think the stalking at Glen Borrodale was much better.

Since any autobiography must be to some extent a confession I must now record one of the most discreditable episodes in my life. Great pressure was put upon me to go out stalking, invitations from the Flemings, persuasion by our keeper, in a beautiful Highland voice; and out of pure weakness and a desire to conform, I agreed. We walked up the hills behind Kentra, sighted some stags, crawled towards

them through the heather (an experience so agreeable as to make me forget my abominable purpose),
and finally came within range. An antlered stag rose
to his feet. 'Now', whispered the keeper; and the stag
fell dead. I immediately realised that I had committed
a murder. I put my head on my arm, and lay there in
an agony of mind. Our dear keeper thought I was in
an ecstasy of joy, but as we walked silently home, accompanied by our pathetic burden, he realised that
something must be wrong. I was sorry to hurt his
feelings. My parents, either from tact or from indifference, never referred to the episode.

My father could not imagine life without a yacht,
and out of force of habit kept one in Loch Sunart.
For some mysterious reason he changed these yachts
almost every year. I suppose he enjoyed building
them, but he gradually ceased to enjoy going on
them, and the yachts would lie idle for weeks on end.
In order to keep the crew out of mischief I was encouraged to take parties of friends from Winchester
or Oxford on cruises round the coast. It sounds like
an ideal holiday, but I don't think that any of us enjoyed ourselves much. Owing to the persistent rain
a great part of our time was spent in sitting in a small
cabin reading and making conversation, all of which
we could have done much more comfortably on land.
When we did arrive at our destinations we would
put on our mackintoshes and walk on that curious
gritty cinder substance of which the streets in Highland villages were then composed, past a few grey
houses with slate roofs, to the village shop, where we
would buy a tin of sardines and a bar of chocolate. I
hardly remember a single fine day; but I must admit
that when the sun does shine on the Hebrides they
are the islands of the blest, and it has never failed to
shine for me in Iona. I have said elsewhere what I
feel about that sacred place. It inspired Dr Johnson
to kneel on the ground after he had waded ashore,
and subsequently to write a passage of prose that Boswell quotes as an example of his style at its most elo-
quent—a passage that ends with these words: 'The man

is little to be envied whose patriotism would not gain force upon the field of Marathon or whose piety would not grow warmer among the ruins of Iona'. When first I visited Iona I had probably never heard the word piety and would not have understood what it meant. But I remember having a peculiar feeling as I walked up to the Abbey and on to the beach beyond. I subsequently attributed that feeling to the lie of the land, the very white sand, interspersed with pinkish rocks, and the colour of the surrounding sea, which really is 'wine dark'. Through some geological accident Iona is not composed of bogs and precipices, but is largely covered with a light, springy turf. To walk on this responsive surface, and to feel free to walk in any direction, was immediately exhilarating. But after repeated visits I began to realise that the purely physical qualities were not the whole reason for my devotion. There are places in the world where even someone as insensitive as I am must feel a vibration from the remote past, an exhalation, whether of good or evil: Delphi, Delos, Mycenae (very evil), Monte Oliveto, Avila, Cézanne's house beside the quary of Bibemus. Among such places I would include Iona, and I was interested to observe, when filming there, that our camera crew, who were not at all mystically inclined, experienced the same sensations. Curiously enough tourists are not always capable of destroying this numinous quality; at least they have not done so in Chartres or Assisi, although they have completely ruined Toledo. In the days when I visited Iona on my father's yacht, tourists were extremely rare, and I dare say that the sense of peace was greater. But tourists are mid-day menaces. In the early mornings and the evenings the sacred spots of the world regain their tranquillity.

After the age of sixteen or so the solitude which I had so much treasured as a child became oppressive to me. I began to suffer from what the French call *accidie, maladie des moines,* a word for which there seems to be no English equivalent, although it must exist in England. Perhaps it is more or less what Burton meant by the melancholy that he so learnedly and fantastically anatomised. It not only leads to depression, but it deprives one of animal faith. Nothing seems to be worth doing. In my own case it developed into hypochondria. For some years I believed intermittently, but with absolute conviction, that I was dying of paralysis. Like the greatest of my fellow sufferers, Dr Johnson, I went for immensely long walks, in hope that the fatigue would comfort me. I also played squash racquets with great agility and considerable skill (I played for Oxford), but nothing could get the idea of paralysis out of my head. I believe this affliction is common among young people, so common as to be almost a part of the regular process of growing up, but they do not like to confess to it, for fear of being thought foolish, and they usually outgrow it. My own hypochondria was deep rooted enough to reappear two or three times in later life. In my early thirties, at the height of my activity at the National Gallery, I thought I had a disease of the heart. I had an 'attack' when staying with Edith Wharton at Hyères and was visited by the local doctor (who turned out to have been the model for Jules Romains' *Dr Knock*). He listened to my heart and said "Ce n'est pas grave. Avec un coeur comme ça vous pouvez tres bien vivre six ans, même sept ans. Pas de sports, bien entendu". He then gave me one of those complicated prescriptions with which French doctors maintain their prestige, one very strong pill to be taken once a day, and sixteen—yes, sixteen—pills to be taken night and morning. He came back after a week and found some improvement. He then repeated his instructions about the pills and I realised that I had been taking sixteen of the very strong pills twice a day and vice versa. I threw them all away and rapidly recovered. The other recurrence was in the 1950's—the fancy of paralysis again. I was sent to see a famous brain specialist called Brain like a character in a Restoration Comedy. He made a number of tests and said that there was indeed something gravely wrong which would involve an examination of my brain. I asked if this meant taking the top off my head. He said that it did. The thought of being treated like a boiled egg on a breakfast table had no appeal to me. I thanked him for his interest, withdrew, and have not had any symptoms of paralysis since. I do not record these experiences out of disrespect for the medical profession, but in order that people who have similar worries may realise how easily one may delude oneself, and even mislead a conscientious doctor.

In the first years at Sheilbridge a number of visitors came to the house, cousins, a few friends of my mother's, the Commedia del' Arte doctor from Bath, and even Tommy Dewar. By this time his great days of dining out were over, and on discovering that our cow-herd (from the great Sudbourne herds we had sunk to two cows named Jetta and Beauty) was called Dewar, he announced that he would take high tea with him rather than come down to dinner. Gradually fewer and fewer people came and, as I spent a good deal of my holidays travelling abroad, one would have supposed that my parents must have had rather a dismal time. But the inertia of old age is such that they probably preferred it that way. In the days when servants existed, elderly people became entirely dependent on them. For over twenty years my mother was dependent on a maid who was one of the nastiest human beings I have ever met. She was married to the butler who was a stupid, narrow man, and in my absence these two odious figures controlled all my parents' decisions. Naturally they loathed me, and did everything they could to make my visits home unpleasant. The butler used to hand me large bills for my laundry every week, although it was done in our own laundry by an extremely pretty laundress, so the bills must have been fictitious. In their chief aim—to make mischief between myself and my parents—they were unsuccessful, but in every other way they succeeded in poisoning the atmosphere of Sheilbridge for almost fifteeen years. But I remember with pleasure a small house in North Devon which we rented for the fishing in spring after I had won my scholarship. Because I felt that I had changed direction, my mind began to work as it has done only two or three times since; and always when I have undertaken something new. I remember reading Carlyle's *Past and Present* and Michelet's history of France, which I thought the greatest piece of historical writing I had ever read. I had conceived a great admiration for Tacitus and hoped one day to write in his style. I planned and sketched great literary enterprises, histories, satires (a form which I now detest), even a novel to be called The Law and the Prophet. My hypochondria vanished, my skill at billiards greatly increased. I felt capable of anything.

A month or two later I arrived in Oxford. Young men of spirit, suddenly released from the discipline of school, are said to burst into bloom in the freer atmosphere of a university. But I was timid and shy, and for some time did not know where to turn. I had not felt altogether at home at Winchester even during my last year, but it provided a routine and an enforced companionship. My first feelings at Oxford were of loneliness and a lack of direction. As I had enjoyed the Shakespeare readings at school and felt within myself a certain talent for acting, I joined the Oxford University Dramatic Society. It had club rooms where one could have a cheap, bad meal, and I went there for lunch several times a week. I sat in the far corner of the dining-room and never dared to speak to any of the other members, who did imitations and laughed at a table by the window. I never dared to put down my name for a part in any of the annual productions. After a time I gave up lunching there, and went to a charming old inn called The Golden Cross, with meat and two veg, and a friendly Dickensian waiter; or to Fullers tea shop, where I ate a poached egg under the eyes of a disdainful, but not hostile, waitress. I occasionally summoned up the courage to dine in Hall (the usual custom among undergraduates), but remember nothing about the evenings except a feeling of insufficiency. In those days one was allowed to give small luncheon parties in one's room, which I greatly enjoyed. In my second year I went to order a meal from the kitchen and, as I left, said to the cook "What's that big room at the back?". "Lor, sir", he said with a mixture of horror and astonishment, "it's the junior common room". I suppose that this inability to join in corporate life was considered by my fellow undergraduates as a sign of snootiness. It arose simply from fear and inexperience. I seemed not to know the magic password that would have enabled me to enter a group, even as its humblest member.

From this rather melancholy situation I was rescued by making new friends. Most of my friends at Winchester had gone to Cambridge; the rest were in New College, where they continued the inward-turning social pattern of the good Wykehamist. The medium through which I made friends was at first the kind, pink man who had watched us do our scholarship papers and advised us to cross out as much as possible of what we had written. He turned out to be a well-known Oxford character named F. F. Urquhart, universally known as Sligger. He was Dean of Balliol and had a large room over the West Gate, an authentic relic of Victorian Oxford, filled with threadbare settees and lined with dowdy-looking books (The Rolls series, Mabillon, the works of Bishop Stubbs) which absorbed whatever light entered through the gothic window. On the shelves stood one or two water colours of the Holy Land by Edward Lear, and an Arundel Club reproduction of Piero della Francesca's *Resurrection* in Borgo San Sepolcro. Into this room drifted every evening a very mixed assortment of undergraduates—earnest young scholars, minor royalty, priests, budding poets, and a few lonely nonentities. They did not have to ask if they could come. They simply walked in and joined in the conversation. I suppose that Sligger must have asked them once in the first place; after that they were free, and

even able to bring their friends. Of course there was
no drink, which kept out the more spirited undergraduates, but it was a reservoir of kindness and
tolerance and I went there most gratefully. Sligger (although he would not have relished the comparison)
was like the perfect hostess. He himself never said
anything of interest, but he encouraged others to show
off. He was often accused of snobbishness. It is true
that, like all hostesses, he preferred those who had
contributed, or were likely to contribute, something
to society. I do not remember meeting in his rooms
any of the earnest young Scots who must have been
fairly numerous in Balliol at this date. On the contrary,
I recall that when I lunched with Sligger, a relatively
rare event, one luncheon was to meet Peter Quennell,
who had arrived in Oxford with the reputation of the
most gifted schoolboy poet since Rimbaud; and the
other was to meet Prince Olaf of Norway. I may add
that neither luncheon produced any lasting benefit.
Peter Quennell soon discovered more stimulating
company, and Prince Olaf was more interested in
games.

The most regular visitors were a group of Eton
scholars, three of them in Balliol and one in Trinity.
This last, the handsome, red-haired boy whom I had
sat next to during my scholarship examination, became my closest friend. Bobby Longden was that
rare and irresistible combination, an intelligent extrovert. He was the son of an admiral who would have
gone to the top in the Navy if he had not suffered
from the same weakness as my own father. Bobby was
by nature a man of action. He had made himself into
an efficient classical scholar, but it was not the chief
interest in his life, as it was in the lives of his fellow
Etonians, Roger Mynors and Denis Danreuther. He
had an immense zest for life, and told longer and fun-
nier stories than anyone I have ever known. Not long
ago I remember someone saying "I haven't laughed
so much since Bobby died"—an enviable epitaph. In
the closed world of the late nineteenth century it was
usual to forecast the future of undergraduates: Cur-

zon was obviously destined to become Viceroy of India, F. E. Smith would be Lord Chancellor. The upheavals of the present day have made these steady progressions seem ridiculous. No one seemed to have any doubt that Bobby Longden would become headmaster of Eton. It was equally assumed that Roger Mynors, his friend and mine, would become Master of Balliol. But Roger was a deep and mysterious character, a great scholar, with an even greater gift of renunciation and self-effacement, whereas Bobby went blithely on until, at an early age, he was made Headmaster of Wellington, for a kind of probationary period. I fancy that he found the human contacts rather more exacting than he had foreseen; he had never developed the knack of placating less well-endowed colleagues, and was too good-natured to dominate them. However, all such speculations were put to an end by a German bomb which fell on his head after the 'all clear' had sounded in the spring of 1941. His closest friend, both at Eton and Oxford, was Cyril Connolly. It was an attraction of opposites. Cyril was not conventionally handsome, and he was certainly not a man of action; but he was without doubt the most gifted undergraduate of his generation. He had read the Greek and Latin authors, including those of the silver age, with a subtle, questioning mind; he had read the French poets and critics of the nineteenth century; he had even read the Christian Fathers. All this learning was almost entirely invisible below a surface of wit and intellectual curiosity. He was a master of parody, who could improvise in anybody's style in the course of conversation. These attributes are usually described as 'brilliant', but this label did not suit Cyril, partly, I think, because his voice had a curiously matt tonality, partly because he never attempted to shine or to assert himself. His talents had not gone unobserved at Eton. Cyril arrived in Oxford with the millstone of promise already hung around his neck. How heavily it weighed on him is declared in the titles of his books, *Enemies of Promise, The Condemned Playground, The Rock Pool.* It couldn't be helped. The young Cyril Connolly really was extra-ordinary. In 1941, when the chances of survival did not seem very strong, I looked through some letters I had received from my friends at Oxford. They read like the letters of schoolboys, or, at least, of immature minds; all except the letters from Cyril. These were brilliant, erudite, original, observant and so perfectly phrased that they could have been published as they stood. I was so much impressed that I put them in a safe place in the cellar of my house. A year or two later it caught fire through an electrical fault and they were all destroyed together with my letters from Logan Pearsall Smith. However, a man need write only one book. Cyril wrote *The Unquiet Grave* and put into it a distillation of himself and of one aspect of our life in Oxford during the 1920's, which will survive.

Sligger's father, I suppose under the influence of Ruskin, had built a chalet on the Prarion, a plateau high up in the foothills of Mont Blanc, and during the summer holidays Sligger used to invite a carefully chosen group of undergraduates to stay with him there. He invited me and as, left to myself, I always accept invitations, I went. It was a mistake. I do not really like mountain scenery and much dislike climbing mountains; I cannot spend a whole day reading; after about an hour I do not remember a word and tend to fall asleep. I hate cold showers, which were all that the chalet provided, and even at that age I was inordinately fond of food. Part of the ritual of a visit to the chalet was to climb Mont Blanc. I was miserably equipped, having no climbing boots, and after a time it became evident that my slender brown brogues from Macafee would not stand the strain; so Sligger sent me home. I went down to the restaurant at the top of the Mont Blanc funicular, ordered *Vitello alla Milanese,* and half a bottle of Chianti. I suppose the food was very coarse, but I have never enjoyed a meal more. I could console myself with the thought that Ruskin would have done the same, only he would have drunk Aleatico. I returned to the chalet slowly. After another week of pulse and stale bread I was suffering acutely from hunger, boredom and constipation, and realized that, however much I might wish to escape from the world, my upbringing had unfitted me for the monastic life. But, paradoxically enough, the most precious and lasting result of my unsuccessful visit was closely connected with monasticism: my friendship with David Knowles, who was staying there at the time. That this great scholar and saintly man should have tolerated a shallow and ignorant worldling, and remained his friend for almost fifty years, I count as one of the great blessings of my life.

Towards the end of my first term I made a friend who was to become, without question, the strongest influence in my life—Maurice Bowra. As with David Knowles, but for very different reasons, it is strange that he should have tolerated me. I was timid, priggish and inhibited. I was not even a scholar, and 'scholarly', repeated several times, was one of the first words of praise in Maurice's vocabulary. Maurice was courageous, warm-hearted, and without question one of the least inhibited of men. He was, which is often forgotten, a great scholar whose book on *Heroic Poetry* (to name only one of his many books) is a feat that no other man of learning of his day could have equalled. In 1922 he was already recognised as the brightest, most vigorous and funniest of the younger 'dons'. I can think of only one reason why he 'took me up'— that we were both uninfluenced by intellectual fads and fashions. He did not think it boring that I should prefer Michelangelo, Rembrandt and Velasquez to Derain, Picabia, or even Picasso. Nobody was less 'petite chapelle' than Maurice, and, although he enjoyed fantasy, he had a hearty contempt for frivolity, in particular for the intellectual frivolity then much in vogue. This, I suppose, is the reason why he never got on with the Bloomsburies, although in other respects he would have been a resonant companion for Clive Bell. I remember a television-interviewer asking Otto Klemperer what he read between his con-

certs: "Oh, Goethe, Schiller, occasionally Shakespeare."
"But Dr. Klemperer, you must sometimes relax;
what do you read then?". "Then I read Nietzsche."
That is in Maurice's spirit. At the back of his mind
were Homer, Pindar, Aeschylus, Dante, Pushkin, Tol-
stoy, Camoens and St Paul, all read in the originals.
These were his standards of judgement. He recognised greatness when he met it and saw no reason
why he should waste time on triviality. After quoting
from one of his favourites, he would say "Big stuff",
and, in a moment of irreverence, I called him 'Big
stuff Bowra', which would not, I think, have dis-
pleased him, because he knew quite well that, unlike
many exponents of big stuff (including, occasionally,
Dr Klemperer) he was never a bore.

That Maurice Bowra was a wit is the first thing that
anyone says about him. He did in fact make some very
funny jokes; he loved puns and had a repertoire of
punning nicknames for his friends and enemies, which
are unforgettable. The chief quality of his wit was its
audacity. He said all the dreadful things one was
longing to hear said, and said them as if they were
obvious to any decent man. It was a riotous entertainment. I was often reminded of two lines from a
poem by W. B. Yeats about Maud Gonne, 'That the
Night Come,' which Maurice was fond of quoting:
'Trumpet and kettledrum, and the outrageous cannon'. For me Maurice's outrageous cannon often acted
as a kind of shock therapy. My priggish fears and
inhibitions were blown to smithereens. As I said in
the first chapter, my father and mother were antitheti-
cal characters. During my lonely adolescence, and unsuccessful attempt to adapt myself to Winchester, my
mother's quakerish character was in the ascendant.
Maurice released the opposite side of my inheritance.
I don't think he ever met my father, but he recreated
him as a mythical personage rather like one of the sea
gods in Böcklin's *Meeres-idylle* and invented for him
extravagant and not altogether improbable adventures. Thus he lifted from my shoulders a load of
shame and resentment which had been deposited

there when, as a child, I had to get my father out of embarrassing scrapes. As well as dis-inhibiting me he educated me. He loved to talk about books, and to read poetry, in what Boswell called 'a loud emphatick voice' (and I may add in parenthesis that, as Maurice grew older, he came to resemble Dr Johnson in several other ways). I enjoyed this hugely. Even when he read Pushkin and Lermontoff, of which one couldn't understand a word, one was buoyed up by his enthusiasm. Naturally it was more exciting when he read something one could understand. He was already considering his essays on the symbolist poets, published almost twenty years later. I was trying to learn German, and it was thrilling for me to be pushed in at the deep end, the poetry of Rilke and George, instead of the usual lyrics by Heine and Goethe (I should add that Maurice had an unbounded admiration for Goethe's *Faust* and would quote large chunks of it). Above all there was his discovery of Yeats. Of course Yeats had long been accepted as a considerable poet, but Maurice was one of the first to recognise that after 1916 (or 1913) he became a *great* poet, and he fired his younger friends with such enthusiasm that we came to know half the contents of *Wild Swans at Coole* by heart. His other idol among living poets, Thomas Hardy, I could not worship unreservedly; I was stuck in the glutinous magic of words and have all my life remained too fond of euphony. But he communicated his enthusiasm to Cecil Day Lewis and John Betjeman, and thus helped to create a whole movement in English poetry.

Looking back on what I have written, I see that I may have suggested a figure rather more serious, or even portentous, than the gay young host who greeted us at Wadham. Our friendship lasted just short of fifty years, and inevitably early impressions have been overlaid. Like everyone else I remember first the sheer enjoyment of those evenings, the noise and funniness and lack of constraint. But I know I am right in thinking that from the start I was deeply influenced by what I can only call Maurice's moral values. Being himself the most warm-hearted of men he hated indifference. "A cold fish" was one of the worst things he could say of anyone. He hated tyrants. He hated hypocrites, sycophants and place-seekers. He had no use for conventional values. All this disqualified him from public life. When the fame of his intelligence began to spread, people used to ask why he did not seek a wider field of action. As well ask Montaigne why he did not leave his tower, or Diogenes his tub. He had imposed his own set of limitations. He refused to speak on the radio or appear on television; and on the telephone would use only two words, 'Yes' and 'No'.* Although he travelled in Germany, Greece, and latterly in Persia, he would not stay for long in London, and much disliked his rare visits to the U.S.A. I must say that he did nothing to conciliate American opinion. He was fond of drawing up 'elevens' of bores, captained by Sir Arthur Colefax, but said that an all-English side wouldn't stand a chance compared with the most modest provincial team of bores from America. When asked by a journalist in Washington how he was getting on in the United States he replied "All right, thanks to food parcels from England". I should add that he was fond of describing a meal that he had eaten in New York which cost him £28: "By no means bad". Ironically the figure whom he seemed most closely to resemble was an American, Edmund Wilson. They both loved literature and hated the establishment. They both dogmatised in a robust Johnsonian manner. Both Maurice and Edmund Wilson enjoyed food and drink to a point that was revealed in their appearances, but whereas Maurice continued to look genial, Edmund Wilson (whom I never met) came to look, in his photographs, rather grumpy. Maurice disliked him intensely, and one can't help feeling that although he knew he was the better scholar he recognized that Edmund Wilson was the better writer.

* Curiously enough, Mr Berenson also refused to have his voice recorded; but he went further and would not speak on the telephone at all, and never made a public speech.

Maurice will reappear frequently in this book, so I must reluctantly take leave of him, and turn to some other aspects of life in Oxford. In those days one went to Oxford to talk, and to educate oneself by conversation with more intelligent people of one's own age, or slightly older. There had to be an apparatus of instruction, lectures, set books and the weekly essay. I hardly ever attended a lecture, except in the hopes of sitting next to a pretty undergraduate named Alix Kilroy,* who, however, remained unaware of my existence. I learnt a great deal from some lectures on the fascinating subject of Aristotle's *Poetics* by a richly patinated character named Farquharson. I listlessly turned over the pages of the set books, and cannot now even remember what most of them were about. But there was no escaping the task of writing an essay and reading it to a tutor every week. By convention these essays were about 2,500 words long and, as they were usually on large and complex subjects, the technique of composing them became an exercise in evasion and bluff. One made a summary of a text book, which was already the summary of another text book. But how else could a young man write in one week an essay on The Social and Economic Consequences of the Thirty Years War? Although it did not stretch the mind, I suppose that the system was useful for future Civil Servants, who have to write summaries for politicians, and it was invaluable to future journalists, especially reviewers. But it taught one the trick of skimming over difficulties of which I am uncomfortably aware when I re-read my own writings.

During my first year the discipline of the weekly essay was relaxed owing to the character of my tutor in Trinity. He was a figure out of Gibbon's Oxford. His purple face, with its disarming smile, retained the traces of good looks, and these had enabled him to marry a lady of an old banking family. Secure in fortune and position he gave up all pretence of fulfilling irksome duties. The first time I went to him for a tu-

* Dame Alix Kilroy, Lady Meynell.

torial (I suppose his other pupils knew better) I found him seated with his feet in a basin of hot water, with cold towels round his head. I withdrew, and thereafter found pinned to his door a notice saying 'Mr——— is indisposed and will not be able to see pupils today'. Since he was in Holy Orders he had a statutory obligation to preach a sermon once a term, and he contrived to get some fun out of it. He had a circle of young bucks who came to drink with him, and they used to bet that he could not introduce certain phrases and allusions into his sermons. He usually won. In fairness to Trinity, I should add that I was tutored in economics by a man of distinguished mind, F. W. Ogilvie,* and, in European history, I was 'farmed out' to a great scholar, G. N. Clark,† who taught me the little about historical method that I know.

But if I didn't learn much about the history of England, I learnt something about the history of art. This was chiefly due to my friendship with a remarkable character named C. F. Bell who was Keeper of the Department of Fine Art in the Ashmolean Museum. I was introduced to him by a handsome, raffish don at Trinity, with whom I suppose he had once been in love, much as the poet Gray (whom he idolised and in many ways resembled) had been in love with Mr Bonstetton. He was a tiny little man, with a slightly humped back, Pope rather than Gray, and a pale magenta face. The red rims of his eyes encircled small and very strong lenses, which, if he wanted to scrutinise a print or drawing decisively, he would remove, and hold within two inches of his nose. He was ageless. In 1922 I believed him to be an old man. He lived till 1966. He was descended from one of the famous Macdonald sisters, and so was a cousin of Baldwin, Burne-Jones and Rudyard Kipling, whom I never heard him mention, although his

---

* Later Sir Frederick Ogilvie, Director General of the B.B.C.
† Later Sir George Clark, editor of the *English Historical Review* and President of the British Academy, who, incidentally, had been Aldous Huxley's tutor when he was in Oxford.

grandfather, Ambrose Poynter, had been one of Kipling's dearest friends. He had the entrée into every great collection and intellectually distinguished milieu in England and Italy. But he had no wish to shine in the great world, only to excel in certain precise and narrow branches of art-history. Through his mother, who was a German scholar, he had been introduced to Dr Bode and had taken up the study of Renaissance bronzes. He had gained a research fellowship at Magdalen by proposing the most futile and laborious subject imaginable—a new edition of Molinier's catalogue of Italian plaquettes. Later his interests widened, without any loss of precision, so that he could expose the errors in other people's books on subjects as diverse as English Watercolours, Italian Majolica, Baroque Bozzetti or Eighteenth-Century Italian Travellers. This he did in notes, rather in the style of A. E. Housman, written in the margins of the offending books, in a beautifully neat hand. In so far as learning is a function of memory he was a very learned man. He was also what was then called a man of taste, which means that his taste stopped short soon after 1810. Up to that point it was infallible. He could just swallow Thomas Hope and early Ingres, but he felt that Beethoven had gone astray after the first symphony. The ninth he thought in very poor taste; the sound of the word Wagner made him feel sick.

Within these limitations he ran his department of the Ashmolean perfectly. It was always spotless and must have been the only museum in the world where the showcases were as beautiful as their contents. He treated it as his private collection, discouraged all visitors, and would have particularly deplored the presence of an undergraduate had one ever entered the department. But, thanks to the recommendation of his handsome friend, I was admitted and even allowed to work in the so-called print room, a very small room with a large safe containing a fabulous collection of drawings. When I say 'work' I mean it. Charlie Bell made me compare every Michelangelo and Raphael with the descriptions in Robinson's ar-

chaic catalogue, and gave me a large paper edition, so
that I might write my own vituperative comments
in the margins. I was also allowed, somewhat reluctantly, to consult Berenson's *Florentine Drawings;*
but as Fischel's publication of Raphael's drawings
had not begun to appear, I had no guide through
that particularly difficult and still debatable, area of
art-history. In any case Charles Bell would never have
allowed me to use it, as he hated all Germans.

To look intensely at original drawings by two of
the greatest draughtsmen who have ever lived, to
spend days in their company, and have to decide on
one's own which seemed to be authentic and which
the work of imitators, was the finest training for the
eye that any young man could have had. One felt, in
all humility, that one was entering into the artist's
mind and understanding the implications of his slightest gesture. One could read his handwriting like a
graphologist. One could also recognise that most inexplicable of all attributes in a work of art—a sense of
form. Looking at Raphael's drawing of a kneeling saint
one could see how this young man of eighteen or so,
open to every visual excitement, had already simplified his experiences so that they conformed to some
pre-ordained plastic ends that had grown up, Heaven
knows how, at the back of his mind. Brooding on
Michelangelo's drawings of muscular shoulders, one
saw how grasp of a single form, with all its understanding of latent power and tension, allowed him to
create a whole world of imaginative relationships.
After Michelangelo and Raphael I went on to German
engravings, Charles Bell rightly thinking that it would
be good for me to work at something that was not
naturally sympathetic to me. But I soon developed
an affection for Schongauer which has increased with
time and, although my Bloomsbury mentors spoke
contemptuously of Dürer, I was bowled over by the
inventiveness and mastery of his woodcuts. Finally,
as a reward for working against the grain, I was let
loose on the Rembrandt etchings. I had loved them
and copied them ever since I was fourteen, but al-

ways from reproductions. Now the magnificent impressions in the Ashmolean showed me how far I had been from understanding the richness of Rembrandt's mind and the life-giving touch of his fingers.

Almost the only people who visited the Ashmolean were collectors of English watercolours. They came to ask the advice of Charles Bell who was the acknowledged authority in this field, and they placated him by promising to leave their 'treasures' to the Museum which, I am bound to say, a good many of them did. I did my best to take an interest in these pleasant provincial works, and even helped Charles Bell to catalogue a newly discovered collection of Cotmans, which was good training in the mechanics of cataloguing. But how they bored me, and do still, except for a few works by Girtin and Cozens, *père et fils*. (Of course I do not include Turner whose genius defies all generalisations.)

When I wanted to escape from this world of good taste, there was always the other half of the Ashmolean, the department of antiquities. In contrast with Charles Bell's department, and perhaps in protest against it, this was arranged with no attempt to please the eye, and very little attempt to instruct the mind. The labels, when they existed, were written by hand and, since archaeologists often change their minds, had become indecipherable from frequent erasures. But it contained plenty to stimulate the imagination, beginning with the Minoan discoveries of Sir Arthur Evans. Evans had been Keeper of the Ashmolean and largely responsible for Charles Bell's appointment; and Bell took me out to call on him in a large house on Boars Hill as ugly as his restorations at Knossos. No one could have charged *him* with too much good taste. He was lively and intelligent, with an impressive range of interests; I remember that we talked about Caravaggio. After tea he said "Something has just arrived that I must show you—I haven't even unpacked it properly". He took me into his study and produced a shoe box full of cotton wool and tissue paper, from which there emerged the ivory snake goddess of Boston.* It was a thrilling moment. I could not help saying (with no *arrière-pensée,* of course) "What an extraordinary modern face she has." He agreed, and pointed out how similar all Cretan decoration is to *art nouveau*. When I saw the goddess in Boston a year or two ago she looked more modern than ever; and when I saw the frescoes at Knossos their likeness to the *style dix neuf cent* was easily explained. Gradually I came to spend more time in the department of antiquities than in the department of fine art. I had read, with immense difficulty, the works of Riegl and had formed the ambition to interpret every scrap of design as the revelation of a state of mind. I dreamed of a great book which would be the successor to Riegl's *Spät-Romische Kunst-Industrie,* and would interpret in human terms the slow, heavy, curve of Egyptian art or the restless, inward-turning line of Scythian gold, and would stand for hours looking at Anglo-Saxon ornament and try to describe how its rhythms differed from the decorations on a Chinese bronze. Needless to say, I had neither the intelligence nor the staying-power to achieve such an ambition, but it has haunted me ever since, and, although I have not written my 'great book', I know what kind of book it ought to have been.

Meanwhile I accumulated experiences. Charles Bell took me to stay with his old friend, Dyson Perrins, who lived in a large Victorian house, also undiluted by any concessions to good taste. On the first visit, when we stayed for several nights, the owner was away and had left Bell the key of his safe. Imagine my feelings when I found I could spend a morning turning over the pages of the Gorleston Psalter, the Oscott Psalter, now in the British Museum, and the exquisite Apocalypse, to mention only three of the manuscripts it contained. And on the open shelves were all the most enchanting illustrated books of the

---

* I cannot swear that it was the Boston figure, but it was one of the same series.

fifteenth century, the famous *Epistolae et Evangelae,* the Tuppo *Aesop* and the unequalled collection of *Sacre Representazioni* with their sweet woodcuts by the artist whom we then called Alunno di Domenico. I used to take a pile of them up to bed, so that I could read their naïve texts as well as enjoy their frontispieces.

We went to stay with Mr. Dyson Perrins in the week's statutory holiday before I took my final examinations, and I remember asking Bell what I should do when my examinations were over. He replied immediately "Write a book on the Gothic Revival". I was taken aback, partly because I didn't really know what the Gothic Revival meant, partly because I wanted to concentrate on one of the great Italians. But it was an inspired suggestion. No book on the subject had appeared since 1872, and no one had taken the trouble to ask why this extraordinary eruption of buildings, sacred and profane, in various mediaeval styles, had taken place. They were accepted as a national misfortune, like the weather. Of course Bell thought that the whole thing was a hideous aberration, but he saw that it ought to be explained and related to the literary and religious movements of the time. He and all my friends expected me to write a sort of satire, and I set out with this in mind. The way in which I was gradually, albeit inadequately, converted to the Gothic revivalists belongs to another chapter.

Charles Bell played a part in my education for which I am eternally grateful. But as a friend he had serious defects. He was inclined to be possessive and wrote me immensely long letters. I am not fond of writing letters and I really dread receiving them. Charles Bell's letters, even when they did not contain recriminations, as they often did, made me feel guilty. I could not bring myself to reply at equal length. And then his dislike of anything painted or written after about 1820 made it difficult for me not to displease him. In life I am deceitful, but where art is concerned I find it almost impossible not to tell the truth. Fortunately during the same years I met a teacher who was in every way the perfect antithesis and antidote to Charles Bell.

I had admired Roger Fry's writings since the publication of *Vision and Design* in 1920, but when I heard him lecture in Oxford on Poussin and Cézanne my admiration turned to idolatry. The wit, the grave, resonant voice and the air of perfect reason with which he would propound incredible theories made him the most bewitching lecturer I have ever heard, and these magical powers were united to a gift of pictorial analysis which, when they were applied to Poussin or Cézanne, was a revelation. One realised how hastily and superficially one had looked at a composition and failed to recognise the complex architecture which underlay it, the calculated intervals, the thrusts and stresses, the changes of direction and the assonance between one form and another. We hardly needed telling that, compared to these abstract ingredients, the subject was of no importance. We had been warned of this in Roger's earlier writing and had seen how he could apply the same critical criteria to a Negro mask or a Chinese bronze. Looking back, I wonder how much I was ever persuaded by the doctrine of 'pure form'. If I had been asked for an honest answer, I suppose I would have admitted that subject matter, with all its implications, was overwhelmingly important to me. And so, perhaps, would Roger, as his earlier and his later writings show. But, in the meanwhile I was content simply to follow the play of his mind. We first met after the Poussin lecture, but became friends after he had held an exhibition of his paintings at the Oxford Arts Club gallery in Broad Street. Roger's paintings and drawings were a severe test for his admirers. Whether working in the style of the early English watercolourists or in that of the post-impressionists his hand was heavy and lifeless and his awkwardness was not confined to the actual touch, but extended, strangely enough, to the whole construction. Yet for forty years he was determined to be a painter and set more store by his laborious canvases than by his hastily written lectures and articles. Paradoxically, the chief merit of his paintings is a naïve earnestness, which is sometimes rather touching. I looked at his exhibition without emotion, but thought there *must* be something there which I had failed to understand, so bought a picture and two drawings. This was the way to Roger's heart. We became friends and, until his death ten years later, I enjoyed his company as much as any man's. He loved to entertain ideas and would listen with apparent interest to the most preposterous suggestions. This made him the ideal companion for Gerald Heard, and the two of them together put on an intellectual circus-act of breathtaking virtuosity. But he was also prepared to listen to the half-baked observations of the young as if they were remarkable discoveries. He made one feel far cleverer than one was; indeed I doubt if I have ever felt clever again since Roger died.

Roger was a Bloomsbury. He had been the lover of Vanessa Bell and his biography was written by Virginia Woolf. You can't be more Bloomsbury than that, unless you are Mr Lytton Strachey himself. He gradually introduced me into that now legendary society and, although I never penetrated deeply (e.g. never met Carrington), I became close friends with Vanessa Bell and Duncan Grant. I had already had a whiff of Bloomsbury, because during my first year at Oxford an acquaintance had taken me out to Garsington. It was exactly as described in numerous memoirs, and the sight of Lady Ottoline's gorgon head turned me to stone. In my embarrassment I wandered among the box hedges till I discovered a timid-looking man wearing a straw hat. As he appeared to be as embarrassed as I was, I spoke a few meaningless words. He answered with some hesitation, in a grave, low voice; he said that his name was Eliot and that he worked in the City. In contrast to the birds of brighter plumage on the upper terrace he was most sympathetic, and I could not help wondering what this kind, obscure man was doing there. A few days later my friend Eddy Sackville-West pressed into my hand a copy of a poem that had just been ·published called *The Waste Land,* and my question was answered.

These pages must give the impression that during my years at Oxford my mind was closed to anything except the history and criticism of art. It is true that this was the occupation for which I was best equipped. But at the same time I was becoming a little more aware of the world around me. This was a by-product of art-history, and I owed it to Ruskin. I believe that when, in 1905, the Labour Party first felt its strength a circular was sent to their members asking what it was that had led them to join the Labour movement, almost all of them replied "Ruskin's *Unto This Last*". It was a revelation to me. Today it is almost impossible to realise how ignorant an ordinary English public schoolboy used to be of the condition of the poor; or, rather, of the working class, for the children of clergymen and retired soldiers, whom they met at school, were probably as poor as miners. I remember that an enterprising master at Winchester invited some members of the local working men's club to come to a debate in the school library. They seemed to us to belong to a different species and we regarded them as figures of fun. Of course it had never occurred to any of us to question the capitalist system any more than we questioned the changing seasons. Even after the Russian revolution our teachers never mentioned Karl Marx, and in the eleventh edition of the *Encyclopaedia Britannica* which, as I have said, was my Bible, the entry under Communism is only a column and a half. Ruskin's beautifully simple and candid examination of the basic truths of economics was accompanied, in my reading, by books like the Hammonds' *Town Labourer* and *Village Labourer,* and Tawney's *Religion and the Rise of Capitalism.* It brought about a complete revolution in my mind. I did not become a social worker; I knew that I had to follow my own line. I did not give away all my money, because I value independence above all things. I am not cut out to be a martyr and am almost incapable of moral indignation. But I have retained from those years of reading a hatred of exploitation that has grown through the years. The sight of a lot of people dining in the Savoy makes me feel sick. This is an emotional, almost physical, response and may seem like hypocrisy, because I am prepared to eat an expensive meal in a small restaurant. But somewhere at the back of my mind is a genuine hatred of Power, Display, Big Business and all that goes with it.

My contemporaries would not have been interested in these questions and I did not mention them. When I read a paper on Ruskin to the College literary society, the only response was one of astonishment that anyone should take him seriously. There must have been some earnest Marxists in Balliol, but they were not to be found in Sligger's rooms, and I never met them, perhaps fortunately, because Marx now seems to me such a marvellous genius that he might have swept me off my feet, and left me suspended in an artificial vacuum, as he did one or two of my immediate successors. My friends and I belonged to the socially irresponsible, post-war generation which was to be succeeded, a year or two later, by the leftist poets; and in so far as my contemporaries were aware of my existence, it was as an uncooperative museum-haunting, music-loving aesthete lacking even the conspicuous absurdity that made other aesthetes a welcome butt to normal undergraduates.

Friends who remember my rooms in Trinity say that what struck them was the vast number of gramophone records that covered the tables, the chairs and even the floor. In collecting them I was encouraged by my friendship with Eddy Sackville-West. He was himself an accomplished pianist, and was to spend years on an exhaustive catalogue of recorded music which was published just after the gramophone companies changed from short to long-playing records, and so became obsolete the moment it appeared. Eddy was a fascinating human being, so full of contradictions that he is almost impossible to describe. He was very slightly built, and seemed to stand permanently on the threshold of death's door, which, alas, he was to cross at a relatively early age. An illustrator, looking for the conventional image of a decadent aristocrat, might well have settled for Eddy. He was not unaware of his *fin de siècle* distinction, and would occasionally dress up in a black cloak with a silver buckle. This gave an incomplete picture of his personality, as he had a strong vein of commonsense, an iron will, great courage and rapid, decisive movements. His hands moved so quickly that he could catch a fly between his finger and thumb. But no doubt a most violent *vie intérieur* boiled under his lighthearted manner and came out in his 'Gothick' novels. He had been in Berlin in 1922 and had found the atmosphere of emotional intensity all too sympathetic. He brought back reproductions of the German expressionists (taboo in Bloomsbury) and hideously printed books by German Symbolists. His interest in Rilke, George and the French Symbolists was a link with Maurice, but he had no patience with 'big stuff'. I, on the other hand, had no patience with *Axel,* and only much later could genuinely admire the *Bateau Ivre.* But we remained close friends, and Eddy spent two years of the war staying with us in Gloucestershire, where he enjoyed being bossed about by our children.

Partly under his influence I made my way to Berlin, where I spent my time in museums and galleries, and so saw nothing of the ferocious depravities which made so great an impression on Eddy, and later on Stephen Spender. I learnt a lot. But I must confess that Germany is very much not my 'spiritual home'. Realising that almost all writers on philosophy and the history of art who had influenced me most deeply —Hegel, Schopenhauer, Jacob Burckhardt, Wöfflin, Riegl, Dvorak—had been German or German trained, I later made a determined effort to soak myself in German culture, and spent almost the whole of one long vacation in Dresden and Munich. Dresden was one of the most beautiful cities in the world. The *Gemälde Galerie,* which still seems to me a model gallery plan, contained the choicest of all princely collections. I went there every day and, like Ruskin, spent hours making notes on the details in the four great Paolo Veroneses. I went to the theatre or the opera every night. At the theatre the *jeune premier* was Anton Walbrook. At the opera Fritz Busch was the conductor, but the tone was set by two old Wagnerian singers named Plashcke. The performances of *The Ring* must have been almost exactly as laid down by Wagner. I went to them conscientiously, picking out the motives on my landlady's piano and reading the text, which is a good deal more interesting than is generally supposed. I was also fortunate in that the revival of interest in Verdi, inaugurated by Werfel in 1922, was well under way, and I was able to see works like the *Forza del Destino* and *Simone Boccanegra* which were not performed in London for many years. Being in the throes of first love with Baroque and Rococo, I was enchanted by the Zwingerhof and, when I got to Munich, was so bowled over by Nymphenburg that forty years later I gave it too much prominence in the ninth programme of *Civilisation.* And yet, in spite of all this, I was unhappy in Germany. 'Only connect'. I never connected, as I did from the first minute I set foot in Italy.

My first visit to Berlin was in the company of a friend who, at that time, played an important part in my life, Leigh Ashton. I had met him with Mr Macdonald while still at Winchester, and he had become my first link with the art world in London. He was a man of exceptional gifts. He played the piano and was surprisingly good at all games (except bridge), and he had rapid and delicate responses to *objets d'art.* He had a good eye for art of all kinds, but what he really loved was a small fragment of Sassanian silk, a Persian pot or a Siculo-Arabic ivory. He had made a collection of such *delectabilia,* to which he had given a perfect setting in a room at the top of his parents' house in Montagu Square. They were quiet, kind people, comfortably off, with portraits of their two pretty daughters by Lavery. There was no indication of the instability that was to afflict at least two of their children. When he visited me at Winchester he was already on the staff of the Victoria and Albert Museum, but he was even less of a scholar than I am. He published a book, practically his only book, on Chinese sculpture, without knowing Chinese or having been to the Far East. Naturally it is full of howlers and received some stinking reviews. But his self-confidence seemed to be unimpaired. He had, what most of his colleagues conspicuously lacked, flair, and when he became Director of the Museum his reorganisation was so imaginative and effective that it has remained the basis of the Museum's arrangement to the present day.

Leigh was* a most generous man and endlessly kind to me. He took me to Paris and introduced me to famous collectors like Raymond Koechlin and famous dealers like Vignier. Koechlin was an exquisite old gentleman who lived in a small apartment surrounded by early Japanese prints, Persian pots and Gothic ivories. It was a refinement upon the taste of the de Goncourts, and remains in my mind when I visit the more opulent collections of the new world. Vignier, who had long been the principal dealer in far eastern art and the first (he claimed) to sell Chinese painting, was an entertaining old ruffian. Hearing that I was a Scot he thumped me on the chest and said 'We are descended from a race of northern pirates who lived by robbery and deceit'. I am afraid I didn't look the part. His boast was borne out by the fact that he chopped off the dated inscription of a beautiful Ming scroll, and sold the central portion to Mr Berenson as the only surviving relic of T'ang painting. In his galleries I met a tall handsome young Frenchman, smoking a pipe, with whom I felt an immediate sympathy. He was called George Salles, and was to

* I use the past tense because, for the last twenty years, he has been in a nursing home, removed from active life.

remain one of my dearest friends till his death in 1966.*

From Paris Leigh took me to Brussels in order to visit the Stoclet collection. It was an expanded version of his own taste, with a superb Khmer figure and cases of Sassanian and Byzantine objects, all housed in a harmonious *art nouveau* house. The Stoclets were dedicated collectors, but their taste stopped short at about the year 1420. They had some fine fourteenth century Italian paintings, but these were kept in a large cupboard and taken out, one by one, only on Sunday afternoons. It was the first great collection† I had visited and remains in my memory as one of the most sympathetic.

Leigh also introduced me to my first hostess, called Mrs Stoop. The husbands of hostesses must be rich and recessive. Mr Stoop (he had some indistinct connection with Dutch Oil) was not very rich, but he had, beyond any other hostess's husband that I have known, the merit of insignificance. He was a small man, with a bottle nose, who, if he had worn a cocked hat, would have been a sympathetic sitter to the old Frans Hals. In later life he had a slight stroke and was told by his doctor to avoid mental exertion. I remember at luncheon someone asking him a question, to which he began hesitantly to reply with the words "I think—er, I think". Mrs Stoop bellowed down the table, "Frank, don't think". The perfect consort for a hostess. Not that Mrs Stoop did much thinking. It was done for her by her companion, a German lady called Weiss who, since 1914, was referred to as

---

* Georges Salles was then an assistant in the Musée Guiment. He became Director of the Louvre in 1945 and President of the Conseil des Musées in 1961.

† Not quite the first, because at the age of fifteen I was so smitten by Velasquez that I wrote for permission to visit Apsley House. I went there with my friend Venables, who looked even more bedraggled than I did. The feelings of the curator, a military man, on seeing these two ridiculous little boys, may be imagined. However, he let us see *The Water Carrier*.

Bianca. She was a cultivated person, with a real feeling for music. She was also selfless and allowed Mrs Stoop to do all the shouting. They were joined by a very odd character, a renegade Bloomsbury named John Hope-Johnstone. He had been tutor to Augustus John's children and is the subject of one of John's best etchings. His real interest was in mathematics and mathematical philosophy. This gave him a tangential interest in music, and made him also a formidable player of bridge and croquet. He could not be described as a sponge, because he lived extremely simply in a bedsitter in Bloomsbury and only accepted money in order to enable him to visit his friend, Gerald Brenan, in Spain. As a young man he had walked to Persia, pushing his luggage in a perambulator. Finally, overcome with fatigue, he got into a fourth class railway carriage. The temperature was in the 'nineties, and the compartment grew fuller and fuller, until finally a goat was pushed in. At this point Hopey rebelled and moved to a first class compartment. The ticket collector asked him what he was doing there, to which he replied that it was against his religion to travel with a goat. The ticket collector considered this a valid reason and allowed him to remain in his first class compartment. Mrs Stoop delighted in his resourcefulness, intelligence and independence. "Isn't it vonderful, I give him money and he never thanks me."

These two characters directed the Stoops' patronage of the arts, and it was of a high order. A Dégas, a Cézanne still-life, a Van Gogh, a blue period Picasso and a Matisse hung on the walls of their small house in Hans Place. Horowitz gave his first concert in their drawing-room, and the musical aristocracy of London walked out saying that Mrs Stoop had picked up another impostor. That she was slightly absurd is unquestionable, but the fact that she took none of the precautions by which a hostess swims upwards in society was exactly what endeared her to her friends and made it easy for a young man to feel at ease in her house.

In the summer of 1925 I hired a boat and crossed the North Sea to Dordrecht (home of the Stoops) with two companions, Leigh Ashton and Bobby Longden. We thought it would be agreeable to visit the chief cities of Holland by going through the canals. England still basked in the sunset of amateurism, and we took no reasonable precautions for what was obviously a complicated project. We had no Dutch phrase-book, not even a Dutch dictionary, one out-of-date chart and a map of the canals. Where we could moor, what dues should be paid for anchorage or the use of canals, was entirely a matter of guesswork. We always paid the same amount, and sometimes were rewarded with blessings, sometimes threatened by shaking fists. Leigh spoke no foreign language correctly but, with his musical ear, he could make noises that sounded exactly like the language in question. He was an excellent cook and did the marketing, wearing very wide and pale grey flannel trousers and a pea-green roll-topped jumper; he was as much a source of amazement to the shopkeepers as a Chinaman (which he somewhat resembled) would have been in the eighteenth century, and was always followed by a crowd of children. We went to all the famous cities—Delft still unspoilt, Gouda to see the stained glass, Utrecht where the episcopal authorities produced without hesitation the famous Psalter to these three very unconvincing-looking scholars, and The Hague where the Mauritshuis (thank God, still unchanged) was the high point of our expedition. Also in The Hague we visited the Kröller Muller Collection, then chiefly famous for an enormous quantity of Van Goghs. They were piled up one above another in a relatively small town house, and perhaps gained, as pictures often do, from being squeezed together. In the next room were a number of abstract pictures by an artist none of us had heard of named Piet Mondrian. Bobby thought them idiotic, and Leigh burbled, but I fell completely under their spell. That a totally abstract picture could give me the same pleasure as a representational picture was a revelation to me, and I looked forward to enjoying this extension of my faculties. Unfortunately I have not got much further; nor, perhaps, has abstract painting.

In Amsterdam (which smelt terribly, as the Rokin had not then been built over) we went to the post office and I learnt that I had got a 'second' in my final examinations. This was no surprise to me; I thought myself fortunate not to have got a 'third', as some of my much cleverer friends were to do in the following year. But Sligger, and other believers in the examination system, were much distressed and sent me letters of commiseration, telling me that John Henry Newman and Mark Pattison had both got seconds (I could have added that Ruskin got an honorary 'fourth'). These consolations did not deceive me. I did not get a 'first' because I have not got a first class mind, only a love of art, a good visual memory and a certain amount of commonsense.

From Amsterdam we went to Alkmaar, which has a pink brick cathedral of ravishing beauty. No tulips: no tourists. We then crossed the Zuyder Zee to East Friesland, and went for a long walk across the fields (walking being still a part of our undergraduate religion), leaping the irrigation canals as we came to them and not noticing that the wind was behind us. On the way back the leaps were more exacting, and at one of them Leigh lost his nerve, faltered and disappeared beneath the waters of the canal. He emerged like a sea-monster, his hair plastered over his face, his pea-green pullover and pale grey trousers a dark brown. He had a long, wet walk back to the boat, which he bore with perfect good humour. No one put up with disasters with greater equanimity and, Heaven knows, he was to have enough of them.

I now had to decide what to do with my next year at Oxford. History courses lasted three years and 'greats'* lasted four, and I was tempted to stay in residence for another year, as most of my friends

---

* Then the most esteemed course, consisting of classical literature, history and philosophy.

would still be there. I began work on the Gothic Revival and determined to go through the illuminated MSS in the Bodleian, many of which were catalogued simply under their author or subject, without any reference to whether or not they were illustrated.

It looked like an attractive prospect, but, except in one particular, it turned out to be a failure. Almost everyone needs some destination, however distant, or some compulsion, however mild. Without the prospect of 'schools' I became neurotic and had a fresh attack of hypochondria, culminating in a genuine attack of jaundice. At that time hardly any doctors were available to Oxford undergraduates, and the only one that any of us knew was a charming old gentleman known as Doggins who got himself up to look like a figure out of *Trelawney of the Wells* and was in fact prompter to the Oxford University Dramatic Society, although when the need for prompting came (as it often did) he was usually asleep. When visiting an undergraduate who believed himself to be ill, he would say "Tell me, laddie, do you drink sherry?". "Yes, Doggins, help yourself". "Then have a good glass of sherry, old man." I couldn't believe that he would recommend this for jaundice, but he did. I became so ill that I had to go back to my parents' house in Bournemouth, where the sight of the yellow curtains in the drawing-room made me physically sick; an experience which may be taken as supporting the physiological theory of aesthetic emotions. It is true that during this year I paid my first visit to Italy, as will be recorded in the next chapter. But the months spent in Oxford were unhappy. I had a pleasant little room in Beaumont Street containing a ravishing Corot, which I had bought at the Leicester Galleries, and my favourite prints by Haranobu. It had the great advantage of a small annexe into which I could put my growing collection of books on the history of art. My landlord, called Hancox, treated me with fatherly care, and when Leigh sent down to call on me (no doubt with the kindest intentions) two ladies of the town he simply said to a visitor "Mr Clark is off his usual". I was much embarrassed by this visit, and rang up Bobby to help me out. It ended with disillusion and boredom on both sides. What I required was not exercise but love and a few months later I got it.

Given my delight in the opposite sex, it may seem extraordinary that I had not fallen in love sooner. But it was practically impossible to meet a girl in Oxford; I saw one or two undergraduates who greatly took my fancy, but they were not allowed to enter my room, or even to lunch with me in a restaurant, without a chaperone. A friend of mine asked me to dinner saying that he wanted me to meet his fiancée. We met in the Moorish Tea Room kept by a character who is fortunately still with us and still lives in Morocco, apparently unchanged. My friend's fiancée, named Jane Martin, turned out to be one of the undergraduates whose appearance, dress and sweet expression had often caught my eye during the last two years. I suppose that I fell in love with her immediately, but banished the thought from my mind. However, I went on seeing her, and when my friend left Oxford for Cairo he asked me to look after her. *Occupe toi d'Amélie*. It was a classic situation. Gradually we saw more and more of each other, and I plucked up courage to ask her to my room. After a few minutes of happy conversation, a step was heard on the stair and I pushed her into my little book cupboard. Sligger walked in and stayed for an interminable time. Jane has retained a slight grievance that I hid her, or would not let her out, but the so-called cupboard at least had a window, and the very sight of a woman would have upset Sligger terribly. Those old Oxford figures must have seen women about in the streets, but the thought of their entering the lives of their friends or pupils would have been extremely painful to them. After a few months it was evident that Jane and I were meant for each other. What she wrote to her fiancé in Egypt I cannot imagine, but he received the news without bitterness or resentment and is still a friend. I was in a seventh heaven of joy. All my hypochondriacal fears left me;

I drove my aged Fiat car at breakneck speed—fifty miles an hour, I suppose.

My parents took the news of my attachment (we were never officially 'engaged') very well. They were completely unworldly and it never struck them that I should 'make a good match'. They had, indeed, received some advance warning of the situation, as my father, to relieve his boredom, used to open and read all my letters. Usually they were from Charlie Bell, and his boredom was increased. A few were from Jane and on one of them he wrote "Don't let the girl catch you". As soon as they met they adored each other. My mother was at first rather worried at the thought of how much sentiment and conventional display a wedding would entail. I doubt if she had been to any wedding except her own; however, she too behaved to Jane with the utmost sweetness and consideration. I think they were genuinely glad to see me so happy; perhaps they were also relieved to have me out of the way.

IV

Italy

IN SEPTEMBER 1925 Charles Bell invited me to go
with him to Italy. He arranged for us both to stay
with his old friend, Mrs Ross, who lived in a Villa
near Florence, named Poggio Gherardo. Many great
writers—Montaigne, Gibbon, Goethe—have described
the excitement of a first visit to Italy; but they had
gone largely to visit the sites and scenes of classical
antiquity, the Italy of Augustus and Marcus Aurelius,
whereas I was going to the Italy of Jacob Burckhardt.
I knew large parts of his book on the culture of the
Renaissance almost by heart, and had had a copy of
his *Cicerone* bound with interleaved pages for notes.

Naturally I was eager to go to Florence, but Charles
Bell insisted that we should break our journey at
Bologna, as he had been brought up in a tradition of
taste that regarded the great Bolognese painters as
fully the equals of the Florentines. I can never be
sufficiently grateful for this decision. The arcaded
streets and apricot stucco of this as yet unspoilt
town, tourist-free, self-sufficient, bursting with life,
were a far better introduction to Italy than would
have been the grim stone walls and the Ruskin-reading
spinsters of Florence. I knew nothing about Bolognese art: in fact in these days it could be studied
only in the original sources. No short cuts existed;
Berenson's little books, and almost all the other introductions to Italian art then available, stopped short
with Paul Veronese. Fortunately I had read Rey-

nolds' *Discourses* in Roger Fry's excellent edition, and had enough sense to recognise that what had seemed the summit of excellence to the artists and connoisseurs of the eighteenth century, was not likely to be negligible. I therefore set off down the arcades in high hopes, enchanted by the shouting, the hooting and the Michelangeloesque torsos of the young men painting the stucco. I needed all my elation, for entering the Museum was like entering a dark, stuffy and loveless mausoleum. Provincial museums in my youth were the most dismal spots on earth (they still are in France). They seemed to be the revenge of the impotent on passion and creative joy. In Bologna the authorities had the advantage of material that lent itself to the gloomiest and most ponderous presentation, and I doubt if I could have kept up my spirits without the enthusiasm of my companion. But before the enormous Guido Reni altarpieces he was in ecstasies that would have satisfied Felibien or Algarotti, and in a few minutes I began to share his feelings. Later in the day we visited the Guidos and Carraccis in the churches and went out to San Michele al Bosco. When, in the 1950's, the Bolognese revival began to gather force I felt like one who, from the laying on of hands, had a direct contact with the earlier faith.

Next day we went on to Florence. In those days the train, burning cheap coal, went through interminable tunnels, and, as we penetrated the Apennines, the windows had to be kept almost permanently shut. My companion, worn out by yesterday's excitement, began visibly to decline, and by the time we reached our destination he was on the point of collapse.

I must say that to visit Mrs Ross at Poggio Gherardo needed courage and good health. The long, dark drive, the crumbling walls, the large abandoned area in front of the door, guarded by a huge, misshapen dog, called Lupo, all produced a chilling effect, which was not lessened when one rang the bell and heard it echoing through empty corridors. After what seemed like an eternity the door was opened by a small, un-

friendly man—the least genial Italian I have ever met
—and one saw that the corridors were even longer
and emptier than they had sounded. By this time my
companion could hardly walk and I had to support
him. Our footsteps, as we staggered along the un-
carpeted floors, made a ghastly confusion of sound.
Finally we reached a small, sunny room, the walls
covered with portrait drawings, the floor thick with
tables on which was a sea of photograph frames. Out
of this rose our tremendous hostess. I introduced
myself, and my companion gave a woebegone smile.
"I'm afraid he is not feeling very well", I said quite
unnecessarily, as I have never seen anyone look iller.
Mrs Ross looked at him with silent disapproval. "I
think he ought to go to bed", I said. "Bed! What
nonsense! I've never spent a day in bed in my life".
However, even she couldn't help noticing his pitiful
condition and told the butler to take us to our rooms.
They were on the north side of the house, huge and
sunless, with the high, square, fourteenth-century
windows overgrown with creepers; between them
was a hideous little chapel, in the middle of which
had been placed a small metal bath. The beds were
hard, the sheets, as always in pre-war Italy, as damp
as dough. I was so much occupied in getting my companion to bed before he actually fainted, that I could
not dwell on the physical miseries of my situation;
but I do remember the unworthy thought crossing
my mind that there was something to be said for
Bournemouth after all.

I dined alone with Mrs. Ross. She was a well-known
terrifier but, after the first formal exchanges, I did
not find her alarming at all. As the numerous descriptions of her may no longer be familiar I must add to
their number. She had been a great beauty, pre-
sumed heroine of many Victorian novels, including
Meredith's *Evan Harrington* and, in a repulsive light,
Ouida's *Friends;* she had also been brought up in a
layer of English society just below the Ducal, but
right at the top of political and intellectual life. She
had frequented Holland House, and thus must have

heard the most intelligent conversation of her day; but there had been no need for her to join in or pay attention. She was a beauty. When I met her she was over eighty but the relics of beauty were still there, a classically regular face, large level eyes, thick white hair, an erect carriage. She always dressed in white, white serge by day, creamy Moroccan silk at night. This progression of whites gave a startling prominence to her fierce black eyebrows. Being interested in history I was anxious to question this living document, and did so at my first dinner. The result was disappointing. "Dear Gladstone, I knew him well", and no more. When pressed she replied "You'll find all that in my books", and after dinner copies of the books were produced, and I read them as quickly as possible, hoping with their help to extract some marginalia from the author. In this I was almost always disappointed, and I suppose that the rather limited number of impressions that Mrs Ross had absorbed in her youthful contact with great Victorians (and pre-Victorians: she had known the Miss Berrys and attended the poet Rogers' breakfast parties) were in fact all included in her books. Needless to say there was nothing in them about her own life and feelings; still less about her passionate rivalry with Ouida, which had split Florence in two during the 1880's. She was the most completely extrovert human being I have ever known, and her passions had passed like water off a duck's back. But, perhaps for this very reason, the books are well-written. She had inherited from her mother, the famous Lady Duff Gordon, a straightforward manner of narration and description, much preferable to a self-conscious style. She was completely without imagination and could not take in an abstract concept. I remember once, when she was translating a book by an early Italian traveller (she knew Italian perfectly, but spoke it with a Churchillian defiance of accent) she came on the word Equator. "Equator, what on earth is that, my dear?" she asked me. "It's an imaginary line drawn round the earth, Aunt Janet". "Imaginary line; what nonsense. I shall leave it out". It is easy to see why she did not recall much of Mr Gladstone's conversation; but her prose-style was better than his.

I went to sleep in my damp sheets, exhausted, but more reconciled to the lack of bourgeois amenities; and when the next morning I went to find Mrs Ross, who, from a vantage point on the terrace, was super-intending the work of her *contadini*, I felt that yearning for the long tradition of Mediterranean life, unbroken, in spite of disasters, for over two thousand years that has fascinated Northern man · since Goethe—*dahin, dahin*.

I gave her the news of my companion, which was bad, but not hopeless. He felt weak and feverish, but thought he would be well enough to accept an invitation to luncheon with Mr Berenson that day. I believe that he did so purely out of kindness to me, because Mr Berenson was leaving for Vienna that afternoon, and Charles Bell know how anxious I was to meet him. He himself had a low opinion of the great man. "He's really only a kind of charlatan, and all that business of attributions is pure guess-work". The Villa i Tatti is less than a mile from Poggio Gherardo, and we contrived to get there on foot. Charles Bell was so delighted by the sight of the white oxen and the vines hanging in swathes that he forgot his mysterious illness, and I, of course, was tremulous with excitement as we entered the Villa. It was a curious contrast to Poggio Gherardo. The en-trance corridor was relatively short and low, and the works of art it contained were arranged with an air of finality, so that they are still in the same places to-day. We were taken into a small room which had been designed for Mrs Berenson by her old friend, Cecil Pinsent. He, and she, were recent converts to the rococo at Nymphenburg, and they had attempted to recreate a room from the Amalienburg, with stucco mouldings picked out in apple-green and pink. The result was a ridiculous parody,* and, as we were being

* After Mrs Berenson's death this decor was removed and library shelves, scarcely less hideous, were put in its place.

offered a thimbleful of vermouth, Charles Bell first shuddered and then began to giggle. Soon Mrs. Berenson appeared, and we were joined by a few Italian guests including a young woman called Pellegrina del Turco who was then the reigning favourite in Mr Berenson's court. He always said that she reminded him of a Ghirlandajo, but I found her more like a niece of Cardinal Mazarin. This little group stood in a semi-circle, nervously awaiting the appearance of the great man. At the last, perfectly chosen moment he entered, small, beautifully dressed, a carnation in his buttonhole. There was an awestruck silence, and he went towards the company, kissing the ladies and extending a small, dry hand to the men. He greeted Charles Bell in the manner of a friendly emperor, both hands on his shoulders. Conversation at luncheon was mainly in Italian, which at that time I did not understand, but after luncheon we went down to a large barn-like structure, full of lemon and pomegranate trees (in fact a *limonaia*) where Mr Berenson liked to sit and talk for about forty minutes, and he beckoned me beside him. By this time I had taken the strongest possible dislike to him. His appearance, and what little I had understood of his conversation, exuded arrogance of a kind that most Anglo-Saxons try to conceal. I am not naturally good at hiding my feelings, and Mr Berenson has left it on record that he was as sensitive as a medium to the aura of criticism. However, we managed to talk for about ten minutes without disaster. Then came an awkward moment when Mr Berenson asked me "Does Charlie Bell still think I am a charlatan?" Fortunately, before I could answer, Mrs Berenson called down the steps that it was time to leave for Vienna, and we all walked up to see him off. He selected a more imposing hat from the collection that always sat on the table at the bottom of the stairs, was helped into a light coat, took a shawl for his knees and advanced towards the door, where a huge Lancia car, containing Mrs Berenson, her maid and Parry, his chauffeur for fifty years, was panting for his departure.

Just after passing the bronze Egyptian cat he stopped, put his hand on my arm, and said "I'm very impulsive, my dear boy, and I have only known you for a few minutes, but I would like you to come and work with me to help me prepare a new edition of my *Florentine Drawings*. Please let me know". He thereupon jumped nimbly into the palpitating vehicle, and drove away.

I am not easily surprised, and usually come to decisions quickly. But on this occasion I was stunned. I had not forgotten the ambition that, as a schoolboy, I had so imprudently announced, and to have it suddenly and accurately fulfilled was rather uncanny—like something out of a fairy-tale. I have a natural distrust of such coincidences, including my own occasional feats of telepathy. I could not help foreseeing how much my parents would dislike the plan. They had, of course, never heard of Mr Berenson, and would suspect that he was another kind of don. Moreover, I had a strong instinct that Mr Berenson's personality would remain foreign to me, and I did not like what little I had experienced of the atmosphere of i Tatti. On the other hand, for a young man setting out on my chosen career, it was the most golden egg that the world of art had to offer, and I would be a goose to refuse it. The conflict in my mind was so great that it gave me a temperature, although there was nothing wrong with me physically.

I had the sense not to mention Mr Berenson's offer either to Mrs Ross or to Charles Bell, and neither of them noticed my perturbation; she because, having once made up her mind on a subject—she had made up her mind to like me—she was impervious to half shadows; and he, poor man, because the luncheon at i Tatti had been the last straw, and on our return home he had retired to bed, where he remained for the rest of our visit. I naturally asked Mrs Ross—or Aunt Janet, as she had now become—to send for a doctor. To my surprise she was fond of doctors and sent for her favourite in Florence, named Giglioli, who bounced through the desolate corridors of Poggio

Gherardo bellowing with true Italian bravura, and roared with laughter at the pitiful spectacle of his patient. But he could not find out what was wrong with Charles Bell, any more than could the numerous doctors whom he continued to consult until his ninety-fourth year. He looked iller than any man I have ever seen. His face had turned pale magenta and his eyelids were so swollen that he could hardly see. His only consolation was to plan my days in Florence, and hear my impressions on my return. He sent me first to the Bargello, partly because its conversion into a museum had not entirely destroyed its true Florentine character, and partly because he recognised that sculpture was the master art of Florence in the *quattrocento*. "You must then lunch in a restaurant beside Or' San Michele", he said, "and see sculpture as it was intended to be seen". I have never really recovered from those first days. Donatello is still at the center of my Pantheon. Every morning I would say "Can't I go to the Uffizi?" "No, not yet; today you must go to Santa Maria Novella. It will take you all day. Tomorrow you must go to Santa Croce and the Badia. It will take you half the day to look at the Renaissance tombs and the Pazzi Chapel, and half to look at the Giottos and Daddis."

The number nine tram to Settignano, which used then to go from the south side of the Duomo, did not keep fixed hours. If I went into the Duomo to enjoy the stained glass or the Bandinelli reliefs it would leave in a flash. There was nothing to be done except wait at the base of the Campanile and try to recall every detail of what I had seen that day. In consequence my reports to Charles Bell were satisfactory, and after a time I was allowed to visit the Uffizi, albeit with many warnings on the gloom of the Botticelli rooms. The Uffizi was, and has to a large extent remained, a depressing gallery, and Botticelli's *Spring,* which must originally have been one of the most beautiful pictures in the world, was barely perceptible beneath its leaden surface. I plodded on till I caught sight of a side-lit room with maps of Grand

Ducal Tuscany on three sides and a view over the roofs toward Santa Croce on the fourth. To step into the daylight out of the *eau de nil* caverns of the gallery raised my spirits, and there in the middle of the room were two sparkling jewels undimmed by time and varnish, Piero della Francesca's portraits of the Duke and Duchess of Urbino. In those days the Piero boom had not begun. I remember that, when Mr Macdonald pulled out of his desk some sepia-coloured photographs of the frescoes at Arezzo, I had immediately felt a sense of pre-ordained harmony different from anything that I had known. Piero's *Baptism* had given me more intense aesthetic delight than any picture in the National Gallery; but nothing had prepared me for the brilliance and sparkle of the Urbino diptych. I fell to my knees, an embarrassing reaction, which, like tears, I cannot always control, and *quel giorno piu non vi leggemmo avante*. Fortunately I was able to report to Charles Bell on the earlier rooms, and satisfied him by my enthusiasm for Gentile da Fabriano and the then neglected (still underated) Lorenzo Monaco.

How I got through a week of dinners alone with Mrs Ross I can't imagine. Every evening as I walked through the suite of dismal rooms, such rooms as the Brownings must have found in Pisa, towards the small dining-room, I thought 'What will happen if I dry up?' Fortunately Mrs Ross made, from a secret recipe of the Medici which she kept locked in her bedroom, a delicious vermouth. She was proud of it, and did not mind how much I drank, so that by dinner time I was quite talkative and managed to extract a few addenda to her books. Like all Victorians of the upper class she resolutely disbelieved that anyone (except the eldest son) was the child of his or her father, and came out with some staggering deviations which would have amused historians of the Holland House set. She was also interesting on the history of the Commune, having been a close friend of Thiers, but when I mentioned the companion of my Cap Martin walks she snorted with indignation. But after a week

Charles Bell guessed that I would need a change, and planned for me an expedition through Southern Tuscany and Umbria. The problem arose who should accompany me, as he himself could not leave his bed, and somebody (I think Mrs Berenson) discovered a Swiss youth called Brown, a few years older than myself and infinitely more a man of the world, who was persuaded that he would enjoy the trip. Naturally Charles Bell gave me detailed directions, which showed his extraordinary knowledge of a school of art in which he had no pretentions to be an expert. "Don't miss the Signorelli in Umbertide; stop at Castiglion Fiorentino to see the Bartolommeo della Gatta stigmatisation of St Francis", etc. etc., all along the line. At Perugia we visited a friend of Charles Bell, who was a defrocked priest. Defrocked Anglicans were common in Italy in those days, but he had the distinction of having been defrocked by the Catholic Church as well. He seemed a mild old pussy-cat, and interested me because he had known Samuel Palmer. By the time I returned to Florence I felt as if I had lived in Italy all my life. The echoing corridors of Poggio Gherardo were no longer alarming; the coarse, damp sheets were like my daily bread; the idea of a bath before dinner was ridiculous. In a few days I had to leave Italy, and my only thought was how to get back. Before I left, Mrs Ross invited me to stay at Poggio Gherardo for as long as I liked and offered me the set of rooms on the upper floor that had been occupied by John Addington Symonds. I had enough sense to say no.

On my way home I told Charles Bell of Mr Berenson's offer. He smiled wanly. "You wouldn't like it, you know. You'd hear nothing but abuse of your friends. They are like crows picking the bones of everyone's reputation." This did, in fact, turn out to be one of the unpleasant features of i Tatti, but I found it more boring then distressing, because the Berensons had so little contact with intelligent life in England that their shots went wide of the mark. I then had to put the proposals to my parents. They were not pleased, chiefly, I think, because they imagined Mr Berenson to be yet another professor, like Sligger, and that working with him would 'keep me back'. They proposed that I should go out there for a month or so to see how I liked the life. This was a sensible suggestion, as I had met Mr and Mrs Berenson for only a few minutes, and during the Easter vacation of 1926 I went for my first visit to i Tatti. It might be better to describe the visit exactly as I remember it; but for two reasons I have taken a different course. For one thing I cannot remember it accurately enough, or, rather, my memories are overlayed by those of later visits; and for another the personality of Mr Berenson was so strange and complex that to introduce him to the reader through the naïve and indistinct memories of his young assistant would be misleading. I will therefore digress to give a sketch of his character and his career, although it contains elements of which I did not become aware for many years.

When I joined Mr Berenson he was sixty years old and at the very height of his reputation as an expert on Italian painting. He had held this position for over twenty-five years, and it had brought him fame and considerable wealth. It had involved the sacrifice of certain gifts and ideals with which he had set out in life, but he was able partially to recapture these attributes in his old age. All that I write of him in this chapter applies to a period before 1935, and those who knew him only in his later and more mellow condition must believe me when I say that in his years of power he was rather less lovable.

He had been brought up in Boston as a poor Jewish refugee from Lithuania, and at an early age had shown amazing intellectual gifts. Like many other great scholars, from Dr Johnson downwards, he said that his mind functioned better between the ages of twelve and sixteen than at any other time of his life, and, thanks to the Boston Public Library and a friendly bookshop, he was able to read enormously. Early photographs show him also to have been strikingly beautiful in the pre-Raphaelite style, and it is not surprising that money was found to send him to the University of Harvard.

At Harvard he studied Oriental languages—Sanskrit, Hebrew, Aramaic—and, though he abandoned the subject in the late 1880's, he was still able to read Hebrew when I knew him, and I heard him discussing points of Hebrew scholarship quite convincingly with the professor of Hebrew in Oxford. The greatest influence on his mind was the philosopher William James, from whom he probably derived his determination to approach aesthetics on a psychological rather than a mystical basis; and William James's racy style, his love of illustrating philosophical points from popular songs and wise-cracks, remained one of the most endearing features of Berenson's conversation.

He was not a student of fine art during his Harvard years. For one thing there were practically no works of art available for study; and for another he had developed uneasy relations with the professor of art, Charles Eliot Norton, who, as an intimate friend of Ruskin and a man of European culture, had an unassailable position in Harvard. Berenson always maintained that it was Norton who prevented him getting a travelling scholarship; but, as he was applying for a scholarship in Oriental languages, this may not be true. At this time his ambitions were not at all precise or, rather, they were so great that he hardly dared to formulate them. It is clear in his later writings, in particular the *Sketch for a Self-Portrait*, that he hoped to become a poet, philosopher and universal man: in short, a second Goethe. He was haunted by this dream all his life and his *Self-Portrait* is fundamentally an attempt to explain to himself why he did not achieve it.

In 1886 a group of friends in Harvard, the chief of whom was a remarkable dilettante named Charles Loeser (probably the first American to buy a Cézanne), raised money for him to go to Europe. He was extremely poor; but he managed to make his way to Greece and Italy, and what he saw transformed him from a student of comparative languages into a student of the visual arts. When he came to look more closely at Italian painting he found a degree of confusion that would have been unthinkable in other disciplines. Only one man, he thought, had applied the kind of scientific tests that had long been current in philology—the Italian scholar Giovanni Morelli. And so he took the first great decision of his life, to develop Morelli's method of saying who painted what picture. He described this moment of decision in his *Sketch for a Self-Portrait*. Sitting at a rickety table outside a café in Bergamo, he said to a friend 'We are the first to have before us no ambition, no expectations, no thought of reward. We shall give ourselves to distinguishing between the authentic works of an Italian painter of the fifteenth and sixteenth century, and those commonly ascribed to him. Here at Bergamo, and in all the fragrant and romantic valleys that branch out northwards, we must not stop till we are sure that every Lotto is a Lotto, every Cariani a Cariani, etc. To this' he adds 'had vaulting ambition, or at least dazzling hopes, shrunk'.

What on earth can have decided a man of Mr Berenson's mental powers to give himself up to the pursuit of Lotto and Cariani? One can find the answer in a note in his diary written almost fifty years later, in Venice, when the first emotions inspired by Venetian art had been rekindled. 'As for Lotto, I went on pilgrimage after pilgrimage, with an almost mediaeval pilgrim's difficulties, anywhere and everywhere, no matter what season and what weather, to see a picture in a church of remote and difficult access. As I left it I was filled with its image and had the leisure to absorb it, to make it unforgettably my own. After three or four years of living with and for Lotto I had him in memory as no bringing together of all his output under one roof could have done'. And later 'In remote villages there was often nothing to eat but hard bread, onions and anchovies, but every morning

I awoke to a glamorous adventure and tasted the freshness of a spring or autumn morning in a Bergamasque
valley. Each altarpiece in its place in the cool or warm,
but penumbral light of a church and its sanctuary
atmosphere I enjoyed like the satisfaction of a vow.'
That is the young Berenson who crossed the St Gott-
hard on foot and walked to Bassae pursued by savage
dogs, in love with art, with Italy and with nature. He
did not want to write a book, only to wander, absorb
and dream. And yet he had to *do* something, and on
the evidence of letters it was his future wife, Mary
Costelloe, who persuaded him to put his experiences
into writing. He struggled against it. 'A picture', he
wrote to her in November 1890, 'inspires in me a feeling so wonderful, so delicate, so subtle, that I can
scarcely define it to myself, not in language, but in
other more usual states of feeling . . . If it were put
into words there would be something *de trop,*
almost indelicate—as we find Walter Pater'. Already
that fear of writing which was to be one of the dominating factors in his life, and which, in his *Self-
Portrait,* he attempts again and again to justify! But
Mary came of a literary family and, to the practical
good sense which made up half her character, talk
and dreaming were not enough. So in the next five
years he forced himself to put his experiences into a
book. He was still in love with Venetian painting,
and in 1894 produced a short list of authentic Venetian
pictures, preceded by an introduction so commonplace that it now reads like a school primer. At the
same time he worked on a book on Lorenzo Lotto.
'The Satisfaction of a Vow': one can account for his
choice of subject only by some such terms, for Lotto
was the last painter to whom his theory of stylistic
criticism could be fruitfully applied. For one thing
nearly all his pictures are signed or documented. For
another, he is unpredictable—the knight on the chess-
board Mr Berenson called him. But the book is written with an air of authority and had considerable
success. While struggling with Lotto, Berenson had
transferred his affections from Venice to Florence, and

in 1894 had gone to live in S Domenico in Fiesole. This move was of crucial importance in his life, because both the art and the intellectual atmosphere of Florence had a bracing quality that Venice and Bergamo had lacked. As a result he wrote the two essays which will probably remain his chief claim to remembrance, one on the character of Florentine painting and one on that of the Central Italians. They are remarkable both for the accuracy of their critical judgements: Botticelli and Piero della Francesca, for example, are, for the first time, given the positions they hold today; and for the aesthetic theories that comprise a great deal more of each essay than is generally realised. Ultimately these theories go back to a dictum by Berenson's hero, Goethe, that art must be life-enhancing. In the visual arts Berenson thought that his 'life-enhancement' could be achieved through what he called 'ideated sensations', and he described a number of these, including ideated sensations of movement, of energy and of space in which we seem to breathe more freely. But the ideated sensation that won him most celebrity, and which he considered his chief contribution to criticism, was what he called *tactile values*. It is the kind of catchy phrase that makes one suspicious, and it does not altogether resist analysis. But it is certain that the ideated sensation of touch heightens our sense of reality in a way that ordinary visual sensations do not, and has a determining influence on our sense of reality. One need only compare Giotto with such a painter as Andrea da Firenze. The accumulation of decorative incident in the Spanish Chapel soon becomes wearisome; Giotto's great forms are inexhaustible.

Berenson's theory of ideated sensations was a brave attempt to put the study of aesthetics on to a new basis, neither the classical academism of the 'middle form', nor the naturalism of the mid-nineteenth century, but something more in keeping with the psychological theories of his teacher, William James. They were capable of expansion, and Berenson often lamented that he had not carried this kind of criticism far further. 'I cannot rid myself', he says, 'of the insistent inner voice that keeps whispering and at times hissing "you should not have competed with the learned nor let yourself become that equivocal thing, an 'expert'. You should have developed and clarified your notions about the enjoyment of the work of art. These notions were your own. They were exhalations of your vital experience." '

Unfortunately, in publishing these 'notions' Berenson follows the same form that he had already employed in his *Venetian Painters*. They were contained in the 'introductions' to lists of authentic pictures. Berenson would have defended this by saying that he did not wish to be a critic or to write about art historically. He wanted people to look for themselves, but look in the right direction, that is to say, look at authentic pictures. It was in the lists, and not in the introductions, that he tried to fulfil the shrunken ambitions arrived at beside the rickety table in Bergamo. At the time it must have seemed to him an idealistic procedure. But there was something dogmatic and authoritarian about the simple lists that was perilous. No argument, no explanation, just a name, pronounced with an almost magical finality. I must add that Mr Berenson's procedure before a picture added to the effect of magic. He would come very close to it and tap its surface and then listen attentively, as if expecting some almost inaudible voice to reply. Then, after a long pause, he would murmur a name. Of course he had tapped the surface to see if the picture were on panel or if the canvas had been relined, but I realise that, to the lay eye, the whole performance looked rather like a conjuring trick, and aroused the suspicions of more laborious scholars.

One can see how much the lists, accompanied as they were by one or two scathing reviews of exhibitions, must have frightened the collectors and dealers of the time. If they were to continue in their agreeable and profitable activities, it was essential to get Berenson on their side.

I have never been able to find out when he took

the second critical decision in his life—to write certificates of authenticity for dealers. On external evidence it must have been about 1895, because by
1900 the penniless scholar was rich enough to rent,
and later to buy, the Villa i Tatti. The sad thing is that
in the same year he wrote to his friends, the Michael
Fields, 'At bottom I no longer care a brass farthing
who painted anything, and yea, the archaeological,
morphological and even historical talk about pictures
is like a wicked stench unto my almighty nostrils'.
Yet he went on saying 'who painted anything' and
was paid increasingly large sums for doing so.

Why should not a man be paid for his expertise?
No one questions the right of a consulting engineer
or a Q.C. to ask a stiff fee for his opinion. The first
answer lies, of course, in the imprecise and unverifi-
able nature of artistic values. A judgement can seldom
be supported by the kind of evidence that would
convince a jury. Add to this changes in fashion, the
charm of rarity, the persuasive voices of critics and
dealers and the desire of rich people to impress one
another, and it is clear that the commercial value of
a picture must be highly artificial. And beyond these
practical considerations, which might apply to other
forms of property, there is a philosophical reason
against this kind of expertise. Works of art are of in-
estimable value to the human spirit, but to become
involved in a process that transposes these spiritual
values into material values, and make money by doing
so, is a kind of Simony. The young Berenson, the
writer of the letters I have just quoted, must have
been painfully aware that he was sacrificing his freedom and idealism and in consequence he was never
able to accept naturally what, to a less evolved person,
would have seemed like an access of good fortune.
To have admitted the simple fact—'I was sick of being poor'—would have undermined that sky-scraper
of high-mindedness which he had been erecting in
his mind since his boyhood. *'Im guten, ganzen,
schönen resolut zu leben'*: Goethe's famous aspiration
reappears in his writings at regular intervals from his

earliest letters onwards. It excludes a consideration of money; and Mr Berenson never mentioned money. Mrs Berenson was more realistic. I remember once saying to them how much I dreaded the impact of letters: I would leave them unopened for days. Mrs Berenson said "Oh, I love opening letters. They might contain a cheque". Mr Berenson shuddered.

Most people would allow that it is nice to have a little money. The trouble was that after 1900 Mr Berenson had a lot, much more than he could possibly have foreseen. He had initially made the mistake of taking a percentage on the price at which each picture was sold, and the expansion of the picture-market in America meant that his fees became enormous. Later on he was to work under contract to Duveen for a fixed fee, but this laid him open to the counter-charge of being in the pay of a single dealer. I am sure that Mr Berenson did not foresee how many deformations a superfluity of wealth involves. There is a subtle corruption which attacks almost everyone when he can no longer be contradicted or prevented from doing things, and when everyone except a few old friends kow-tows to him. Mr. Berenson used to say that he liked people who contradicted him. I never saw any evidence of this. Mrs Berenson and his old chauffeur, Parry, were almost the only people who did so. More formidable opponents, like Croce or Santayana, were still spoken of as old friends, but were not invited to i Tatti. The only person to argue with him with impunity was the great American judge, Learned Hand. Mr Berenson admired him more than any man alive. Judge Learned Hand did not admire Mr Berenson.

And then we may charitably suppose that when he began working for dealers, Berenson did not realise what kind of a jungle he was entering. Perhaps he imagined that, with his superb intelligence, he could look after himself, just as (to continue the metaphor) a great rifle-shot might believe that he could penetrate the Matto Grosso. He could not have foreseen the density of the forest, the hidden pitfalls and the

My father before his marriage

My father at Kinaird

My mother and friends at Sudbourne

My father and my two godfathers

Sudbourne Hall before and after

The staircase at Sudbourne after transformation

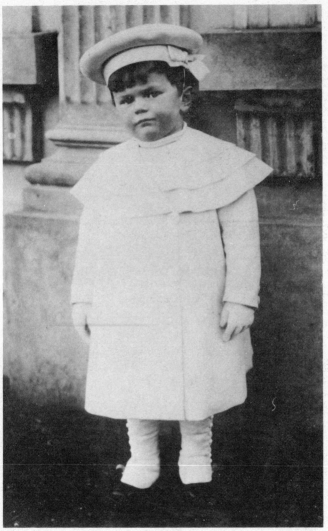

At Kinaird

Sudbourne Araby

My father shooting

Shooting party after lunch. Tommy Dewar (*centre standing*),
Lam (*right*)

The game cart

On the yacht

My mother in my fat cousin's Rolls

My mother on the first *Katoomba*

My mother on the second *Katoomba*

Dressing up at Cap Martin

With my grandmother at
Sudbourne

The man who broke the
bank at Monte Carlo

Posing for a portrait by Charles Sims at Iken

At Bath, photographed by Herbert Lambert

Jane at Oxford

Janet Ross at Poggio Gherardo

Bernard Berenson, circa 1926

Jane with twins

Mr. Gulbenkian in Egypt, circa 1950

Jane, 1939

The Director of the National Gallery in 1939

poisonous tendrils that were to enmesh him, and make freedom of action almost impossible. Although he did not like to talk about dealers, he never ceased to speak with contempt and indignation about his colleagues in the field of art criticism and expertise; and of course they spoke with equal venom, although with less grotesque imagery, about him. It is true that in the thirty years preceding the depression of 1929—30 the world of art dealing was in an unusually depraved condition. The new collectors, chiefly in America, refused to buy any picture that was not certified as authentic. Most of the pictures were quite worthless—it was the certificates that counted. The nearest parallel is the authentication of relics in the late middle ages, and just as I have seen a sacristan sweeping into the corner, with his rubbish, a heap of unauthenticated relics, so, in 1930, I was taken to the cellars of banks and shown pictures on which the bank had advanced a loan of over half a million pounds but which would not have fetched £250 at auction. Almost every critic and art historian on the continent wrote these certificates, often for quite small sums, paid in cash. Their audacity knew no bounds. I remember a rubbed down copy of an old man's portrait by some follower of Bassano, which was sold with a certificate by the great historian of Italian art, Adolfo Venturi, stating, with much eloquence, that it was a portrait of Michelangelo by Titian. Mr Berenson's position must be judged against this background. He was perched on the pinnacle of a mountain of corruption. The air was purer up there. He would not have kept his position if he had done anything flagrantly dishonest; on the other hand, he could not get down.

All this the thirty year old Berenson could not have foreseen and the eighty year old Berenson would never admit. But he could not forget it. In his *Self-Portrait* he asks again and again why he feels himself to be a failure, and gives many fascinating answers. Amongst other things, he blames his decision to write the *Florentine Drawings,* which is in many ways his masterpiece. 'I dared not resist the chance offered of proving that I could toil and plod and pedantise and bore with the best of them.' This is what psychologists call a substitution. The fact is that for almost forty years after 1900 he did practically nothing* except authenticate pictures, sometimes by short articles which were afterwards collected to make a reputable-looking volume, more often by a mere signature. Naturally this false position made him touchy and irascible. He was never a modest man, and the authority he wielded in the world of art-dealing made him extremely arrogant. The extraordinary thing was how much of the young Berenson, the poet, philosopher and sensitive companion he managed to preserve. This complex man retained a sensibility to nature comparable to that of the poet Clare.

Above all he never lost his passionate curiosity about the interaction of art and history. For some years, as an escape from his irksome position, he concentrated on Chinese art, and even considered going to live in the Far East. By the time I came to stay at i Tatti his chief interest was in the decline of classical art—what he called the deformation of form. His travels and his reading were directed to understanding the catastrophic changes that came over European art between the fifth and seventh centuries. He disliked the theory of Oriental influence, and the scholar who had proposed it, Josef Strygowski, became a subject of vituperation second only to Mussolini. It was marvellous that a difference of opinion on a complex historical problem, which is still unsettled, which have driven him into such paraxysms of fury. If I could have worked with him on this splendid subject, which already held great interest for me (I had read the infamous Strygowski with admiration),

---

* The *Florentine Drawings* was finished before 1900, but its publication delayed for some years owing to difficulties with the German State printing press, engineered, Mr Berenson believed, by his only serious rival, Dr Bode. The beautiful essay on Sassetta was written in 1903, and some excellent pages in the *North Italian Painters* as late as 1904.

it would have been exactly the opportunity for which I was hoping. But unfortunately he was also committed to the revision of his earlier works, the *Florentine Drawings* and the lists.

Of course it was inevitable that he should do this. The first lists contain errors of judgement which seem to us now as incredible as those of Crowe and Cavalcaselle. There are also astonishing omissions.* All this Mr Berenson had discovered almost thirty years earlier, and it was galling for him to be continually criticised for mistakes which he had been the first to detect. Then there was the question of certified pictures. The owners, who, indirectly, had paid for their certificates, naturally wanted to see the results confirmed in print. He had to do it; but what a disaster it was for him, and what a cruel punishment for the hubris of those first unqualified statements!

When I joined Mr Berenson in March, 1926, I was, of course, unaware of these complications. I knew only that he had written some books that I admired, that he spoke with authority and was thought to know everything that was to be known about Renaissance art. (Incidentally, I could not, to the end, make up my mind how much he *did* know. That he was enormously well-read in world history is unquestionable; but I came to feel that a distaste for his means of livelihood had made him pay less attention to the Italian Renaissance than to any other historical period.) I knew also that Mr Berenson had grown rich by certifying the authenticity of Italian pictures, but this did not disturb me. In my family making money was considered a laudable activity. I had been 'brought up rich', and was not at all put off by the fabled luxury of i Tatti, which, to a large extent, was

---

* Including Sassetta, a few of whose works appear under the name of the then better known Sano di Pietro. The 'discovery' of Sassetta by a disreputable critic named Langton Douglas was one of the events that gave Mr Berenson the most pain in his life.

a myth. On my first visit I stayed in what was called the Ritz Suite, but any American visitor who expected the kind of conveniences to which he (or more probably she) was accustomed in a Ritz hotel would have been disappointed, and might justifiably have complained that there was practically never enough hot water to fill the small archaic bath. Perhaps my only qualification for working at i Tatti was that I was not overawed by its grandeur.

The social situation into which I had been plunged was as complex as the character of my master, and was based on ancient histories which I was not to recognise for many years. The chief actors, in addition to the great man, were Mrs Berenson, her brother, Logan Pearsall Smith, and Nicky Mariano. I had met Mrs Berenson for only a few minutes, and had received the impression of a tall Giottesque figure, with a very large face and a pleasant Chaucerian commonsense. Aunt Janet assured me that she had been a beauty in her youth, but of this I could see no trace. In London I had called on her sister Alys, the first wife of Bertrand Russell, who certainly had been a beauty. I had been almost stifled by her sweetness and goodwill, and this had led me to expect the same kind of benevolence in Mrs Berenson. But she was a far from simple person. Passions boiled under her huge, impassive-looking exterior. Perhaps in unconscious reaction against her Quaker ancestry she loved strong flavours. She was like those dyspeptics who drench their food in Worcester Sauce and if, in life, a situation was not dramatic enough for her taste she would enliven it by her powers of imagination. She had been brought up as a Quaker (her mother was a well-known religious teacher in Philadelphia), had become a Catholic on her first marriage to a don at Balliol named Costelloe, and had subsequently lost all belief in Christianity. She filled the void with obsessions, sometimes for people, sometimes for architectural projects or certain tasty dishes, always for her children and grandchildren. For them she would do anything, and as both her daughters were married to Bloomsbury intellectuals of modest means, she was anxious to give them as much money as possible. When Mr Berenson's interest in authenticating pictures began to flag, she revived it (under his influence she had become an enthusiastic attributor, and had published a Morellian study of the pictures at Hampton Court), and she welcomed the appearance of art dealers, especially of Lord Duveen. "I love Joe's visits" she said to Mr Berenson, "it's like drinking champagne". "Gin" he replied. In any case, this intoxicating personality gave her a kick and relieved her fundamental melancholy.

Her brother, Logan Pearsall Smith, was an entirely different character. He had no vestige of his sisters' religious or charitable instincts, and must have taken after his father, who was always said to have built himself a house up a tree to escape from the earnest and strong-minded ladies who surrounded him. His whole aim in life was to get to a small top room full of books (there was one at i Tatti, which is still called Logan's room), lie down on a sofa and read. His tall frame, hunched up, with head thrust forward like a bird, was balanced unsteadily on vestigial legs which seemed to have lost their sense of direction through long disuse. But he made expeditions into the world, which he observed with cynical amusement. For a short time, as the result of the success of *Trivia*, it was the 'great' world, and Logan revelled in it. He coined for this experience—he loved coining words —the word 'swimgloat'. His swimgloat had lasted only a few months. Then they dropped him for Wyndham Lewis or Ezra Pound and Logan retired to Chelsea, where he enjoyed the company of Desmond Mac- Carthy and of a number of sharp-tongued spinsters of independent means who had taken up painting and had become pupils of Jacques Emile Blanche, but no longer took their vocation very seriously. I remember attending a luncheon for Blanche where three of these ladies were present in addition to Logan and Edmund Gosse. I suppose I was the only person present under sixty. The flow of commentary and reminiscence seemed to me as brilliant as a page of Proust, but as we left Logan said "You ought to take us all out and drown us in a bucket".

Mrs Berenson had given me an introduction to Logan before my first visit to i Tatti. He had learned to view her enthusiasms with suspicion, and was huffy and silent, but I suppose that my genuine admiration for his work, not only for *Trivia*, but for his incomparable anthologies of Donne and Jeremy Taylor, conquered his prejudices, for he suddenly thawed, and became my friend and mentor. He had always dreamed of meeting a young man who would be like himself when he first went to Balliol, talented, devoted to literature, and as yet without direction. This golden youth (Logan was very fond of the word golden, and his writings had first appeared in a privately printed volume called *The Golden Urn*) would help him in his own researches, and in return would be instructed in the art of Fine Writing.

The trouble about literary apprentices is that if they have talent they want to be independent, and if they have not, they become bores. I introduced Logan to the most talented youth of my acquaintance, Cyril Connolly, but he certainly had no need of instruction from Logan, either as a literary critic or a stylist, and so the apprenticeship didn't last very long. However, Cyril always remained grateful and loyal to the memory of his mentor, which is more than can be said for his immediate successor.

During my first month at i Tatti I enjoyed Logan's company very much more than Mr Berenson's. We spoke the same language, the language of Oxford and the fringe of Bloomsbury, whereas Mr Berenson spoke the language of pre-war Paris. And then, Logan was extremely amusing, whereas Mr Berenson's stories were incomprehensible to me, although he seemed to find them irresistibly funny and would continue to laugh at them when even his Italian and American companions were exhausted. Logan had created in his mind a picture of i Tatti like a little Renaissance court, and he greatly enjoyed all the rises and falls from grace, the denunciations and rages, which are a

feature of court life. Considering the clouds of in-
cense that were burnt every day under Mr Berenson's
nose, Logan, in the background, showed very little
jealousy. He could always console himself with the
thought that he could write and BB couldn't, and he
always recognised that BB had a far greater mind; in
fact, he was the first man I ever heard compare him
to Goethe, and his mockery was coloured by admiration. Mr Berenson, on the other hand, had a low
opinion of his brother-in-law and if, by some accident, Logan began to tell the company a funny story
(and it *was* a funny story), BB would become extremely restive and finally break in with a withering
comment in another language. As we left the dining
room he would say to me, in grieved tones, "Dear me,
what a smutty old clown Logan is becoming". Alas,
as time passed, this description came nearer to the
truth, as poor Logan suffered from the illness named
by its discoverer, Charcot, *folie circulaire*. His periods
ran for about six months. At the height of his euphoria
he really did become a gobbling old clown; at the
bottom of his depression he could not put up with
human company and retired to his little room to read.
The time to see him was when he began to come
up from one of his 'lows'. For three months he would
have been reading about a single subject—Coleridge,
the Carlyles, Fitzgerald or whoever, and he would
have come to inhabit completely their world. His
affliction did not seem to impair his memory, so that
'on the way up' he could remember everything that
Carlyle said and thought about week by week and
relish the human comedy revealed. I suppose that the
Donne and Jeremy Taylor anthologies were done under those circumstances. At those times he was one
of the most enchanting companions I have ever
known. Then he would gradually ascend to euphoria
and one wouldn't know where to look.

The third inhabitant of i Tatti, Nicky Mariano, who
was, in effect, the second Mrs Berenson, must have
been one of the most universally beloved people in
the world. She had not been present when I went

over with Charles Bell; perhaps she had been sent to Vienna in advance to make sure that Mr Berenson's hotel was quite comfortable. But during that time, and in the following six months, I received accounts of her, from Aunt Janet, from Alys Russell, from everyone who had ever stayed at i Tatti. Carmen herself did not have such a build up; and unlike so many Carmens, when she entered the Tatti library, with her sweet smile, her blue slavonic eyes and her jolly nautical gait, I was not disappointed. She seemed to me one of the most completely lovable people I had ever encountered. Alas, the impression I made on her was very different. 'When the young prodigy Kenneth Clark arrived after Christmas to stay for a fortnight, what so often happens when somebody has been praised in superlative terms happened to me. I found him not too easy to talk to, rather standoffish and cutting in his remarks, also not free from conceit for one so young.' It is a proof of Nicky's sweetness of character that I never guessed her feelings about me, and was astonished to read these words in her reminiscences, to which I had agreed to write an introduction. I think she grew fonder of me as time went by, but never quite got over her first impression. Her great complaint was that I lacked a sense of humour—a proposition which the reader must judge for himself. The real reason was that she idolised Mr Berenson, and knew that, although I greatly admired his intelligence and came to have an affection for him, I stopped well short of idolatry. As for the disagreeable impression I made on her—I am afraid that what she says must be true, because I have found it corroborated in unexpected sources. Whether from shyness or from a lack of human warmth in my upbringing, I evidently had what the French call *un abord horriblement froid,* and appeared to be conceited.

When I arrived at i Tatti the working day was devoted entirely to the revision of the lists. This was done with the help of bulging cardboard folders of photographs which were taken into BB's room, artist by artist, for him to examine. Most of the photographs were very old, and many of them were stained by a disease which had provided one of the most terrible of all Tatti dramas. Old silver-print photographs were on thin paper and Mrs Berenson had laboriously stuck them down on to cardboard. She had used a paste made of flour, which was still germinating, and soon produced a culture of brown fungus. Someone lunching at i Tatti said that the only way to cure this was to put the infected photographs into the sun, and Mrs Berenson, with her usual credulity, filled the garden with photographs, which curled up in the heat. When they were straightened again it was found that the fungus had profited by its treatment and spread all over the surface. In consequence, a number of precious prints had to be destroyed. In addition to these blotched, but honest, photographs, there were the enormous glossy prints, sent in by dealers, which looked as unreliable as photographs of fashionable beauties. Nicky was in charge of this unscientific collection as well as of the library. She sat in a small room outside the library, and gave instructions to a number of young women, flustered and untrained, who were sent to look for lost photographs or missing books. Most of them were in a panic, a few hysterical. I was often reminded of Yeats' lines, 'I saw a staring virgin stand/where holy Dionysus died'. Nicky's work as librarian was largely taken up with comforting them. She had already read to Mr Berenson for an hour and helped him dress; and of course throughout the morning there were continual telephone calls from eminent visitors to Florence who wished to come up and lunch at i Tatti and had somehow to be fitted in. Her stamina and good humour were amazing. At about 11 o'clock Mrs Berenson would come lumbering out of her bedroom and make her way to the dining room, where she would interview the cook and insert some richer dishes into the menu. If she met the hysterical young women she had a calming effect on them. She had inherited some of her mother's gifts of spiritual authority, and told me that once when a cook had gone mad (not surprisingly) and threatened her with a meat axe, she had said "I am the Virgin Mary, and I command you to give me that axe", which the cook had done. Mr Berenson seldom appeared in the library, and it was a dreadful moment if he did so, for it meant that all attempts to find an important book or photograph had failed. On these occasions his rages were really magnificent. He was a great admirer of the Old Testament prophets, whom he could quote in the original Hebrew, and would draw on this unrivalled repertoire of vituperation until everyone within earshot was trembling and a few were in tears. Mrs Berenson took these rages quite calmly, and Logan loved them. Twice a week there would be another terrible uproar in the corridor outside Mr Berenson's bedroom. This was made by a huge and hideous Swedish masseuse who was in love with him and thought she was being slighted if he did not make love to her after every treatment. As this occurred on regular days, one could avoid it, but in order to pacify her, Nicky (because of course she ended by making a scene with Nicky) used to ask her to dinner, which ruined the evening.

I remember an old American lady standing in the library and saying "Well, what I say is, where there's books there's peace". We all had difficulty in controlling ourselves.

In the mornings I was left to my own devices. Mr Berenson had not the faintest instinct to teach or impart knowledge; indeed I hardly ever heard him talk about art-history. He said that I would learn far more by browsing in his library than by any settled employment. He himself with his power of application and prodigious memory had learnt in this way; but it didn't suit me, because the riches of the i Tatti library were a kind of intellectual debauch and I flitted from one beauty to another, like Candide in the harem. Mary Berenson saw that I needed direction and set me to work on preparing material for the lists. The artist she chose was one of the most difficult and debatable of all—Giovanni Bellini.

Earlier in this chapter I wrote about the more disreputable aspects of connoisseurship. I must now write a word in its defence. To say whether a picture is, or is not, by Bellini or Botticelli involves a combination of memory, analysis and sensibility, which is an excellent discipline for both mind and eye. The nearest analogy is the textual criticism which was considered the ultimate end of classical scholarship from Bentley to Housman. No one complained that they were wasting their time when they emended, once again, the text of a third-rate author like Manilius. They were not even judged by the correctness of their emendations, but rather by some combination of memory, patience and elegance of mind which gave these minute revisions a quality of intellectual beauty. In connoisseurship memory of facts and documents is replaced by visual memory, not only of the Morellian criteria of ears and fingernails, but of spatial and compositional elements, tone and colour; all of which must be related to what was happening in the rest of European art at the time (hence the necessity of dating) and even to mere fashion. It is an exacting discipline. Also involved is a feeling for the almost indescribable way in which a line evokes a form and for the equally mysterious relationship of tone and colour. A serious judgement of authenticity involves one's whole faculties. It also keeps alive or revives the enjoyment of a work of art, which is the most defensible purpose of all criticism. The first aesthetic shock lasts only a few seconds, and in order to discover in a picture a fraction more of what the artist put into it, there must be some ritual, some telling of beads or reciting of sutras, which keeps one's attention fixed on the work till one's powers of appreciation revive. Perhaps iconological studies may achieve this, but in so far as they are concerned with subject and not form, and may be pursued as well from a line engraving as from the original, they are less rewarding than stylistic analysis.

This must be my excuse for having spent several

years in learning and practising what Mr Berenson had called the rudiments of connoisseurship. But it would be hypocritical to pretend that it was my motive. The fact was that the game of saying who painted what was being played all round me and seemed to me for a time to be the only game worth playing. It never entered my head to play it for money, and, to my chagrin, I have never been offered a bribe, except a box of chocolates by a Viennese dealer. But I thought that to make a smart, unexpected and convincing 'attribution' was the cleverest thing one could do. I made two or three very good ones and thought I was going to the top of the league. I now see that this was a false direction; and Mr Berenson, on one of the very rare occasions when he spoke to me about my future, warned me against it. He said "My dear boy, you have a certain faculty for seeing things vertically instead of horizontally; that is what you should cultivate". On the other hand Mrs Berenson, whose interest in art-history had stopped short at the name-giving stage, kept me engaged in connoisseurship. I remember that she even gave me the Titian folder to prepare. At that time I had not been to the Prado, nor Vienna, nor even Venice. Nothing could show more clearly the hollowness of the system of art-historical studies then fashionable, and still, I believe, current in certain institutions, than that I should have been expected to determine from photographs alone, the authenticity of works by a supreme colourist.

At the end of my morning's occupation, which could not be described as work, I would go down to the sham rococo room to await the luncheon guests, and there was repeated the ritual that I have already described. There were usually about eight or ten guests, and in spite of Nicky's despairing efforts to invite people who would get on with one another, there were always a few American millionaires, Roman Princesses or Spanish Duchesses who could not be refused and who fitted uneasily into a party of Italian intellectuals. The luncheons were very seldom harmonious, but this did not matter much, as most of the time was spent in listening to Mr Berenson. Sometimes two celebrated Italian monologists, Ugo Ojetti and Carlo Placci, were allowed to come on and do short turns; and occasionally a rich old American lady, having got over her first feelings of awe, could contain herself no longer and would give us her impressions of Florence, which Mr Berenson would listen to with perfect courtesy, nodding in agreement and patting solicitiously her hand. But in general Mr Berenson talked without interruption, except for shouts of laughter and applause. What did he talk about? Chiefly politics. He told me that he had never thought about politics till after 1914, and the early letters certainly show no interest in public affairs. But the war had shaken him out of his isolation; at the end of it he believed that he had played an active part in the intrigues and discussions accompanying the Treaty of Versailles. This experience, real or imaginary, had given him a profound distrust of politicians and a hatred of authoritarian government in general. In consequence he had recoiled from the triumph of Mussolini at a time when the European and American upper classes were in ecstasies of admiration. Three years later, when I arrived at i Tatti, anti-Fascist diatribes took place at every luncheon. They were laudable, but monotonous. At that time I knew nothing at all about politics and scarcely listened. Later on, when I had spent some time on the perimeter of public life, I came to feel that a man who had never sat on a committee, never bargained with an opponent, never tried to reach a compromise and never had to make a ruthless decision, could not have much knowledge of the day to day problems of politics; and many of his judgements on English politics were grotesquely wrong. But with his vast knowledge of world history he sometimes made far-sighted judgements, and I remember on the first emergence of Hitler at the time of the beer cellar *putsch* in 1929, he said "This will turn into something that will make Mussolini look like a fairy tale".

One might have supposed that Fascism and the British Foreign Office would have exhausted Mr Berenson's powers of vituperation, but he always had some left over for colleagues, especially Roger Fry and Tancred Borenius and, of course, the execrable Strygowski. I can hardly ever remember him talking about art, except for an occasional swipe at Picasso. Finally he would tell some of his remarkably unfunny stories, and we would rise from the table in gales of laughter. We would then walk down to the *limonaia*, where Mr Berenson would continue to talk, but in a more subdued manner. Then at about 3 o'clock he would go up for an hour's siesta. This meant that in winter he did not set out on his afternoon walk until the sun was beginning to go down, but no one, not even Mrs Wharton, could persuade him to change his routine. For the afternoon walk we drove up the hills behind Vincigliata, often for several miles, and then walked down to find the car at an appointed place. Mr Berenson had spent thirty years exploring these hills and he knew every path. Each walk had its own name, often that of some friend who had discovered it, and Mr Berenson had only to mention the name to old Parry, for us to be catapulted up to the point of departure. Parry was a bad driver and after an enormous lunch would be half asleep all afternoon, but Mr Berenson was impervious to fear or discomfort. How he loved those walks: more, I believe, than any work of art. On my first visit there were usually more eminent people to accompany him, but whenever I did so I discovered a changed being. Gone were the vituperation and the arrogance of the all-powerful expert, and there reappeared the youthful aesthete who had tramped through the valleys of the Veneto. Every hundred yards he would stop in ecstasy, sometimes at a distant view, more often at a group of farmhouses, or the roots of an old olive tree, or at a cluster of autumnal leaves and seed pods. He would be completely absorbed in what he saw, speechless with delight. His conversation on these walks was often about the strange characters who had lived in the villas and farms, or about old friends. Occasionally he spoke of books, and anyone who knows his book *One Year's Reading for Fun* can imagine the depth, enthusiasm and unpredictability of his comments.

Tea at i Tatti took place in the large, joyless library, with a vaulted ceiling, which was then used as a living room. It had been Scott and Pinsent's first job, and they had achieved the remarkable feat of totally excluding the beautiful views that, in those days, stretched away from i Tatti on every side. In the middle was a recessed fireplace in the *quattrocento* style and, on either side, above the book cases, were two enormous blank lunettes. These had led to one of the classic i Tatti rows which, as usual, was initiated by Mrs Berenson. She had taken a fancy to a showy and conceited French painter named René Piot, and one day at tea (this at any rate is Mrs Berenson's version of the story) had said "Monsieur Piot, quel dommage que nous n'avons pas des fresques sur ces murs". As she spoke all foreign languages very badly she may have put it slightly differently. At all events, M Piot thought he had been commissioned to decorate the two empty lunettes, and appeared next morning saying that he had been up all night and made sketches for this vast decoration which would be the masterpiece of the century. Mary protested that this had never been her intention, whereupon M Piot said that if he could not paint the frescoes he would commit suicide that afternoon. Mary relented; but of course the project had to be kept a secret from BB, and M Piot had to contain himself till the Berensons had gone on one of their expeditions. He started work immediately they left and, like Michelangelo in the Sistina, made it a condition that the room should be kept locked, his food carried up to the roof and pushed in through a high window. Cecil Pinsent, who had had to be let in to the secret, became alarmed when enormous bills for lapis lazuli appeared by every post. Clearly there was not going to be anything recessive or self-effacing about M Piot's frescoes and, when Pinsent was at last allowed to see them, his worst

fears were confirmed. In front of a sky of the strongest lapis lazuli blue were groups of almost life-size
naked figures in poses indicating strong sexual excitement. M Piot, inspired by the antique wall-paint-
ings of Herculaneum, in style no less than subject,
had painted the male figures a rich orange brown
and the women pink and white; beyond them, in a
different style, was a view of the Tuscan countryside,
as it might appear in a tourist-agent's brochure. Mr
Berenson returned from his journey slightly fatigued,
entered his beloved library and immediately fainted.
He is said to have fallen flat on the floor, rigid with
horror. He was carried to bed, where he remained for
a week. When he had sufficiently recovered the rows
began. Of course he insisted that the decoration be
instantly painted over. M Piot replied that if this was
done he would institute a lawsuit and apparently he
would have won it. In the end there was a compromise,
the frescoes were photographed (which is why I
can describe them) then covered by vast pieces of
linen on wooden frames, so that the tea-time visitors
to i Tatti never knew what an explosion of vulgarity
had taken place over their heads.

The tea guests were usually less grand than the
luncheon guests and included some art historians and
pretty, middle-aged women. Mr Berenson sat in a
large leather chair by the fire with the principal lady
on his right. I usually sat on a stool in the fireplace
recess, so that I could be at hand to pour out tea and
put logs on the fire. This position gave me the advantage that I could overhear his conversation. Several times in his *Self-Portrait* he says that he could
talk his best only to people who listened to him with
unquestioning appreciation. His best talk was seldom
addressed to me, but I often overheard it when a
sympathetic lady was seated beside him, and I was
buttering his toast. It was indeed a remarkable performance, of which the reader of his later journals
can form a faint impression. The flow of ideas, the
range of historical reference, the intellectual curiosity
and unexpected human sympathy were certainly be-

yond those of anyone I have met. Add to this the intense gaze of his beautiful grey eyes, with their long lashes, which can be described only by one of his favourite words 'caressing', and one can easily see why his companion was hypnotised, even when she did not understand a quarter of what he said. I must add that he sometimes talked a good deal of nonsense, either out of pure self-indulgence or in order to see how far he could go without arousing opposition. At six o'clock he retired, and we all began to chatter. At eight-fifteen we met for dinner and were offered tiny glasses of vermouth, with some lemon juice. Sam Behrman, in his book on Duveen, refers to cocktail time at i Tatti, but this is a playwright's sense of the dramatically appropriate. What wouldn't we all have given for a cocktail to get us through a sticky dinner; especially as the wine from the village was almost undrinkable. Mr Berenson, whose physical responses to form, colour and space were so acute, took little pleasure in food and drink. Mrs Berenson, on the other hand, loved food so much that when we were motoring in north Italy she would plan our expeditions by memories of meals. "I must go to Feltre", she would say. "Why, there is nothing much to see there". "I remember eating excellent *lassagne verde*". "But, Mary, that was thirty years ago". Most sympathetic to me. (Actually what she wanted to see in Feltre was the lunatic asylum, which she visited with great satisfaction, while we were looking at a picture attributed to Morto da Feltre.)

My visit to i Tatti was not an unqualified success. I believe that most people shared Nicky's disappointment, and Aunt Janet went so far as to say that my character had deteriorated since the preceding autumn, which may well have been true, as I had had another attack of hypochondria, culminating in jaundice. I did, however, make one friend whose sweet character, intelligence and absolute sincerity have been a joy to me ever since, Umberto Morra. His father had been a general, a close friend of King Umberto I, and later Italian ambassador at St Petersburg. Owing to an accident his son was lame, and thus disqualified from the life of action, which must have been a tragedy for the General, but was a blessing for everyone else, as Umberto Morra's gifts of sympathy and sensibility could hardly have survived a military training. He was to become the translator of Virginia Woolf. But some inheritance from the man of action remained, and made him a tireless opponent of Fascism, which was one reason for his friendship with Mr Berenson. The thought of meeting Umberto again was one of the factors which made me look forward to returning to the world of i Tatti in the following autumn.

I joined the Berensons in Milan in October 1926. We stayed in the Hotel Cavour, one of the most agreeable hotels in Europe, long since demolished. At that time it was full of notabilities who had assembled to hear Toscanini conduct the nine symphonies of Beethoven in the Scala. I went to most of the concerts, and have been a little sniffy about other performances of Beethoven's symphonies ever since. Among the guests in the Cavour was Diaghilev, whom I met only twice; but it was enough for me to experience the feeling of his overwhelming physical potency which, in my experience, was equalled only by that of Mr Calouste Gulbenkian. I suppose that Lloyd George had it, but by the time I met him it had evaporated. It is a most disturbing quality and explains a good deal in history which is incomprehensible on documentary evidence alone.

With BB and Nicky I visited the chief galleries of Milan, the Brera, as portentous and dismal then as it is now, the Poldi Pezzoli as charming, the Ambrosian library as welcoming and as dark. After a week or two we moved off to the cities of northern Italy, checking the lists as we went from place to place. At Brescia I had the disagreeable experience of being arrested. Two days earlier we had passed through the featureless market town of Treviglio, and stopped in order to see an historically important, but not very exhilarating, altarpiece by two Milanese artists named Zenale and Butinone. As visitors to Treviglio are rare, two enterprising townsmen took the number of my car (I had driven out to Italy in a chic, but impracticable, Sunbeam), stole the church treasure and then went to the police describing how I had entered the church empty-handed and emerged carrying a large brown paper parcel. They must have been very simple to imagine that anyone would believe such a story. I was locked in my room for the day, which saved me a few more hours' exposure to grey Brescian painting, and by evening the thieves were caught at the frontier and the perfectly hideous church treasure was duly restored to Treviglio. The only other incident that I can remember in Brescia was that BB's shawl, which he always carried on his arm to put over his knees in a church, was stolen in S Giovanni. Nicky went to the priest, who preached a sermon describing how someone had stolen a poor old man's shawl, knitted by his mother (which in fact was true) and the shawl was returned. We then drove on to Bergamo, which I loved, and we explored in greater comfort BB's fragrant valleys and penumbral churches. Our chief quarry was Lorenzo Lotto, and I began to understand BB's early obsession. Unpredictable, vulnerable, uneven and painfully conscious of the spiritual malaise of his time, he aroused my northern conscience. I was crushed by the intolerable confidence of Titian, but Lotto's uneasiness was sympathetic. Forty-five years later I have come to appreciate the greatness of Titian, and to feel slightly impatient at Lotto's instability.

Mrs Berenson came with us on part of our journeys, then returned to i Tatti on secret business. She must have been with us in Verona, for I remember her seated in the sacristy of S Domenico reading over and over again the inscription on the architrave *Credo vita eterna,* and adding "I do *not* believe". Spiritual hunger transformed her vast, jolly face, so that she looked like some monument of the late Roman Empire. At this time I found her company far

more congenial than that of Mr Berenson, on account
of her candour and humanity. To tell the truth, I
cannot remember a single word of Mr Berenson's
conversation during the whole three months of our
travels together. When looking at works of art he was
silent and absorbed, at meal times he was exhausted
and distressed by the soggy rice and hard *pasta,* which
at that date was the usual fare in Italian hotels. And
then there was no one there to spark him off. In
each town we had to meet the gallery director, inspector of monuments and more self-important local
savants. By this time I had learnt a little Italian, and
so was able to realise how boring they were. Mr
Berenson listened to them with inexhaustible patience.
Whatever he might say about the famous scholars in
London or Vienna, he was always courteous to their
humble colleagues, partly because he hoped that their
interminable harangues might contain one grain of
useful information. He would question anyone whom
he thought might remember a tradition. Once, in
front of some feeble fourteenth-century frescoes in
Verona, he insisted on asking a very vinous sacristan
who was the painter. After much head-scratching and
hiccoughing the sacristan replied rather dubiously
"Un certo Zocchi-Giocchi, non so." BB was delighted
that the fame of Giotto had spread so far.

Much of the time BB and Mary quarrelled, like
old sparring partners. She was bored by his interest
in the nameless art of the early middle ages; he was
annoyed by her constant preoccupation with her family and with food. But they retained warmer feelings
for each other than most people realised. I remember
driving in the Lancia down some side road in the flat,
featureless Lombard plain, looking for Heaven knows
what obscure addition to the lists, when we came to a
ford. Old Parry pulled up. BB, who always said that
he put himself into a motor car like a good Catholic
into the hands of God, said "Drive on Parry". "If you
like it that way", said Parry, and we drove into the
river, which immediately flowed over the engine and
the car remained stationary with the water just cov-

ering the floor of the back seat. It was getting dark and we had no idea where we were, but BB was not in the least put out. He held Mary's hand, and they began to sing old Harvard songs—'My name is Solomon Levi' and 'The waiter bellowed down the hall, "We don't serve bread with one fish ball" '. Meanwhile Nicky and I walked up and down the bank, looking for help. As always in Italy, men sprang up from the ground, and in half an hour a team of oxen had towed the Lancia to the other side. Of course it would not start, so Nicky and I had to leave the Berensons sitting side by side, upright and impassive, like Egyptian figures, while we walked to the main road and thumbed a lift to Parma. Next day they both seemed rejuvenated by their humanising misadventure.

At Parma there were the Antelamis and the Correggios. I loved equally the austere figures on the Baptistry and the golden hair of Correggio's Magdalen in the *Giorno*. I also remember another moment of vision which was to lie dormant in my imagination for many years—a realisation of the ecstasy of martyrdom, which came to me before Correggio's picture of S Placida and S Flavia. It was the moment at which I became capable of writing the chapter on the Counter-reformation in *Civilisation*. At Padua I had my first real experience of Giotto (for the Giottos in S Croce were obviously so restored that only a distorted echo was audible). It was strong, but not nearly as strong as my response to Giotto has since become. I suppose that I was still looking for 'significant form' and 'tactile values', and did not understand how these pictorial qualities arose out of Giotto's desire to make me believe more intensely in the truth of each episode. I do not know how many times I have been to the Arena Chapel since then, certainly more than a dozen, and each time I am more deeply moved. Clive Bell's *Art* may be two thirds rubbish, but at least it had the merit of stressing the greatness of Giotto.

I also saw for the first time, and under favourable

conditions, which the Antonini monks do their best to prevent, Donatello's bronze reliefs of the miracles of St Anthony of Padua. They seemed to be equal to the Giottos and, with the Masaccios in the Carmine, to be the bed-rock of European art.

Mr Berenson was condemned to spend many hours in the dismal gallery of Padua where there seemed to be an exceptionally large number of *ispettori* and local *savants*. But he was cheered up by the presence in the town of what he used to describe, in sacramental tones, as 'a very great lady', the Countess Papafava. She was a nice, noisy old creature, who bellowed at a crowd of local sycophants in a powerful contralto voice. The furniture in her drawing room was designed by Canova. The whole scene reminded me of Stendhal, then one of my favourite authors, and I absorbed it with silent pleasure. Under these happy circumstances Mr Berenson became quite his old i Tatti self. She owned a large picture of St Jerome in the Wilderness, which had appeared in 'the lists' as a Basaiti. Mr Berenson had no hesitation in pronouncing it a Bellini. Mrs Berenson, who had rejoined us, was delighted. "Little do they know" she said, "how much money BB has put into their pockets". It was not long before the Papafava Bellini was sold to Duveen and is now in the National Gallery of Washington.

After Padua we went on to Bologna; but by now it was late November and the apricot light had faded from the streets. We stayed in one of those old-fashioned Italian hotels, a converted palazzo, the wide corridors hung with old pictures, landscapes in the style of Salvator Rosa and minor Bolognese painters whose work would now be sold for many thousands of pounds by art dealers in Jermyn Street, but at that date was considered worthless. There was no Countess Papafava in Bologna, so our stay was short; but we did get to the Gallery. The huge sagging canvases were barely visible in the winter light, and dear Guido made a melancholy impression. Mr Berenson walked round in silence with folded hands. Nevertheless he had the intelligence to recognise that the fashionable neglect of the *seicento* was ridiculous. "You will live to see it come back, my dear boy", he said, "and I hope you may do for it what I have done for the *quattrocento*". By the time Bolognese painting came back into fashion and editors were prepared to publish articles on the subject, my own interest in art-history had taken an entirely different direction. Fortunately there were several scholars who were prepared to become the Berensons of the *seicento,* and have carried on the same kind of controversies that took place between Berenson and Bode.

We then returned to Florence, and there ensued an i Tatti drama, less catastrophic than M Piot's mural paintings, although in the long run more regrettable. Mrs Berenson's frequent absences from our trip had worried Nicky and BB, but were attributed to some secret anxiety about her family. In fact they were concerned with the erection of a clock tower on the roof of i Tatti. i Tatti was a plain Tuscan manor house and its extensions for working purposes had all taken place at the back. Under the influence of Cecil Pinsent Mrs Berenson had constructed an imitation baroque garden, which Mr Berenson always disliked. But it was below the rustic *limonaia* where he sat and talked after luncheon; and between the *limonaia* and the front of the house were the unproductive flower beds and the glass frames that might have been found in any villa. It was a pleasant, unpretentious ensemble. Mrs Berenson thought it was not imposing enough, and she determined to add a central clock tower. She had already confided in me that she and Pinsent were motoring round Florence to find a suitable model, and of course they didn't find one, because houses with clock towers were much grander and had façades into which the clock tower was incorporated. So she secretly instructed Pinsent to design one and jam it on somehow, while Mr Berenson was away. She had also ordered Pinsent to replace the charming *intonaco* floor of the entrance corridor with inlaid marble. When we returned home, at night,

Mr Berenson was confronted with this slippery and pretentious substance, which put him in a bad frame of mind. His feelings next morning, when he went for his 10.30 walk in the garden and saw the clock tower, in all its agggressive novelty, may be imagined. As usual, he went to bed after ordering that the tower be immediately removed. Of course this proved impractical—the tiles on the roof could not be matched, and he would have had to endure two months of hammering and scaffolding in front of the study window. So the tower is still there and is accepted by pilgrims to i Tatti as one of the most attractive features of the villa.

After this drama it took some weeks for the i Tatti ritual to be reestablished. Mr Berenson was *incommunicado,* and I sat turning over photographs of Florentine drawings without much profit. Logan was in London, so I stayed in his room and followed his example of spending most of my time reading on his settee. I seemed to be a fixture, pushing in chairs and buttering toast, like a *jeune fille de la maison.* Much of the conversation at i Tatti was concerned with people's sexual relationships: not surprisingly, given Mr Berenson's own Jove-like exploits. And naturally there had been many arguments and discussions about my own sex life, some of which had come back to me by an indirect source. BB naturally hoped that I would form a liaison with an older woman, if possible a 'great lady', in Florence. Nicky hoped that I would have a series of passionate love affairs that would provide subjects of conversation for a year or two. Mary hoped that I would marry one of her granddaughters, Mrs Ross that I would marry her great niece. Unfortunately I showed no sign of fulfilling any of their hopes. The inhabitants of i Tatti were puzzled and frustrated. Finally they came to the conclusion that I must prefer boys. Boys—yes, of course: it was usual among young Englishmen. But when did I see them? The whole thing was tiresomely obscure. Finally Mrs Berenson could bear it no longer and thought of a way of broaching the question. She said, quite reasonably, that it would not be good for me to live at i Tatti any longer. I must have independence. She therefore proposed that I should stay with Cecil Pinsent, who had a spare bedroom in his apartment. Whether she had ever put the plan to Pinsent I very much doubt, but Mary was always optimistic. The proposal indicated a final acceptance of the theory BOYS, because Pinsent's tastes were known to incline in that direction. Driven into a corner by this bizarre proposition, I had no alternative but to come out with the truth. "Mary", I said, "I want to get married!"

This announcement pleased nobody. Nicky said to me, almost with tears "But Kenneth, we hoped you would have such wonderful affairs". Mrs Ross said "I don't know what he wants to get married for when he can live with me", to which Mr Berenson replied "There's no accounting for tastes, Aunt Janet". Mrs Berenson, with her strong family feeling, behaved in a kind and practical manner and arranged for a house in which we should live when I brought my bride back to Settignano. Mr Berenson never mentioned the matter. This did not strike me as peculiar because he did not speak to me much in the ordinary way. But long afterwards I learned that he had been deeply hurt, and considered that I had (in his own words) 'betrayed him'. A few days after my announcement I wired to Jane asking her to marry me on January 10th, 1927, to which she agreed. I stayed on at i Tatti, perhaps tactlessly, till after Christmas. When the hour of my departure came Mrs Berenson led me round to say goodbye to her husband. He was in the bathroom and could be heard through the thin door brushing his teeth. "Bernard", she said, "Kenneth has come to say goodbye. He's going to get married". Brush, brush, brush. "Very well, Mary", brush, brush, brush, "I don't mind". Being used to the undemonstrative behaviour of my mother, this did not seem strange to me.

V

Growing Up

BEFORE GOING home to be married I paid my first visit to Rome. I was overwhelmed and bewildered. Impossible to take it all in. Where should I begin? Ancient Rome? Early Christian mosaics, Baroque Churches or the Vatican? The mosaics won. Of course I went to the Sistine Chapel and to Raphael's Stanze, which, as Reynolds says, means very little to a young man. But my heart and mind were concentrated on S Maria Maggiore, S Constanza and SS Cosimo e Damiano. When I visit Rome for the last time, I hope I shall return to them.

The night before going home I dined with Lytton Strachey and Arthur Waley in Alfredos. We must have been a queer-looking party, Arthur with his beautiful Franciscan face emerging from a black turtle-neck sweater, which somehow suggested Missions to Seamen; his friend Beryl de Zoete with hair like a Japanese doll, dressed in Balinese costume. Lytton's appearance need not be described. Perhaps because we looked so odd, we were chosen as a target by the evil-looking little man who sang indecent Neapolitan songs into the ears of the diners. He made a set at Lytton, who covered his head with his long thin hands and moaned "Can nobody get rid of him?" But nobody could, and he is still there, singing the same songs, forty-six years later.

I arrived back in London the day before the wedding to find that Jane had just had a tooth out and was feeling much the worse for wear. I had very meanly left it to her mother to make all the arrangements, stipulating only that I did not want bridesmaids or a wedding dress. I was still the victim of a Quakerish fear of ritual, and was also influenced by the thought of how much my mother would dislike any form of display. This was unfair on Jane who loves dressing up, and it turned out to be a dreary compromise. St Peter's Church in Eaton Square was almost empty. A few old servants sat at the back with an air of mournful resignation. My fat cousin from over Christie's came in a silk hat. Our best man was Leigh Ashton because he was the only person I knew who seemed to be a 'man of the world'. After the ceremony no one knew what to do. Of course my parents should have given a wedding luncheon, including Jane's parents, the best man and other friends, but my father 'couldn't be bothered' (his favourite phrase), and my mother was afraid that there might be some display of emotion. So we walked back to a hideous hotel called St Ermins and lunched alone with my parents. For some mysterious reason my mother had taken a fancy to this dismal building, and had rented a service flat there. When I decided to get married she handed it over to me. I decorated it in a conventional style, my only independent stroke being to commission Bernard Leach to do the tiles round the fireplace. The apartment had nothing to recommend it, not even a kitchenette, but we were in no mood to be critical.

After about a week of uneasy existence in St Ermins, we thankfully entered the Rome Express, Florence portion, and rattled out to our future home, the Chiostro di San Martino, near Settignano, which Mrs Berenson, seeing my helplessness, had rented for us. It adjoined a beautiful, unspoiled Brunelleschian church, one of the few to retain all its original altarpieces, and was itself basically a *quattrocento* building, although a plaque on the wall informed us that the blessed Andrew the Scot had died in our bedroom in the year 682. The owner had left us her old French maid, her cook and her housemaid. What a perfect way to begin married life! But less than a mile away loomed two ogres' castles, i Tatti and Poggio Gherardo. I was so much alarmed at the thought of taking Jane up to i Tatti that, before doing so, I felt genuinely ill and had to lie down on a chaise-longue. Jane had more courage, and we set out in good heart; but I cannot say that the visit was a complete success. BB was still furious at my 'betrayal', and treated Jane with a lack of sympathy to which she was not at all accustomed. Convention ordained that, as a bride, she sat next to him at every meal, and he talked across her in German or Italian, neither of which she understood. This was, in fact, his normal mode of conversation, but Jane thought it was deliberately insulting and formed a dislike of Mr Berenson which she never entirely lost. However, on one occasion she had to admit that he behaved well. This arose as a result of our first visit to Mrs Ross at Poggio Gherardo. The old dragon, in her best Ouida form, would not speak to Jane at all, but led me off through her long suite of rooms, leaving Jane alone with a canary. I suppose I should have protested, but I wanted to get out of the house as quickly as possible and a row might have gone on for ever. When Mr Berenson heard the story he was shocked. He put on a tail coat and silk top hat and went up to Poggio Gherardo to administer an official rebuke. I can't say it had much effect; but it was kind of him.

Various investigators were sent down—Umberto Morra, R. C. Trevelyan and the Japanese scholar Yukio Yashiro. Umberto was gentle, natural and understanding, and soon became as much Jane's friend as mine. Bob Trevelyan behaved with rustic chivalry and gave Jane a book, priced 1/6d., one of our few wedding presents. Yukio Yashiro brought her a roll of pink Japanese silk in which to wrap our first-born who he assumed would be a daughter. All three became friends; and although I have seen 'Yuki' all too seldom, the fortnight I spent with him in Japan showed me how foolish it is to assume that distance and a different cultural background are bars to friendship. Lady Colefax also called, but was not much impressed. The days when we were referred to as 'my young people' were yet to come. Our Oxford friends came to stay with us, and were a relief after the formalities of i Tatti. Naturally we took Maurice Bowra and John Sparrow up to visit the great man, but it didn't go at all well and, as far as I know, Maurice never crossed the threshold of i Tatti again. They were succeeded by Cyril Connolly (at that time on bad terms with Maurice), who delighted Mr Berenson and soon left San Martino to settle in for a long stay at i Tatti.

A joyful time; and the greatest joy of all was to find that Jane liked pictures. It had never occurred to me to ask if she enjoyed works of art and if she had not our life together would have been very different. But she turned out to have an unusually good eye, and learnt her lessons in art-history with enthusiasm. We visited the galleries and churches of Florence, skipping from picture to picture, from chapel to chapel, in a frenzy of excitement.

In April we paid our first visit to Venice. Charles Bell had made me promise not to go there by train, but to stay in Padua and take the slow, ancient boat that twice a day chugged over to Venice from the village of Fusina. As usual, his advice showed his impeccable sense of values. We saw Venice rising out of the sea as Ruskin and Whistler had seen it. When we arrived there were no tourists and the touts had lost heart except for a man who tried to sell us a monkey. We lived very frugally, as I was under the impression that, until I could make some money, I ought not to spend it; also I am by nature exceptionally mean. All the time I was courting Jane, the only present I gave her was a paper bag of peppermint bullseyes. In Venice the weather was warm, and Jane had brought only one thin dress. She wore it for a fortnight, as she thought it would be rude to ask me to buy her another, and of course it never occurred to me to do so.

In between these enchanting expeditions I continued my work on the revision of the *Florentine Drawings*. From the Chiostro di San Martino I could run down the hill to Ponte a Mensola and catch the 9.20 tram to Florence, arriving at the Gabinetto del Disegni as it opened. I checked the sizes and mediums of the drawings in Mr Berenson's catalogue, but I seldom criticised his attributions, and made practically no new discoveries. I was to do the same thing, with the same results, in nearly all the printrooms of Europe. The only question on which I dared to disagree with him was his thesis, derived from Wickhoff, that some of the greatest of Michelangelo's drawings were done by Sebastiano del Piombo. He shook his head sadly, but remained silent; it was his favourite child. In the end (although not in the book) the Sebastiano hypothesis was abandoned. He handsomely acknowledged my help in the preface to the new edition, but all I contributed could have been done by a hack. I was the gainer, being received in printrooms as the disciple of the great Berenson.

We made a few friends in Florence—one of them, more of an *objet trouvé* than a friend, Miss Paget, who, under the pseudonym of Vernon Lee, had written a book on the completely neglected subject of eighteenth-century Italy. It appeared in 1881, and had an enormous *succès d'estime*. She was lionized by the late pre-Raphaelite set and praised by Walter Pater. She was said to be the most brilliant talker in London; one can still form some impression of her brilliance from Sargent's portrait in the Tate. She gave offence to her friends, was pro-German during the war and, by the time we met her, was isolated, querulous and deaf. She looked somewhat grotesque, as she wore men's clothes, had short grey hair and her jaw had a sideways thrust. In spite of all this I found her company irresistible, as she had a mind of rare tenacity. "Never be afraid of being a bore" said Desmond MacCarthy, thinking of the society in which he moved, where bird-like talkers hopped lightly from one subject to another. Miss Paget went grinding on like an old machine, and out of it came a few grains of gold dust. She was glad of an audience, everyone else having long ago given up and, as I had read and admired several of her books, I could keep the machine in motion.

The other character I would like to recall was a real friend. His name was Edmund Houghton, and he was the most unworldly and disinterested man I have ever met. He was an old Fabian and thought it wrong to have any more money than was absolutely necessary to support life. His suits were worn out, his shirts full of holes round the neck, but he always wore a clean white stiff collar and a blue knitted tie that matched his eyes. He lived in the attic of a Florentine *palazzo*, entirely filled with fragmentary works of art which he had been given by local *antiquaires* who thought them worthless. In one corner were two little iron beds for himself and his wife. It was a mistake to admire one of his fragments, as he immediately gave it to one, and nothing would stop him. When I was at the Ashmolean he gave the museum a very 'important' and valuable majolica figure. He went back to England in the summer on a motor-bicycle and side-car combination, which he said was the cheapest way of travelling, and sometimes he had to sell a table to raise money for the petrol. In England he lived in a house by the Thames of which he was very proud. We drove out to see it one dark night. We went down a lane which seemed to run straight into the river and at the last moment Edmund said, in his courteous voice, "Turn in here, please". I turned into a field and slithered along for about a hundred yards. "Now, here we are", in tones that Lord Egremont might have used when arriving at Petworth. We got out and could just see the outline of a small, ruinous fifteenth-century house. The water gurgled all round us as we followed Edmund to the door. Inside it seemed to be totally dark but after a minute we could make out the figure of Mrs Houghton, in a long cloak and long grey ringlets, sitting beside the embers of a fire. "Give us some light my dear", said Edmund, and she threw some old newspapers on the fire. That was all the light there was. It lit up the beams of the ceiling and the puddles on the floor. "But I must show you our bedroom", said Edmund, and he found the stump of a candle. Upstairs the pools of water were larger, and over the two little beds were open umbrellas. "You see", said Edmund, "it's really all one wants". I have spent most of my life among worldly and ambitious people; and, although not at all ambitious myself, must be reckoned a worldling. The memory of Edmund Houghton has become increasingly precious to me.

I seemed to be totally dedicated to the study of Italian art, and one day, walking up the cypress avenue to i Tatti, I said to Jane that I thought I would give up the project of the Gothic Revival. She stopped dead in horror and indignation. She hardly knew what the words Gothic Revival meant, but to abandon a work of which I had already written over a third, and which was, in a sense, a moral obligation, shocked her profoundly. I saw that she was right, and went back to work on my book. I had just reached the most interesting section, the chapter on Pugin, and for the first time was able to escape from the 'prize essay' style in which the earlier chapters are written. I wrote it quickly. Logan had given me a piece of advice, unexpected from him. "If you feel that your pen is running away with you, let it run". I had been brought up on the opposite principle ('Easy writing makes hard reading', etc.) but I have learned from experience that Logan was right. If words come tumbling out it gives to one's style an energy and a rhythm that cannot be achieved by deliberation, and one can enjoy the pleasures of polishing later.

Having made up my mind to the Gothic Revival, I saw that I had to do a good deal more research, and, when we left Italy in the summer, we took a house at Oxford so that I could work in the Bodleian. Cramped, slippery and ill-proportioned, it was a painful contrast to the Chiostro. An abandoned university in a wet English July is not exhilarating, and Jane felt ill. The only thing I remember with pleasure is a visit to Robert Bridges, to whom, when I was an undergraduate, Logan had given me an introduction. He was finishing *The Testament of Beauty* and read to us with great relish the lines: 'by rambling lanes, with hazel and thorn embowered woodbine, bryony and wild roses; the landscape lure of rural England, that held glory in native art until our painters took their new fashion from France'. "I put that in to annoy Roger" he said (Roger Fry, who was his wife's cousin, habitually referred to Bridges as 'That chaste, cantankerous old man'). He talked scornfully about French poetry, and in particular about the claim that La Fontaine was a major poet. I remained silent, and as we parted at the gate (which he always came out to shut) he added "I'm so glad that you agree with me about that French fellow". I drove off rapidly before my love of La Fontaine began to show.

There remained one more ordeal—taking Jane to Sheilbridge. We went by sleeper to Oban, where one of my father's yachts was to convey us to Loch Sunart. Jane hates all boats, and yachts in particular, and on this occasion her position was made even more embarrassing because, in honour of the bride, the crew had decked out the yacht with flags. The journey to Sunart takes about five hours and includes one or two rough patches. We arrived in very poor shape. It rained every day, and the salmon showed no inclination to swallow a fly. I remember only two episodes: Jane standing on a chair to thank a small group of woebegone tenants for a hideous rose-bowl that the poor people had given us; and me thanking a group of dear old fishermen at Strontian for the gift of a barometer. It was my first public speech, and our factor (Scotch for 'land-agent') had confided in my parents that he didn't think I would be up to it.

After our visit to Sheilbridge, we returned thankfully to San Martino and resumed our former way of life, except that Jane was expecting a baby in the spring and could not take bumpy rides in the Tuscan hills. I continued to work in the Gabinetto dei Disegni, and Jane read Gibbon's *Decline and Fall* in a sunny bedroom. As spring approached it was thought that Jane should have a nurse to take her home, and one was sent out from England. After two meals of agonising boredom we paid her passage home, and returned a fortnight later. Our son was born on April 13th, 1928.

I like to think that I finished *The Gothic Revival* on the day that Alan was born, but in fact I was too worried to work, and it took another fortnight. By the end I had come a long way since the first pleasant chapters on Ruins and Rococo, and I had escaped from the infection of Stracheyan irony that influenced my chapter on the Ecclesiologists. The chief reason was that I had immersed myself in Ruskin and, in trying to separate the grain from the chaff, had recognised a genius that towered above the idols of my boyhood. My chapter on Ruskin does not go very deep but it is (if I may be allowed to boast) rather nearer the truth than anything else that was being written at the time. I was able to amplify it thirty-four years later in the notes to an anthology called *Ruskin To-day*. My enthusiasm for Ruskin had one drawback. It prevented me from including in my book two or three of the gothic revivalists whom he, for complex reasons, despised, but whom I had recognised as great architects. It was a gross injustice to represent the movement only by the energetic Gilbert Scott (who, although a shameless go-getter, was a better architect than I realised). And the sad thing is that I had already begun to recognise the qualities of Street and Butterfield. One chapter on each would have made *The Gothic Revival* into a pioneering book of some value. But it would have meant delaying publication by a year. And how it would have annoyed, or even estranged, my friends in the world of good taste!

Having delivered the book to a publisher recommended by Logan, I was free to turn back to my true centre, Italian art, and instead of studying the kind of modest minor artist who is thought appropriate to a beginner, I plunged in at the deep end. I concentrated on Leonardo da Vinci. This may now sound both commonplace and ambitious. But in 1928 there were very few books on Leonardo worth reading. Stylistically there was still much uncertainty; the Uffizi *Annunciation* was thought to be by Verrocchio, and the Ginevra dei Benci was not accepted as a Leonardo. More important, nobody had made a serious effort to relate the vast corpus of Leonardo's writings to his drawings and paintings. For example, Muntz, whose book on Leonardo gives a good account of life at the Court of Milan, does not reproduce a single authentic drawing, whereas Mr Berenson, whose list of drawings is impeccable, makes practically no reference to Leonardo's thought. Fortunately there was one invaluable (if misnamed) piece of scholarship, Richter's *Literary Works of Leonardo de Vinci* and a good short book by de Séailles on Leonardo as a thinker and scientist. This had furnished M Valery with the only sensible paragraphs in his *Discours sur le Méthode de Leonardo da Vinci*. I was irritated by M Valery's metaphysical embroideries, and wrote a somewhat jaundiced note on Leonardo which Desmond MacCarthy published in *Life and Letters* in 1929. It does not bear re-reading but at least it was an attempt to see Leonardo in relation to the intellectual life of his time, and not as a semi-mythical anachronism.

At about this time I paid my first visit to the Library at Windsor Castle, and met the newly appointed librarian, Owen Morshead. We became fast friends, and a year later he invited me to catalogue the great collection of Leonardo's drawings in the Library. This was one of the most interesting and responsible jobs that any scholar could have been asked to undertake, and in offering it to a young man of 26, who had not even published a learned article, Owen showed a rashness, or perhaps an innocence, unthinkable today.

I worked for about three years on the Leonardo

catalogue, happy, excited, confident that I was gaining new ground. I made one major mistake in my historical account of the collection, and several minor mistakes in transcribing Leonardo's notes, because, although his writing is not (as is usually said) difficult to read, he uses certain abbreviations that only an Italian scholar could have understood. On the other hand, my dating of the drawings is usually correct and was a step forward in Leonardo studies. The catalogue remains my only chance to be considered a scholar.

My article on Leonardo had another curious and less fortunate result. A character named Arthur Hungerford Pollen, who had made a name for himself as a writer on naval strategy in the 1914 war, had bought at auction a tiny drawing of the Virgin and Child with a Cat, which was unquestionably an authentic work of Leonardo da Vinci. He was a rich and forceful man, and wished to have his drawing published with maximum glory. He planned a short book on Leonardo's drawings of the Virgin and Cat, to be printed by Bruce Rogers, in which his discovery would naturally be given due prominence. He asked me to write this book, offering a substantial fee, and invited us to dine with him in order to discuss the details. We dined in a large house in Wilton Place, and drank a quantity of very powerful burgundy. Towards the end of the meal Mr Pollen asked me what I thought of Sargent. I gave a fuddled, but conventional, answer: he was a brilliant portrait painter, whose success had sometimes led him into superficiality. "You are quite wrong" said my host, "Sargent was a mystic (he pronounced it 'mythic') visionary. He painted a portrait of a man possessed by the devil. You Protestants don't believe in diabolical possession ('I do', I said feebly), but we Catholics know that it exists and that a great artist can perceive it." We waited breathlessly for the revelation of who the sitter could have been. "Sargent", said Mr Pollen very solemnly "painted a portrait of Woodrow Wilson, and it was hung in the Royal Academy. Fortunately nuns and other holy persons do not go to picture galleries (totally untrue), but if one of them had seen this picture their souls would have been mortally wounded. I offered" he continued "any pure young woman a hundred pounds if she would sit for five minutes looking at the picture, and they all ran screaming from the room." In the course of this monologue I had caught Jane's eye, and I suppose that our host, who was no fool, had noticed and interpreted our exchange of glances, for when it was over he became noticeably less friendly. In spite of enormous goblets of brandy, our discussion of the projected book was somewhat formal, and when I finally staggered into the fresh air, saying that I would think it over and let him know, he said goodbye very curtly. He was not surprised, although very angry, when he received my letter saying that, owing to previous engagements, etc., I could not accept his generous offer. This was the first letter I wrote of a kind that I have had, alas, to write rather often; and the first, although by no means the most bizarre, of my encounters with collectors.

Experiences of this kind were soon to become more usual. I had agreed to take a part in the famous, or infamous, exhibition of Italian art that opened at Burlington House in January 1930. I say 'infamous' because it grew out of a friendship between Lady Austen Chamberlain and Mussolini, and so was basically a piece of Fascist propaganda; also because it was a wicked risk to send so many of the world's greatest pictures in a single ship to a single exhibition. None of this occurred to me at the time, but naturally it occurred to Mr Berenson, and the news that I had become one of the organisers of the exhibition widened the gap between us. Indeed it speaks very well for his kindness of heart that he ever forgave me.

An exhibition of this kind is a policy decision made by busy and powerful public men. They then find idle elderly men to form a committee, and take the credit. These men then have to find someone to do the work. For the Italian exhibition they had found an industrious official at the National Gallery named W. G. Constable, but it was thought (not by him) that he could not manage so large an undertaking alone, and in desperation they turned to the untried youth who had just returned from Florence. In this way I entered what was known as the London Art World.

It was like a battlefield at nightfall. The principal combatants were exhausted and had retired to their own quarters, surrounded by their attendants; but their enmities continued unabated. Berenson and Fry had not been on speaking terms for over twenty years; both disliked and distrusted Ricketts, and all three had a low opinion of Sir Robert Witt. D. S. MacColl had, and showed, a lofty contempt for them all. Lord Lee of Fareham, the most detested figure of the museum world, must be the subject of a separate section. All these once famous and ferocious figures treated me very kindly. One could say that they wanted to get me on their side, but they never seemed to bear me any ill will when I saw their enemies. I think they were glad to have a new member of their circle who was not influenced by their old feuds, and could sympathise with their various points of view.

Roger Fry was already a friend and, of my new acquaintances, far the most captivating was Charles Ricketts. He was a painter, sculptor, book illustrator and stage designer of real distinction, and much of his work, especially his sculpture and his costume designs, will be 'rediscovered' with astonishment. The quintessence of the nineties, he came at the exact point of juncture between the pre-Raphaelities and the Symbolists, the point at which Beardsley emerged corruptly from the virtuous Burne-Jones. When he was offered the post of director of the National Gallery he made it a condition that all the pictures must be reframed, the floors covered with Persian rugs and the rooms filled with flowers. Naturally this was not accepted, and the post went to his nominee, C. J. Holmes. In the 'art world' he was thought of less as an artist than as a collector; and, if the words 'perfect taste' mean anything, then Ricketts and his friend Shannon had it. Greek terra-cottas, white *lekythoi,* prints by Harunobu, drawings by Watteau, all displayed with the utmost discretion; it was a strange contrast to Roger's room in Bloomsbury, with its dusty African mask and the pictures by Juan Gris and Derain so dirty that they melted into the mud-coloured wall. I once said to Ricketts about some writer that I thought him too precious, to which he replied "Can one ever be too precious?" Quite right, and Ricketts's exquisite interior was the result of love as well as 'taste'. An invitation to dine was in Rossettian language "Come and grub with me", but the dinner was more Beardsleyan: one sat at a lapis lazuli table, with a huge bank of madonna lilies at one end, and drank vast quantities of Orvieto, while Ricketts's stories became more and more scandalous. Shannon hardly spoke, but his gentle, distinguished presence prevented the evening from degenerating into an aesthetic mad hatter's tea party. The only penalty was that the meal traditionally ended with quantities of Strega, which gave one a sore head the next day. Ricketts was said by his enemies to be an intriguer and conspirator of the most Machiavellian kind. Of this I saw no evidence, except in his appearance, which was that of a sixteenth-century cardinal. He was of about the same size as Mr Berenson, with a slightly longer beard and fine drawn temples, and I used to think that it would be interesting to see those two small, beautiful bearded men together. They could have complemented each other: Berenson had the greater mind, Ricketts knew how things were made. When they did meet (I was present) they were so suspicious of each other than they hardly spoke. BB was heavily sarcastic, Ricketts screamed the aesthete's scream of embarrassment.

Lives devoted to beauty usually end badly, and that of Ricketts was no exception. Shannon had a stroke while hanging a picture, fell off the ladder and became insane. He developed a passionate hatred of

Ricketts, who died heart-broken some years before his life-long friend.

Another friend we made in the art world was Henry Harris, known to his friends as Bogey. He was one of those figures that appear in memoires of all ages and mystify historians. Why was this man, who did nothing, and said nothing, the friend of all the great, with an entrée into every salon? There was a certain resemblance to Swann, and it would take the genius and the prolixity of Proust to give the whole answer. But a short answer is that in a society composed of bursting egos anyone who is recessive without being dull is always welcome. Bogey was entirely without ambition. Although he had grown up with the 'leaders of society' he was the least snobbish of men. Far from pressing himself on people, he was a master of evasion, and gave us the good advice, "Always pretend to have left your engagement book behind". He had a vein of melancholy and told me that after dining with the Londonderrys he would spend most of the night walking through the East End. He was a wit, and his comments had more sting than people realised till they had got home. But, unlike Oscar Wilde, whom, of course, he had known,* he never made a single witticism that could be quoted. All his jokes were 'throw away lines'. His wit depended on his quizzical response to an immediate situation.

He had been a rich and handsome young man and had inherited a large estate in Hampshire. At Eton he had made friends with all the swells, and when he launched out into society he was sucked into the Marlborough House set. He became friends with the Prince of Wales, and inevitably (I am sure very reluctantly) had to play baccarat with him. In a short time the greater part of his patrimony had vanished. He sold his Hampshire estate and decided to live in Italy. He was a Catholic, and obtained a small post at

---

* A light on Victorian values: I said something to Bogey about Wilde going into society. Bogey replied "Wilde was never in society. He never dined with the Devonshires".

the Vatican, where he made friends with Pope Pius X, "the wittiest man I have ever known", he said. But his real home was in Florence, where he made friends with that remarkable scholar, collector and typographer, Herbert Horne, perhaps the most distinguished man to be omitted from the *Dictionary of National Biography*. Horne had made an excellent collection with very little money. When someone asked him for a photograph of one of his pictures he said "Why have a photograph? It's cheaper to buy an original". Under his influence Bogey began to collect in the same frugal manner. He was a relentless bargainer and used to say "I hate waste. I'm Scotch, you see". He had no other Scottish characteristics. Bargainers lose golden opportunities, and dealers are naturally hostile to them; but Bogey made a collection of Italian art which, when installed in his house in Bedford Square, gave one as much pleasure as any collection that I can remember. Things seemed to have come together by a happy accident.

Owing to his genius for detachment Bogey had managed to keep on good terms with all the warring factions of the art world. It was he who brought BB to call on Ricketts, and he attempted the yet more formidable task of bringing together Mr Berenson and Roger Fry. It was even more unsuccessful. Everyone who loved Italian art went to his house, and came away delighted. But he kept up with his society friends who came to play bridge with him in spite of the religious pictures, marble reliefs, bronzes and majolica which would have made them feel uneasy if they had noticed them. I remember an exception. Mrs Cavendish Bentinck noticed a *dugento* panel of the Last Supper* in which the Apostles were sitting round a table, with square plates in front of them. She was puzzled. "Look at all those old tramps", she said, in Royal accents. "I vonder vot they are playing".

Bogey will appear frequently in the next chapter, and I must now return to the event which brought

* Now in the Barber Institute, Birmingham.

us together—the Italian Exhibition. As so many of the pictures were coming from Italy, the most important influence on its preparation was the Italian commissioner, Ettore Modigliani. He was a ridiculous figure by any standards and must have risen to his high office by sheer volubility. He never stopped talking for a second, and hardpressed officials must have given him anything he asked for in order to get rid of him. He had no claims to scholarship, but sent us over catalogue entries for all the pictures coming from Italy, which were to be translated and checked, but not altered. The rest of the catalogue was written by Constable and myself (except for the drawings, scrupulously catalogued by A. E. Popham), and it must have been, by a long chalk, the worst catalogue of a great exhibition ever printed. By modern standards it was puerile. Constable left the larger part of it to me, and I simply did not know enough. When the Italian pictures arrived at the docks Modigliani went down to receive them. The strong-room of the ship was locked, and he had the only key. As he approached the door a look of agony came over his face and his hands beat the air. "La chiave, dove!" (Where is the key!) Only those who have had long experience of Italian sacristans will enjoy this story. The key was found in his hotel bedroom.

With my love of *coups de théatre* I asked the Academy attendants to keep Botticelli's *Birth of Venus* on one side until I could collect everyone working on the hanging to watch her rise from the basement into the gallery; and it was an unforgettable moment. The hanging of the exhibition was extremely exhausting, and I can remember very few episodes. One was meeting Ricketts with an enormous bunch of Parma violets in his hand. He said "Witt is being so horrible to one of the secretaries that I went out and bought her these violets; but I can't find her. You take them"; and he gave them to Jane instead. Another was showing Giorgione's *Tempesta* to the President of the Academy, Sir William Llewellyn. He looked at it for a minute and then said, sincerely "We would have rejected that if it had come up before our hanging committee".

In general Royal Academicians of this date were hostile to what were known as Old Masters, rightly supposing that if the public took a fancy to that kind of painting their own degraded realism would be at a discount. I was glad to see my old friend David Murray leading round a group of colleagues and saying about the Titans "They're really no' sae bad. Ye can learn a lot from these old fellies!" His friends grunted in disapproval.

In order to get the exhibition ready for the press on December 30th we worked over Christmas. I remember going into the Academy to work on Christmas Eve, tiptoeing past the attendants and guardians of this priceless collection, all of whom were slumped in their chairs or on the floor, dead drunk. I felt as if I were entering the Sleeping Beauty's castle.

Absurdly enough I do not remember anything about the opening day. Was there a ceremony? Who performed it? I cannot even remember who was the chairman of our committee. It was a fabulous success. The crowds were so great that one couldn't possibly see the pictures, and people would sink to any subterfuge in order to get in on a Sunday morning. As I had been one of the organisers of the exhibition it was thought that I could produce tickets and I enjoyed a sudden popularity. Lady Colefax asked us to lunch almost every week and her letters, with their frenzied writing, looking like a bicycle-race, poured in by every post.*

As a by-product of the Italian Exhibition I was asked to give some lectures. The first, on Botticelli, was given in the house of my old friends the St John Hornbys in Chelsea. I had never lectured before but

---

* A note on Lady Colefax's writing: she wrote frequently to the London Library for books, and Mr Cox, that unforgettable character who for fifty years sat at the issuing desk, used to keep her letters stuck with drawing pins to the shelf behind him, and glanced back at them from time to time hoping that light would dawn.

the prospect did not alarm me at all; indeed, I found it ridiculously easy. I also lectured on Giotto and Bellini. These lectures were well received, and thus I was set on a course that I have followed till the present day. Considering that lecturing has brought me some reputation and a fair amount of money, it may sound ungrateful to suggest that I had much better never have given a lecture at all. The lecture form encouraged all the evasions and half-truths that I had learnt to practise in my weekly essays at Oxford. How can a talk of fifty minutes on Giotto or Bellini be anything but superficial. I was conscious of this at the time and wrote two serious lectures on Wölfflin and Riegl which I gave, at the instigation of Tancred Borenius, in an enormous hall in London University. When I mounted the rostrum there were about fifteen pupils in the hall. "Wait", said Tancred, "the students will come in the thousands". In fact no one else came. This sobering experience cured me temporarily of my itch to lecture, but not for long. The fact is that I enjoy imparting information and awakening people's interest; and in the arts this can be achieved more successfully by a lecture than by the printed page. But historical truth is usually complex and frequently dull, and anyone with a sense of style or a love of language is tempted to take short cuts and omit the qualifications that would make a statement less telling. The practice of lecturing not only ended my ambition to be a scholar (this might never have succeeded, as I am too easily bored), but prevented me from examining problems of style and history with sufficient care. On the other hand, lecturing on Giotto and Bellini forces one to clear one's mind and sort out the evidence, and a few striking statements may awaken in the listener an interest which a rigmarole of qualifications would not. Education involves a balance of effort and delight. So I am left not knowing whether my career as a lecturer, which began so modestly in the spring of 1930, was a mistake or not.

For me the best thing that came out of the Italian

Exhibition was my friendship with the other youthful member of our committee. David Balniel. I had met him before, but came to know him only when we worked together. He is, and has always been, one of the most lovable of human beings. His gentleness, sweetness and courtesy are irresistible, and he also has a wideranging knowledge of art history. In 1930 he knew much more about Italian art than I did. Heirs to a long line of cultivated and scholarly ancestors often rebel against such a burden of civilisation; but David took it naturally. He was glad that an ancestor, Lady Anne Lindsay, should have been poet laureate of Scotland in the fourteenth century; that his great grandfather should have written the first book in English on Christian Art—the book from which Ruskin derived his scanty knowledge of the subject. He regretted only that, during ups and downs of the family fortunes, tons of books had been sold from the enormous library at Haigh, including the manuscripts, in their jewelled bindings, that now lie unseen in the Rylands Library at Manchester. But what a library remained! One of his ancestors had a prejudice against reading any of the classics except in the first editions, which meant that the Latin authors were practically all in incunabula. He was brought up surrounded by such books, and by a collection of pictures from Duccio to Rembrandt; they had entered his blood stream. All this scholarship and understanding of art has been spent in public service. He has been chairman of almost every institution connected with the arts, except the British Museum, of which he is the senior trustee, and brought to his tasks human understanding as well as expert knowledge. I will not deny that certain aggressive personalities arouse his highland instincts. But they are very rare.

After the exhibition closed, and the final horrifying days of taking down and packing the pictures were over (horrifying, because, when an exhibition is over, everyone loses interest in it, and the pictures are piled up and thrown about like tea-trays in a hotel pantry), it was decided that there must be a massive

catalogue commemorating the great event, and David
and I were instructed to prepare it. It was to be
printed by the Oxford Press, who take no account of
time, and the plates were to be by Emery Walker,
who was over eighty, and whose workshop was in a
state of confusion I have never seen equalled. I suppose that David and I were also rather dilatory. The
original catalogue had been so bad that there was a lot
of work to do; and even after our efforts the catalogue
was amateurish, by modern standards. A curious fact
—our handwritings were so similar that we could not
tell which of us was responsible for notes on the
proofs. Finally we sent in our proofs to the secretary
of the exhibition who, as a 'practical man', had been
chosen to deal with the business side of the publication, and some mysterious episode took place which
delayed the publication by another six months. By
this time the famous Italian Exhibition was forgotten,
or had aroused, as such outbursts of hysteria often do,
a reaction; hardly a copy was sold. Naturally the guar-
antors were not at all pleased.

During this episode we were living in a nasty little
house in Westminster which we had bought as a stop
gap. We put William Morris paper in the bedroom;
in other respects it was irredeemable. We had wanted
to live in the country, where both of us had been
brought up, and naturally I had begun by looking for
houses near Sudbourne. But my parents thought it
would be a mistake to cut ourselves off from the
world and, as things turned out, they were right. We
were both blissfully immature, and in the happy isolation of Ufford or Iken we should have never grown
up.

What did Jane do while I worked in the Windsor
Library? Looked after Alan, or rather after Alan's
nurse, engaged in a grisly and degrading struggle with
English servants, whose taboos, after our dear Italians,
seemed incomprehensible. She had another more
agreeable occupation. I wanted to have her painted,
and had thought of turning to Wilson Steer who, although he was a landscape painter, had painted two

or three beautiful portraits which were without the vulgarity of Augustus John and were above the dead level of the professionals. I used to meet the famous Professor Tonks in the Burlington Fine Arts Club and he undertook to recommend us to Steer. I never mentioned my earlier visit. Steer said he would consider it and we went round to see him in his house at the far end of Chelsea Embankment, looking up the river towards Lots Road Power Station. Steer was a large placid bow-fronted man and less like the romantic image of an artist than anyone I have known. He was a kind man but when he saw Jane's neat figure and Eton crop he could not help exclaiming "But there's nothing to paint!" However he was won round by her charm and set to work. He chose a plain yellow silk dress and allowed her to wear the first piece of jewellery I gave her, a silver-gilt impression of the Rawlins medal (it was later stolen by a burglar who thought it was gold).

Steer had a studio at the top of his house but he never entered it and did all his painting in his first floor sitting-room. He sat Jane in the corner, beside the fireplace, surrounded by the pretty odds and ends that he loved to collect in his walks in Chelsea (never more than half a mile, I suppose). And in a few weeks he had produced a rather charming sketch. I had supposed that this would be turned into a life-size picture; but at this point Tonks intervened. He had himself been painting a number of small conversation pieces of his friends—George Moore and the Hutchinsons, Steer and Sickert, and Steer's old maid Mrs Raynes entertaining her cronies to tea—and they are the things by which he is most likely to be remembered. He thought it would be amusing to see if Steer could do the same. He was a commanding personality, and he succeeded in persuading Steer not to enlarge Jane's portrait, but to 'finish it'. As a result Jane had to go for dozens more sittings. The yellow dress was duly aired by Flo, Steer's maid, but it became slightly grubby. The paint surface became more and more lifeless. Jane's face came to look like that of an old-fashioned doll, with buttons for eyes. Only the little objects that Steer had collected south of the King's Road retained any life. It must be one of the worst portraits ever painted.

We spent as much of our time as possible away from our house in Westminster, travelling or staying in the country, taking with us the infant Alan, his nurse and all the paraphernalia of infancy, cots, pots, a large weighing machine (very hard to pack), a folding bath, a folding pram and a mammoth pram with which the nurse could outshine any nurses in the district. We went to Romney Marsh, and had our first sight of Hythe, which was to become our future home; we went to stay in a charming cottage on the Solent, lent us by Logan where, for a second time, my mind was in working order; and we went to Sospel, a town behind Mentone in the first valley of the Alpes Maritimes. Down this valley flows a river with a picturesque bridge, much beloved by amateur artists, and on either side of the river was light, springy turf which some enterprising speculator had made into a rather primitive golf course. After a successful evening at Monte Carlo my father had been persuaded to buy the golf course and to build a large hotel at the far end of it. After the war he was bored with it and gave the hotel to me. I loved it. The drive up was hell—ninety-two hair-pin bends—but once there the clear stream full of trout, the cows, the smell of hay and the magnificent hills, like the approach to Delphi, were a merciful escape from the poison strip of the Riviera.

I was fond of golf and I much enjoyed the drama and complications of hotel management, which go further than most guests would imagine. I remember, for example, an evening when one of the *clients,* returning rather late, broke into the *commissariat* and took all the eggs, which he proceeded to throw at the night porter, the Swiss manager and, when I emerged, at me. A lot of clearing up and no eggs for breakfast. The great thing about owning an hotel is that one has no domestic worries; and wily millionaires, like the late Lord Rothermere and Mr Bulbenkian, have recognised this. When we went there with Alan he was not quite a year old and crawled happily in the sun. Maurice came to stay and, for the only time in his life, set foot on a golf course, and brandished a club with immense determination; but, after two or three unsuccessful attempts to hit the ball, returned to Pushkin.

We needed the rest, because in the winter we had had a very exacting visit to Italy. In Rome the weather was cold and our bedroom at the top of the old, unreformed Hassler was unheated. The service was non-existent and the food uneatable. We thought that the view over Rome would compensate for our discomfort. But the visit provided two experiences that greatly affected my life. The first was a visit to the Capella Paolina in the Vatican. We were taken there by a highly-strung Austrian scholar named Anny Popp, who had written the only tolerable book on Leonardo's drawings. As we looked at Michelangelo's frescoes we both felt, as so many lovers of Renaissance art have felt, a deep sense of disappointment. After a long silence Jane said "They are tragic"; Anny Popp proceeded to expound their meaning. In half-an-hour we had come to see that they are two of the most sublime works of art ever created. It was like a religious conversion; and to this day, when I study the Paolina frescoes, I seem to come nearer to an understanding of man's relations with God.

The other episode in this Roman visit that changed my life was a lecture by Aby Warburg, given in a German institute called the Herziana. Warburg, the eldest son of the famous Hamburg banking family, had handed over to his brothers his share in the family business, on condition that they would buy books for him. This was the origin of the famous Warburg Library, now a part of London University. How it got there will be related later in this chapter. Warburg was without doubt the most original thinker on art-history of our time, and entirely changed the course of art-historical studies. His point of view could be described as a reaction against the formalist or stylistic approach of Morelli and Berenson. But I am sure that this was not his intention, because from the first his mind moved in an entirely different way. Instead of thinking of works of art as life-enhancing representations he thought of them as symbols, and he believed that the art-historian should concern himself with the origin, meaning and transmission of symbolic images. The Renaissance was his chosen field of enquiry, partly because Renaissance art contained a large number of such symbolic images; and partly because he had the true German love of Italy. He accumulated vast learning, but his writings are all fragments. He should not have been an art-historian, but a poet like Hölderlin. He himself said that if he had been five inches taller (he was even shorter than Berenson) he would have become an actor, and I can believe it, for he had, to an uncanny degree, the gift of mimesis. He could 'get inside' a character, so that when he quoted from Savonarola, one seemed to hear the Frate's high, compelling voice; and when he read from Poliziano there was all the daintiness and the slight artificiality of the Medicean circle. Symbols are a dangerous branch of study as they easily lead to magic; and magic leads to the loss of reason. Warburg went out of his mind in 1918, but by 1927, under the nun-like care of Dr Byng, he was sufficiently recovered to visit Rome and give a lecture. Dr Steinmann, the director of the Herziana, knowing that my German was imperfect, arranged for us to sit in the front row, and Warburg, who preferred to talk to an individual, directed the whole lecture at me. It lasted over two hours, and I understood about two-thirds. But it was enough. Thenceforward my interest in 'connoisseurship' became no more than a kind of habit, and my mind was occupied in trying to answer the kind of questions that had occupied Warburg. The parts of my writing that have given me most satisfaction, for example, the chapter in *The Nude* called 'Pathos', are entirely Warburgian.

At the lecture Jane, who was already unwell, sat

next to a lady with bad influenza, and was out of action for ten days. We then went on to stay with Umberto Morra at Cortona in his lovable nineteenth-century villa, with its frescoes in the *style troubadour,* and its study modelled on Napoleon's 'tent' at Malmaison. Cortona is one of the coldest places in Italy and even in the house we had to carry round little pots of embers (*scaldini*). Jane was laid up in the largest bed and the coldest bedroom I can remember. No doctor was available, but Iris Origo* called in the local vet from Montepulciano who prescribed a remedy which, as it was strong enough to cure a cow, cured Jane immediately.

In 1929 the Berensons paid one of their rare visits to England. London was distasteful to Mr Berenson for two reasons; first that he was not received in intellectual society—or any other society—as he would have been in Paris and Rome, and secondly that Mary's Bloomsbury relations were in the offing, and she was always cadging money for them. However, he took a charming house from Lady Horner (one of the inheritors of the Graham collection of *quattrocento* pictures), full of Burne-Jones relics including a piano with Burne-Jones paintings inside the lid, where for once he let himself go. The purpose of the visit was to work on the drawings in the British Museum, Windsor and Oxford. BB had spent a year in Oxford as a young man, but had hardly been there since. His sentimental feelings were so strong that on the way back he insisted on travelling third class; to remind himself of old times he even demanded a cup of tea, and drank it, saying "How exquisitely revolting". The compartment filled up, fortunately with friends of mine. The first was the painter called Maresco Pierce, the second was called Isaiah Berlin. BB was delighted by these peculiar names, and even more by

---

* The Marchesa Origo, that most distinguished writer, the biographer of Byron and Leopardi.

Isaiah's conversation which lasted all the way to London.

I remember one high-powered luncheon in Lady Horner's house. Augustine Birrell, the most genial wit I have ever met, Sydney Cockerell, Logan and the Berensons were all assembled, awaiting the arrival of their dreaded guest—Sir Edmund Gosse. Gosse was the last reviewer who could make or unmake a reputation and he did nothing to disguise his love of power. He came at last, looking like a cross between an old tom cat and an octogenarian pirate, and was greeted by Mary Berenson with the words "Sir Edmund, we've met before". "Oh no, dear lady, it ill becomes me to contradict my hostess, but really I must protest that such a delightful encounter would not have faded from my memory," etc. "Oh yes, we have", said Mary "and I'll tell you how it happened. I was crossing on the ferry at Camden when a young man wearing a straw boater got on board, and I thought 'That must be an Englishman, and he'll be going to call on Walt'. So I went up to you and said 'If you're going to visit Walt Whitman I'll come with you, because the boy is out today, but I can get you in'.* So we went off together, and I led you round to the larder window at the back, which was always kept open, but it was rather high up, so I said 'You'll have to give me a boost', and you did, and I squeezed through, and let you in by the back door." I shall never forget Gosse's face. It turned white with rage, and his jaw began to work in an alarming manner. Of course the thought of this shaky old creature giving a boost to the enormous Mrs Berenson was rather ridiculous, or even macabre. Mary was quite oblivious to his rage. Then after a minute he had composed himself, and said in icy tones "Dear Lady, your picturesque narrative is entirely untrue. I remember my visit to Walt Whitman perfectly. I recorded it that night and printed the account in one of my books. I rang the

---

* Walt Whitman by this time was paralysed and could not go down stairs.

front door bell; it was answered by a smart parlour maid (this is not improbable), and facing me, at the head of the stairs, was your great poet, who raised his hand and said 'Is this my friend?' " Historians, please note.

At some point in 1929 we went down to lunch with A. E. Popham, who lived beside the river at Twickenham. The house was full of reflected light and children, and when we returned we were more than ever depressed by our squalid little house in Westminster. We decided to look for a house by the Thames and, as the depression had just set in, we had no difficulty in finding a beauty. It was called Old Palace Place, on Richmond Green, and was a large red brick house of the early eighteenth century which had been built round the remains of the Tudor palace of Sheen. At last we had a house which would be a good setting for the pictures, drawings and furniture which we had been collecting for the last two years.

By now we had both become passionate collectors. I described in an earlier chapter how, while still at school, I had collected Japanese prints; but I very soon began to branch off into other directions; a Corot, some Sung pottery, a sixteenth-century French ivory. Collectors are basically of two kinds; those who aim at completing a series, and those who long to possess things that have bewitched them. The former, of whom stamp and coin collectors are the obvious examples, enjoy the pleasures of a limited aim, and its comforting certainties. The latter may suffer ups and downs, changes of heart and deceptions, but they have several great advantages. They never know when some new love will inflame them; they learn a great deal more about themselves from their possessions; and in the end they are surrounded by old friends, with long love stories which they must try hard not to tell to their friends.

Why possess works of art when one can see much better ones in a public gallery? One might answer that (unless one is a museum curator) this is the only way to have the direct, daily contact with an object which no amount of gallery going can supply. But this is not the whole truth, because, while the impulse to collect is strong, it becomes an almost totally irrational obsession; and it has given me as much pleasure as almost any form of self-indulgence I have known. I write in the past tense, because about fifteen years ago the urge to collect left me entirely; evidently it was largely a physical impulse.

There were other elements. One of them was the excitement of discovery, which was associated with a feeling of rescue. It was exhilarating to find two Pisanello medals in a tobacconist's shop in Tunbridge Wells, or a Cambodian lacquer hand in a postcard shop in Cromer, and one felt a sentimental satisfaction at the thought of repatriating them into their own world. Unfortunately, the excitement of discovery is not far removed from bargain-hunting. This, too, is amusing, and appeals to the gambler's instinct in all of us, but from the collector's point of view it is a mistake. The great collections were not formed by bargain-hunters. In our youth, however, it was customary for Christian collectors to boast of how little they had paid for their prizes. "Picked it up for a few coppers", was the usual phrase. Jewish collectors, on the other hand, were proud to tell one what sacrifices they had made to obtain their treasures. Henry Oppenheimer, one of the most lovable of old-style collectors, used to say "Ven I tell old Lippman vat I pay for it, he says 'Mein Gott, Oppenheimer, you are crazy".' There can be no doubt which of these two standpoints denotes the greater love of art; and it is also probable that the Jewish approach leads to more material advantage. Anyone who followed Herr Oppenheimer's advice "Py de pest" would have had a far greater return on his money than the bargain-hunter. I can truthfully say that I have never in my life bought something because I thought it would go up in value; to do so is to become an art-dealer *in petto*. I have never bought a picture thinking that I might sell it, and, although I have sold a number of pictures that once hung on my walls (and given away over a hundred), it has always been because they didn't fit into a new house, or that I had fallen out of love with them. With one exception, I have no regrets and am only sorry that I made such small profits. I have gradually discovered the difference between a picture one admires and a picture one wants to live with. A striking example is Matisse's large picture *L'Atelier,* which I bought from the Gargoyle Club. It is a masterpiece, and was the subject of a whole television programme. But it is a most troublesome picture to have in the house, and I would much rather see it in the Duncan Phillips Gallery. I suppose that one bought such pictures partly to show off, whereas our first purchases, in Italy and London, were made purely out of love. As a result, our present rooms in Albany contain almost exactly the same drawings, in the same frames, as hung in our sitting-room in Richmond in 1930. We bought most of them in Florence in 1928 from the heirs of Fairfax Murray; we also bought some admirable Italian furniture for £10 or £15 a piece, all of which we still use. On our return to England in 1928 the sale of Samuel Palmer's son took place in Christie's, and we bought, among other things, *The Cornfield,* which is now the most reproduced picture we own, although at the time no one took the least interest in it. We also bought two little round pictures by different artists, one of which I felt convinced was by Raphael. Can collectors' megalomania go further? But it turned out to be true. It is the portrait of his friend, Valerio Belli, the famous engraver of crystal; and the other portrait is of his son, Elio Belli, by Fasolo. I discovered the confirmatory documents about a year after buying them.

The first rule of collecting is never buy anything because it is fashionable or because it makes one feel one up on other collectors. I broke this rule disastrously in 1930 by buying (or, rather, asking my father to buy for me) a large, heavy portrait by Tintoretto of a young member of the Gonzaga family, with a scene of David and Goliath in the background. It was an admirable work, but entirely without charm—as much a 'gallery picture' as the Matisse *L'Atelier*. At first I thought it grand to own such a thumping example of Renaissance painting, but I soon recognised my mistake and suffered agonies of remorse. It was an expensive lesson.*

The pleasures of collecting, while the fever lasts, do not lie in such weighty purchases, but in darting from one antique shop to another and eyeing the contents as greedily as a small boy looking into a sweet shop. We would zig-zag across streets, giving cries of triumph, usually followed by groans of disappointment. When motoring to Oxford I saw two Roccatagliata candlesticks on the opposite side of the road in a modern furniture shop at Shepherd's Bush; I pulled up, to the public peril, darted through the stationary traffic and returned with them before it had moved on. As a matter of fact they are not particularly attractive, and I would not have dreamt of buying them under any other circumstances.

I had incredible pieces of luck, partly because of the economic depression, partly because rich people had not yet begun to think of art as an investment but only as a way of entering society: and for the latter purpose they bought the pictures one would least like to possess—eighteenth-century English portraits. Collecting has now become, like the Stock Exchange, a form of gambling and of tax evasion. Even pottery and porcelain, which made one pull up one's car and flatten one's nose on a village shop, is subject to monthly quotations like a share index. Blake said 'The springs of pure delight can never be defiled'; but the simplest pleasures can be commercialised and destroyed.

On the first floor of Old Palace Place there was a long room, with seven tall windows looking over Richmond Green. We hung it with old red silk and

* I finally sold it, and it is now in the Gallery of Western Art in Tokyo.

painted the woodwork green and gold. At one end was the stolid, unenviable Tintoretto; at the other a perfect facsimile of the Dyrham Park book-case, made by Mallett when he sold the original. On the ground floor, opening on to the garden, Jane had a white panelled sitting-room, hung with our drawings. In our dining-room, which was part of the old Palace, there was the original sixteenth-century chimneypiece, and on either side of it, let into the wall, were two marble angels in the style of Mino da Fiesole. I believe they are still there. We were proud of our house and began to entertain. People were willing to take the tiresome journey out to Richmond to see us, including W. B. Yeats whom we had known in Oxford. We had been present at dinner with Maurice when Yeats was given an honorary degree, and had listened enthralled to the marvellous flow of his talk—anecdote, fantasy, moonshine and profound aphorisms. At dinner Maurice made a short speech saying how glad he was that Oxford had at last atoned for the disgrace of sending Shelley down by giving an honorary degree to the greatest poet of our time. Mr Yeats nodded in agreement. After dinner he read some unpublished poems, including 'Byzantium' and the prophecy that I quoted at the end of *Civilisation*. Mr Yeats had a rich Irish accent and read his poems with a rhythmic rise and fall that gave them their full value as incantation. He told me a story which, in case it has not been recorded elsewhere, I will set down, as it is a good example of elaborate Irish wit. He had been reading his poems to a school audience, and at the end a lady (who turned out to be the teacher of elocution) said "Will Mr. Yeats kindly tell us why he reads his poems in that extraordinary way?" Yeats replied "Madam, I read my poems as all great poets have read their poems from the time of Homer". Undefeated, the lady said "And by what authority does Mr Yeats assert that Homer read his poems in this way?" To which Mr Yeats replied "I must give the same answer as the Scotchman who claimed that Shakespeare was a Scot —'The ability of the man warrants the assumption' ".

On this occasion Mr Yeats was staying at the Mitre Hotel and we were told off to look after him. Next morning we met at breakfast at about 9 o'clock, and Mr Yeats began talking as eloquently as on the preceding night. We were joined by John Sparrow. The dining-room emptied. Mr Yeats continued to talk, saying in parenthesis "I can't talk for long; my voice tires easily these days." At about 11 o'clock we had to catch a train for London, leaving John to look after the poet who barely interrupted his monologue to say good bye. The waiters began to lay the tables for luncheon. Mr Yeats still talked. As the first luncheon guests began to trickle in he was sublime.

Richmond was on the way to Windsor, so that I could walk across the Green and be down in the Library in half an hour. The catalogue progressed. Alan was old enough to walk in Richmond Park and we developed a fondness for taking walks together which has lasted for forty years. I seemed set for a peaceful life of scholarship, friendship and collecting. One day I received a telephone call from Brigadier-General Sir Harold Hartley asking if he could come down to see us. I knew and liked him, and invited him to luncheon. After the meal he made the astonishing proposal that I should take the place of Charles Bell at the Ashmolean. I had made up my mind not to join the staff of a museum because I believed that administration would prevent me from writing the great works that I already had in mind. On the other hand I knew that my mother was constantly worried by my not having a proper job—"But what does your son do, Mrs Clark?" To say "He is a writer" was like the old police-court description of "Giving her profession as actress". With the callow egotism of youth I never asked what was happening to Charles Bell: as he appeared to be immensely old, it seemed natural to me that he should retire. In fact he was only 56 and was being pushed out. This alone should have made me refuse. Vanity and filial piety made me accept. Goodbye happy days in Windsor Library, good-bye our London friends and our beautiful house. It was a turning point in my life, and I am certain that I took the wrong turning.

As Harold Hartley had said, the administrative part of my post was not very onerous, as it was done by the Keeper of the whole Museum named Leeds, who looked, as an archaeologist should, like a tousled Irish terrier. I was Keeper only of the Department of Fine Art. But a job of this kind always involves interruptions from 'friends' of the Museum, would-be donors, local ladies of importance and mere busybodies. One has very little free time for work, except for an hour after lunch, when, owing to my early residence in Italy, I am always overcome by sleep. Fortunately I had appointed as my assistant a young man who, whatever his shortcomings as a scholar, was a wizard with old ladies.

We rented a featureless modern house on Shotover Hill, about three miles outside Oxford. We did our best with it, but it remained irredeemably commonplace. It had only one merit. It was so planned that every room had a good view over the Thames Valley which pleased our Oxford visitors more than any architectural qualities would have done.

The Oxford establishment behaved well to me; but there were painful dinner parties with heads of houses. Being at the bottom of the top class we were always put next to the penultimate couple; Jane sat next to the Public Orator, I sat next to his wife. We went to dinner arm in arm, falling over footstools as we passed from one small room to another and sat down to a seven course meal, beginning with grapefruit and stuffed eggs, and ending with Scotch woodcock. In spite of these gastronomic drawbacks, which have always weighed heavily on my mind, our short period in Oxford was a happy time. Charles Bell had treated the Ashmolean as a private collection, and, for better or worse, I did the same. My trustees, known as the Visitors, did not interfere with me at all. I was not even required to consult them before making a purchase or spending money. With the help of the National Art Collections Fund I bought Piero di

Cosimo's *Forest Fire*; and out of my tiny grant I was able to buy the ravishing ivory of Venus and Cupid by Peytel which we had been watching for years, waiting for the price to go down. The thought that it could now be in the Garden House still gives me a twinge. I even persuaded the University to build a new gallery, by advancing the cost interest free. I hung it with 17th- and 18th-century pictures, including the *Ascanius and the Stag* by Claude Lorrain, that dream-like poem of old age, which had been presented to us, together with a Watteau and a Chardin, by a North Oxford lady named Mrs Weldon.

From childhood onwards hanging pictures has been my favourite occupation. It has been a substitute for being a painter and a concrete illustration of my feelings as a critic. It is a curious art. One never knows what pictures are going to say to one another till they meet. Like two placid babies passing each other in their prams, they may either stretch out their arms in longing or scream with rage. People who hang galleries 'on paper', with measured squares representing the pictures, have never heard those cries of love or hate.

I was not allowed to forget the more exacting duties of my new profession. For nearly the whole time I was there Campbell Dodgson, almost the only English *kunst forscher* of the date who was respected on the Continent, came to the Museum every day to work on German engravings. Most of them had been bought by an early 19th-century collector called Douce, who was interested in the macabre and the grotesque and bought anything that contained a skeleton. On this basis he had formed a priceless collection of 15th-century German prints, which he had left to the Bodleian. These had been transferred to the Ashmolean but had never been catalogued. The unflagging zest and thoroughness with which Dodgson studied these horrible images should have been a lesson to me. Charles Bell had taken my appointment very well. He never complained of the way in which the University had treated him, and allowed me to talk to him about purchases and problems in the department. He wrote generously about *The Gothic Revival,* and was pleased that I had dedicated it to him. Then suddenly he turned against me. I suppose it was inevitable. Oxford was full of gossipy old women. He never saw me or spoke to me again and his letters no longer lay unopened on my desk. I should have been much more sorry than I was.

One reason may have been my friendship with Roger Fry. Bell naturally hated his opinions and had a personal grievance against him as he had written disrespectfully of Sir Edward Poynter P.R.A., who was Bell's cousin. He had personally prevented Fry from becoming Slade professor at Oxford—"The Old Spider did it" he said with glee—and he had caused to be elected a man named Gleadowe, who took less trouble about his performances than any lecturer I have ever heard. His text seemed to consist of only three words "Next slide please", although sometimes he said "No, not that one." We invited Roger down to lecture on Cézanne. Gleadowe was naturally indignant at this infringement of his role and would not allow Roger into his lecture room. I therefore asked Sir Michael Sadler, the Master of University College, if it could take place in the Hall of his college. Sadler was a remarkable man. He had formed a very good collection of post-impressionist pictures, including three magnificent Gauguins, six Matisses, five Bonnards, and the best pictures Segonzac ever painted,* all bought under Roger's influence. So he immediately said we could have the Hall. I did not realise that, like Logan, he suffered from euphoria

---

* To illustrate Michael Sadler's uncanny foresight: he rang me up one evening in 1933 saying "I've discovered a new painter. He's called Francis Bacon. I've commissioned him to paint my portrait for Hall. It will be like an X-ray photograph of my nut." This was one of his 'up' periods, and alas the commission was cancelled when he went 'down'. He also persuaded the Fellows of University College to hang Gauguin's *Christ in the garden of Gethsemane* over the altar in Chapel; but withdrew it later.

and was amazed when, three days before the lecture, he sent word that the Hall would not be available. He had passed into a 'low'. I managed to win him round, but it was a near thing. In the end Roger had influenza and was only just able to croak his way through the lecture. He then went to bed with pneumonia and nearly died in our house.

At about this time it became evident that Jane was about to have another baby. Shortly before it was due she turned herself upside down in a rather too lively car (called a Wolseley Hornet) and demolished a lamp post conveniently outside the Radcliffe Hospital in Headington. The patients sitting on the lawn were delighted. She thought that she was going to have twins, and an X-ray proved that this was correct. They were born on April 9th, 1932. I happened to be lunching that day with Lady Cunard (who will play a large part in the next section) and bounced into the room delighted with myself. "Emerald, we've just had twins". "Oh, Kenneth, how wicked of you. To bring more people into this world is terrible." Ned Lutyens, who was standing behind her, said "Boys or girls?" I said triumphantly, "A boy and a girl". "Always means two fathers", he said, and continued to scratch out his pipe.

I say 'they were born on April 9th', but as a matter of fact I don't know when they were born, because a few days after they had entered the world my father left it. His superb constitution had finally collapsed, and every organ simultaneously refused to function. I was torn between being in London with Jane and her two enchanting new creations, or in Sheilbridge with my father. There was no one to look after him but the local doctor, who spoke English haltingly (his normal language being Gaelic) and seemed to have no idea how long my father could hold out. But I discovered that the butler had been told to give him glasses of cold tea, pretending that they were whisky, and he was accepting them; so I realised that he could not have long to live. I was able to tell him about the birth of the twins. He said "That's good, but there'll never be another—," he meant to say "Alan", but instead he said "Roddy", the name of the gentle ghillie who had looked after him every day as he fished. These were his last words. My mother was in a pitiful state. Her life's work was over, and her long determination to repress her feelings could no longer be maintained. She was quite intelligent enough to realise this, and said to me "It's like having lost the use of a limb". Her atrophied feelings turned to hysteria, and she could relieve her own misery only by making everyone around her miserable. When, after my father's funeral, I could finally leave my mother and return to Jane, I realised that the birth of the twins had not been registered. In the general confusion no one could remember when they had been born.

Growing old is not a gradual decline, but a series of jumps down from one ledge to another. The same in reverse is true of growing up. When I married I was thoughtless, unimaginative and completely self-centred. The birth of Alan had done something to shake me out of my aesthetic carapace; and the birth of the twins, followed in less than a week by the death of my father, gave me, for the first time, some sense of responsibility. I had to think of other people. I had to deal with my father's affairs; I had to deal with my mother, who had been left the Ardnamurchan estate, but refused to make any decisions or consider any plans. From the gloomy and frustrating atmosphere of Sheilbridge I would return to London to visit Jane and the two little souls which she had so miraculously brought into this world, already complete with their own characters, and as different as they could be from one another. We took them to Oxford, and I asked that quintessence of old Oxford, Dr Blakiston, if he would christen them in Trinity Chapel. He was at first reluctant, but finally agreed, giving as his reason that he had never christened twins. Jane ordered in flowers, and I, with my usual cowardice, did not like to tell the President. Finally, the day before the ceremony, I went to ask permission for the flowers, and received a classic Oxford reply: "I'm prepared to oppose it." I pleaded with him and he gave in. In the event he was the hero of the occasion, because Colin's godfather, Owen Morshead, lost his nerve and answered the question 'name this child' with the words 'Colette Elizabeth'. Blakiston had discovered that the boy twin should come first, and held his ground. In the end the twins got their right names, and were taken back to Shotover amidst general rejoicing.

During my time at the Ashmolean two characters began to play an increasing part in our lives, so that they became almost like elderly relatives. They were Edith Wharton and Lord Lee of Fareham. I had met Edith on one of my first visits to i Tatti, and had been given the frozen mitt for which she was famous. I bore no resentment, because there was no reason why she should bother about an unknown youth to whom Mrs Berenson had taken one of her inexplicable fancies. But when I met her again *The Gothic Revival* had been published, and Edith (it is one of the greatest compliments I have ever been paid) saw in me a fellow craftsman; and we became friends. The transition between being 'in' or 'out' with Edith was very sudden. She seemed to live in a social fortress of which the doors were occasionally opened for a second to admit a newcomer. This was not a matter of snobbishness; the fortress contained people of all kinds, including some who seemed to me quite uninteresting, and at least one positive bounder; and I have long speculated on why certain people gave her a feeling of reassurance. She had retained from her early days of loneliness in plutocratic New York an absolute horror of dinner-party society. On the other hand, she had also retained a dislike of bohemianism and disorder of all kinds. She was, on many counts, a formidable person, extremely intelligent, immensely well read in four languages, witty, self-disciplined. All her best stories—*Summer, The House of Mirth, The Custom of the Country,* are based on disillusion and a sense of the cruelty of life. Indeed

The Custom of the Country was considered so cynical by the Nobel Committee that they finally refused to give her the Nobel Prize for literature. To know that under a perfectly conventional surface there lay this unfathomable depth of pessimism was somewhat daunting; but to her friends Edith was so funny and so warm-hearted that the author of *Ethan Frome* was forgotten. After one or two meetings she invited us to stay at her pretty villa in the Old Castle of Hyères; and when I had to go to Paris I stayed regularly at the beautiful Pavillion Colombe. The first night I would tell her of all the extraordinary human situations that had developed since we last met, and she would giggle like a girl. Novelists live on material of this kind, and, although Edith had an enormous store of memories, I fancy that they had lost their sharpness of impact. Her old cronies told her stories that she had heard too often.

I must not conceal the fact, so elaborately described by her first biographer, Percy Lubbock, that Edith could be tiresome. She was fidgetty. Every few minutes she rang the bell in order that her servants, whom she treated angelically, should find her glasses or her bag, or let in her beloved dog. She relaxed only after dinner, when she liked to read aloud. She loved Walt Whitman, saying that she had learnt how to read him from Henry James, whose reading of Whitman was one of the greatest literary experiences of her life. Like all Victorians she felt a mysterious urge to go on picnics, which were preceded by endless fuss and usually went badly. And, of course, when she felt obliged to invite the local *gratin* of Hyères to luncheon, she became once more the *grande dame* of Newport, and listened with icy contempt to the endless stream of platitudes that makes up French provincial conversation, her mouth shut like a trap.

It is often said that she never spoke about her work, and almost pretended not to be a writer at all; but this was not my experience. When she came down from her morning's writing—she always wrote in bed till about eleven o'clock—she would talk, as we walked in the garden, about the problems of language and construction that had confronted her that morning, and one realised what a master-craftsman she was. As she lived in great style and was exceedingly generous to all local charities, her considerable fortune began to dwindle; and finally it turned out that she had been misinformed about her income tax and owed a very large sum. A capable friend took over her affairs, and virtually controlled her life for the last six months. When she died we found that she had bequeathed her library to our son Colin, who was her godson.

Lord Lee of Fareham was in a very different category, and in retrospect I see that he represented the side of my life that has given me least satisfaction. He was a man of action. The younger son of a poor country clergyman, he had joined the army determined to succeed. He had bluffed his way out to Canada as a professor of tactics, and had later managed to strike up an acquaintance with Theodore Roosevelt and became an honorary 'rough rider' in the Cuban war. Roosevelt evidently took a fancy to this adventurous young Englishman and asked that he should be made British Military Attaché in Washington. His push and tenacity must have been equal to that of the young Churchill. He fell in love with an American girl named Ruth Moore, whose father was known as 'the diplomat of Wall Street.' She loved her father and kept Arthur waiting seven years, but in the end she married him, bringing with her a sizeable fortune. He was thus able to stand for Parliament and entered the House of Commons on the same day as Winston Churchill. Rich, ambitious and methodical, he seemed sure to succeed. But for various reasons—some circumstantial, some due to his own tactless and overbearing character—his political career was a comparative failure. He had a brief period in office when he was the *creato* of Lloyd George, but he is remembered chiefly as the man who had the vision and patriotism to give his house, Chequers, to the nation.

This frustrated man of action had turned his attention to the arts. His first collection, including some fine Constable sketches, had been left behind at Chequers; when he started collecting again it became his chief interest. He had genuine feeling for craftsmanship, and bought some admirable pieces of goldsmith's work, which in a panic he presented to Hart House in Toronto in 1941; but he was a less perceptive judge of painting, and his political instincts made him keen to get the better of the dealers. When we first knew him he lived in White Lodge, a large palladian house with curved wings like the villa Mocenigo, set in the middle of Richmond Park. The main rooms were beautifully furnished and decorated (Lady Lee had the finest Edwardian taste), and meals there were a pleasure; but at the end of one of the wings were picture galleries to which, after a good lunch, one's reluctant steps were directed. Lord Lee had installed his 'discoveries' in rooms hung with grey velvet, and almost all of them were placed in large velvet-lined boxes (known as 'shadow boxes') which were then believed to enhance a picture's value. There were a few genuine discoveries, like the Botticelli Altar-piece from S Spirito, but many of the pictures were totally repainted and a few were positive forgeries. The general effect was of a dealer's exhibition. Arthur always went round with one, standing very close and breathing hard; if he had been six inches taller he would literally have breathed down one's neck. He hoped for confirmation of all his labels, or even a measure of expansion. He had a dossier for all his pictures in which the case in favour of an attribution was argued like a lawyer's brief, with frequent underlinings in blue and red.

He was completely lacking in detachment and, like many people with a taste for power—headmasters and headmistresses are prime examples—he was always extolling the virtue of 'loyalty'. How he put up with my love of irony I can't imagine. His incursion into the world of art galleries was bound to lead to trouble.

Arthur Lee, with the push and twist learnt under Lloyd George, had no difficulty in achieving a dominating place, and when I first came on the scene he was Chairman of the National Gallery. Of course he was high-handed, bullied the staff and tried to force the Gallery to buy 'discoveries' that he could not afford to buy for himself. The result was one of those classic rows that rocked the museum world and must seem completely ridiculous to outsiders.

As Arthur Lee was exceptionally kind to me for over fifteen years I would be a monster of ingratitude if I did not record some of the actions that may be remembered in his favour. Here is one of them. In 1933 he and Ruth were staying with us in Oxford when, during dinner, the telephone rang. The call was from Fritz Saxl, director of the Warburg Institute in Hamburg, whom I had never met, but who had presumably heard from Dr Bing that I had been present at Warburg's last lecture. He said, in guarded terms, that the time had come for the Institute to leave Germany, and wondered if there was any chance of its being established in Oxford. I knew enough about University politics to realise that this could not be done without several years of lobbying, during which time the Library would have been seized by the Nazis and the Library staff sent to concentration camps. But I said I would do what I could. When I came back to the dinner table Jane asked me about the call and I explained. Arthur said "This could be something for the Courtauld" (he had persuaded Sam Courtauld to found an Institute for Art History bearing his name), and when I described the marvels of the Warburg Library (which I had never visited) and the devotion of the staff, Arthur was convinced and moved into action. First of all he had to persuade the University of London to accept the Library, but, as time was running short, Arthur somehow bullied the Hamburg authorities into sending over the whole Library as a personal loan to himself. He then took a floor of Thames House, which was entirely empty, and had the Library arranged there. Only someone with his will and obstinacy could have done all this, and it showed that men of action are sometimes useful in the world of scholarship.

No parts of an autobiography are more boring than those that describe feuds and squabbles. These usually arise from trivial issues or from the clash of long-forgotten personalities, and the writer, who still feels some pain or indignation, dwells on them at inordinate length. I must, however, say a few words about the great National Gallery rows of 1932—33, because nothing else can explain the extraordinary decision to offer the directorship of the National Gallery to an immature man of 30.

Early in the 1920's Arthur Lee had been struck by the lectures given at the Wallace Collection by an earnest-looking man named W. G. Constable. He was seeking employment at the Bar, but in 1923, no doubt under Lee's influence, he joined the staff of the National Gallery. During the next ten years this body was in a state of rebellion against the trustees in general and against Arthur Lee in particular, and Constable must have been in an uneasy position. He therefore accepted the offer to become the first Director of the new Art Historical Institute which, although it had been paid for by Samuel Courtauld and bears his name, had been brought into existence under the impulse of Arthur Lee. I would suppose that Constable accepted this appointment reluctantly because it took him away from the National Gallery. He consoled himself with the thought that ultimately he was bound to be appointed Director—there was no one else. He would keep on the Courtauld and thus have the kind of commanding position in the art world that Eastlake had enjoyed in the nineteenth century. Meanwhile there had appeared on the Board of the Gallery an active antagonist to Arthur Lee, then called Ormsby Gore.* He was a hard-working man with a

* Later Lord Harlech.

good memory but somewhat lacking in tact.* He espoused the cause of the Keeper and staff. There was a stop-gap director, named Augustus Daniel, a friend of Tonks and Steer and a most lovable man, but he would take no part in all these feuds and wisely bought only two modest Dutch still-lifes during his three years of office. In 1933 Director Lee's term of office expired, and Philip Sassoon became Chairman in his place. This did not greatly worry Arthur, because he thought that, if he could get me appointed as director, he could soon come back, and I would be 'loyal'. He broached the matter to me several times in the spring of 1933; indeed this was probably his reason for staying with us in Oxford. But I had always said that I was far too young and that I could not leave the Ashmolean after only three years.

In June 1933, when I was still under thirty, I received a telegram from Mr Ramsay MacDonald offering me the directorship. It would be hypocritical to deny that I was flattered. But on reflection I saw that this apparent stroke of luck had come to me too early. I had no administrative experience, and did not know how to deal with people, least of all people with grievances. In my sheltered life I had met with nothing but kindness and good will since I had left school. If I had known the true state of affairs in the Gallery I would have refused. As it was I temporised and wrote for advice to a few trusted friends, including Edith Wharton. They all advised me to accept; but, of course, they did not know the situation any more than I did. Finally I accepted, because I thought I could buy some good pictures for the Gallery which I take to be a director's first duty. I often regretted my decision; but the pictures are there.

---

* I cannot resist quoting verbatim the speech he made to Giles Gilbert Scott when he had been elected President of the R.I.B.A. "Mr Scott is a moderate architect and a moderate man, a sort of architectural Baldwin". The diners began to move uneasily in their seats. "Well", he continued, "when I was young I was always told that a moderate man was like a moderate egg, useful at elections."

VI

Innocents in Clover

I COME NOW to the strangest period in our lives: what can only be described as the Great Clark Boom. It lasted from about 1932 till 1939, and was as mysterious as a boom in Australian gold shares. That it existed is unquestionable. For seven years we were borne along on the crest of a social wave. We were asked everywhere, and almost everyone of note came to lunch or dine with us. In one week Walter Lippmann dined with us to meet Winston Churchill, and three days later flew back to Paris to lunch with Mr Neville Chamberlain. As a contemporary wit said "Jane and the K is all around I see". This episode is hard to explain. It had as little to do with talent as Australian gold shares have to do with the precious metal in a mine. Although we were quite presentable there were far more handsome couples. We were comfortably off, but far richer people were trying to make their way into society, in vain. Our home contained some good pictures by artists who have since become fashionable—Cézanne, Renoir, Seurat, Matisse and Bonnard—which we had been able to buy at modest prices; but the high-powered people who visited us (other than Americans) never noticed them. Absurd as it sounds, I think that the real explanation was our innocence. We were obviously not trying to get on. We took people at their face value. We thought that they were being kind to us, and were grateful. Jane's warmth and sympathy, and my enthusiasm for the arts, were fresh ingredients in a group of people most of whom knew each other's weaknesses too well. The reader of this section may think that it is like an article in a glossy magazine: 'These names make news'. I can't help it. These were our daily companions, and in some cases became real friends. They were, for the most part, interesting people and I am glad to have known them.

Since I have used the metaphor of the Stock Exchange, I will sustain it, and say that the brokers who kept an eye on social values were the hostesses. I am not thinking of the great political hostesses, Lady Londonderry or Lady Wimborne: we visited their houses, but as we took no part in politics we were not of interest to them. Of the freelance hostesses the most indomitable, although in a sense the humblest, was Sibyl Colefax. She has already appeared in the previous chapter as a by-product of the Italian Exhibition, but she deserves to be described at greater length. The need to collect celebrities was for her an addiction as strong as alcohol or drugs. If in some way she was thwarted—a guest fell out at the last minute or a celebrity left early—she would suffer a physical change, and the upper part of her face would turn black. She literally gave one a black look, and it was very alarming. When we first knew her she lived in Argyll House, a beautiful eighteenth-century building by Leone which still stands in the Kings Road. She had a husband. This is always a drawback for a hostess, and except in financial terms, Sir Arthur Colefax was not an asset. He was a successful K.C., a heavy man with a very large face, who was thought by those who had never visited the provinces to be the biggest bore in England. He sat at the far end of the table, with two loyal or docile guests beside him, and repeated the week's news in a slow, solemn voice. The only one of Sibyl's celebrities to seek his company was Max Beerbohm, who said that as he lived out of England and never read the newspapers, he was glad to be informed. Max himself spoke slowly, and I daresay had known many figures like Sir Arthur in his youth.

Sibyl's programme of entertaining must have involved a prodigious amount of administrative skill and energy. She spent every weekend staying at a friend's country house, and before going to bed would make sure that the drawer of her writing table was full of notepaper and envelopes. She would wake at five, and for the next three hours would write dozens of letters of invitation. As I have already indicated they were very difficult to read, but the important part, the date of the luncheon or dinner, was always clear, and sometimes one could decipher the name of the principal attraction, say H. G. Wells or Granville Barker. This huge bundle of letters was posted on Sunday afternoon, and woe to him who declined. In fact it would have been a mistake to do so. Sibyl was an excellent hostess. Her house was pretty, and the company nearly always amusing. She was a well-read woman, who would stimulate the conversation of her literary guests. One met people one would never have met otherwise. Two of them I have named already, Max Beerbohm and Granville Barker. Although Max had a great reputation as a wit I never heard him say anything amusing. He was sweet and gentle, much older than his years, and looked like a precious pink Christmas present that had just been unpacked, so that some of the cotton wool still clung to its surface. By this time he had said all that he had to say and did absolutely nothing except read Edwardian memoirs. Granville Barker was a different proposition. A brilliant actor, an able dramatist, a master of theatrical production, he had been persuaded by his millionairess wife to abandon the theatre and live in retirement in Devon in order to write a masterpiece. What a fate for the original of John Tanner in *Man and Superman!* The result was foreseeable. He grew stout and torpid and did practically no writing. Occasionally the call of the theatre was too strong for him. He would come to London to direct a production of Shakespeare, and John Gielgud (who knows more about Shakespeare than anyone I have ever met) tells me that Granville Barker's direction was that of a supreme master. I must admit that he also wrote several prefaces to Shakespeare's plays, which are excellent. But it was a waste. Activists should not isolate themselves before the age of seventy. For thirty years kind friends have suggested to me that I should retire into the country and write a book: to which my reply has been "Granville Barker". (Not that I would compare my limited abilities with his glorious talents.)

For a time we stood very high in Sibyl Colefax's hierarchy, and were known by the proud title of 'my young people'. We lost this distinction as the result of a dirty trick I played on her. I was lunching in Wheelers restaurant with Vivien Leigh, then rehearsing *The Doctor's Dilemma,* when Sibyl came out of the back room. I greeted her, but some naughty instinct prevented me from introducing my exquisitely beautiful companion. As soon as I got home the telephone rang—it had been ringing all afternoon—and Sibyl's voice, hysterical with fury, asked "Who was that? Who was that?" "Vivien Leigh." "Oh, of course, how stupid of me." In ten days we were asked to luncheon to meet the Oliviers. "Have you met my young people?" said Sibyl as we entered.

The climax of Sibyl's 'my young people' was a shade too ambitious, being nothing less than the Prince of Wales and Mrs Simpson; and the summit of her career was an evening when her 'young people' (the Prince of Wales now King) came to dinner. It did not go well from the start but the real misfortune came after dinner, when Sibyl had persuaded Arthur Rubinstein to play the piano. He announced that he would play the Barcarolle, meaning, of course, the work of Chopin. As the piece proceeded the King looked bewildered, then irritated, and finally said "That isn't the one we like": he was thinking of the popular intermezzo in *The Tales of Hoffman.* Rubinstein then played a Chopin Prelude. The King looked even more irritated, and at the end rose to leave. It was 10.15. Consternation. Sibyl on the verge of tears.

Lady Diana Duff-Cooper took command, and asked Nöel Coward to play one of his songs. Nöel very properly refused. Arthur Rubinstein, seeing that he was no longer needed, returned to the dining-room, and philosophically consumed the whisky and soda that he had denied himself before. We accompanied him, filled with anger and humiliation. By this time the King had reached the front door, but by good fortune Mr Churchill was arriving, which delayed the royal departure. At this moment there came from the drawing room the strains of 'Mad Dogs and Englishmen': Nöel, like the kind man he was, had put his artistic scruples in his pocket in order to save his friend's evening. And it *was* saved. The King returned to the drawing room and stayed, I believe, to a late hour. We went out with Arthur Rubinstein, found a taxi and took him back to his hotel.

Perhaps, in the end, Sibyl's greatest claim to gratitude was her wide circle of friends in the United States. No eminent American came to London without visiting her, and, at a time when there was much less rapport between English and American society than there is today, she did a great deal for trans-Atlantic understanding. We owe to her friendships that have lasted a lifetime. With her we first met Tom Lamont, Walter Lippmann, Lynn and Alfred Lunt, and many others. When we first went to the United States in 1935 she gave us over twenty letters of introduction, and, as my American friends have played a great part in my life, I cannot forget her kindness. But even they could find her maddening. I remember Alfred Lunt describing how he took her to the theatre. Sibyl, as usual, stood up, looked round with hunting eyes, and fidgeted at the sight of unexpected combinations. Finally Alfred could bear it no longer. "Sibyl, you have been taken to the first night of a very interesting play by one of the greatest living actors. You will sit down, talk to me and listen to the play, or I shall leave." Sibyl obeyed.

Diarists, except for Harold Nicolson, have been malicious about Sibyl Colefax, and the Bloomsburys in particular shuddered at her name. But they went there. In fact almost the only time I met Virginia Woolf was in Argyll House. After the death of Sir Arthur, when she moved to a small house in Lord North Street, where conditions were not so agreeable, they still went, and the house was packed to bursting. One sat round the table on little gilt chairs and had to eat by the action of one's wrists, as one's arms were pinioned by one's neighbours. Sibyl genuinely loved people, and bringing them together was her life's work. One should have loved her more than one did. The trouble is that there is something dehumanising about any sort of addiction. One cannot help thinking about people in terms of their obsessions, and until the last few weeks of her life one could not quite believe Lady Colefax was a real person. In this she was the complete counterpart of the other famous hostess of our youth, Lady Cunard.

Sibyl came from a serious upper middle-class background; Walter Bagehot and the Wedgwoods were somewhere amongst her ancestors. By standards of conventional morality she was irreproachable. Maud Burke, later to become Lady Cunard, came from San Francisco and had spent her youth wandering about Europe with her mother in search of adventures. It would be wrong to call her an adventuress, because this would imply that she was 'on the make', which she never was. But she moved in 'a whirlwind of passionate love affairs' (her own words). She must have been enchantingly pretty, neat as a Clodion with tiny bones and brilliant blue eyes. In 1894 she met George Moore, who conceived a passion for her that lasted till his death forty years later. How much she cared for him it is difficult to say, as so many of his early letters to her have been destroyed. He was rather a ridiculous figure, and physically inept. But he was the friend of Manet, Mallarmé, Huysmans, and Maud Burke, who had already developed her love for music and literature, may have been glad to feel that she was so close to the centre of European culture. They travelled together in France and Germany, but decided that they must not marry, believing, in George Moore's words, that they must "stint their desires to blessed adultery". In 1895 she married a shipping magnate, Sir Bache Cunard, who took her down to Market Harborough, where she rode to hounds and must have dazzled the county. She also had a daughter, named Nancy, whom she neglected and who wrote a bitterly vindictive book about her mother. Nancy Cunard was a menacing figure in the intellectual world of the 1920's, disturbing many lives, including, for a year, that of Aldous Huxley. I never met her, but have the impression that she had a good deal in common with her mother, with the difference that she liked black people and squalor, whereas her mother liked pink people and luxury.

Maud's whole interest lay in London, in the conversation of intelligent men, in the theatre, and above all in opera; and after a time she left Market Harborough for Grosvenor Square and changed her name from Maud to Emerald. Bogey Harris was the only person I know who still called her Maud. George Moore had receded into the background, but still adored her, wrote her hundreds of letters and bequeathed to her his pictures, including two Manets and a Monet that he had bought with the profits of *Esther Waters*. She had many lovers, but only one who influenced her life, Sir Thomas Beecham. Between them they managed to finance seasons of opera at Covent Garden in the days before state subsidy; he by spending a large personal fortune, she by bewitching and bamboozling rich people, who sat at the back of her box and talked about hunting or the stock market. She had a remarkable knowledge of opera, and would intersperse her conversation with arias from Bellini, Verdi, Puccini and even Wagner, very accurately sung. She also loved the art of acting, and would go alone to a theatre in the suburbs if the play contained an actor whom she admired. She slept badly and read half the night, so that she was exceptionally well read. Unfortunately she had the habit of ringing up her friends in the small hours of the morning to discuss a character in Balzac or the implications of one of Madame de Sevigné's letters. She remained devoted to Beecham for at least thirty years, and bitterly resented his marriage. I actually saw her faint in his arms. I should add that by this time she looked an agelessly old lady, fearfully bedizened. Curiously enough, the nearer one got to her the younger she looked; from a distance one could see only paint and wrinkles.

I must have met her in about 1930 because I remember that when I was first at the Ashmolean she came down to a concert in the Sheldonian given by Beecham. As usual she was late. The audience had been kept waiting, and when I led this painted Jezebel, chattering like a parakeet, to her place in the middle of the auditorium, Sir Thomas turned round and said "You're late, sit down." Not a good moment for a twenty-seven year old member of the University staff. She was in fact always late, and at lectures one would see, a third of the way through, the shadow of osprey feathers bobbing up and down on the lower part of the screen, and know that she had arrived. I have already recalled that I was lunching with her on the day that our twins were born; by that time we had become fast friends. I have seen it stated that she used to take people up and drop them. I can only say that I have seldom had a more loyal and devoted friend. But she was a reckless character and sometimes made unwise experiments. She had been impressed by Wyndham Lewis's *Time and Western Man,* and paid him a call. "What was he like, Emerald?" "It was terrible. He was in an empty room, absolutely empty. I don't know how anyone can live under £10,000 a year. He was sitting on a barrel holding a pistol." "Was it loaded?" "He said so, but it didn't matter because he seemed to be almost blind." "What did he say?" "Oh, I couldn't repeat *that.*" Emerald, whatever her behaviour, was easily shocked by bad language or *gros mots*. The word 'bloody' would have upset her as much as it did the teaparty in *Pygmalion*.

Her luncheon and dinner parties were a curious mixture of handsome young men, accepted wits like Lord Berners, a few writers like Sachie Sitwell and Peter Quennell; clever, spiteful women, and ambassadors. I remember, early on, going in to lunch decorously following two eminent politicians, who automatically took up their places either side of our hostess. "I'm not interested in politics," said Emerald. "I love art. Kenneth, come and sit beside me." And she really did love music and poetry, although her taste in visual art was limited. Conversation was what is known as 'brilliant', but, as everyone was afraid of being a bore, they never stuck to a point long enough to follow a train of thought. It was a diet of *hors d'oeuvres*. This does not suit me, and I sometimes talked for about a minute on end, to the fury of the other guests; but Emerald forgave me.

She was at her best when she had some heavy public man to tease. She would whizz round him like a humming bird till he became completely dizzy and began to doubt his own identity. I remember an evening, rather late in her life, when the principal guest was a rich, monolithic American named Myron Taylor. "Now, Mr Taylor, what do you think about incest?" "Well, er, ah, well, there seems to be no doubt at all that biologically the results are deleterious. In some of our small prairie towns statistics show . . ." "But, Mr Taylor, what about Siegmund and Sieglinde?" and Emerald began to sing in her small sweet voice, with impeccable diction, the end of Act I of the *Valkyrie*. Mr Taylor, only slightly shaken, continued inexorably ". . . and it proved conclusively that in some Near Eastern countries . . ." "Kenneth, what do you think about incest?" "I'm in favour of it, Emerald." "Oh Kenneth, what a wicked thing to say! Think of the Greeks." Putting her head back and closing her eyes she recited, with a triumphant smile, a longish quotation from Gilbert Murray's translation of the *Oresteaia*. "Beautiful" (K.C.) "But all the same it was just a silly taboo, like Pythagoras saying that it was wicked to eat beans." Emerald was delighted. "Mr

Taylor, do you think it wicked to eat beans?" Emerald's rooms were always very warm, and by this time the wretched Myron Taylor was sweating profusely. All he could do was to cover his large senatorial face with a table napkin.

I only once saw her put out. We were on the dangerous topic of resemblances between men and animals. "What am I like?" asked Emerald. There was an uneasy silence while we all tried to think of substitutes for the word 'parakeet'. Golden Pheasant? No, too bright. Bird of paradise? Too obvious. I was just about to say "Lady Amherst's pheasant" (which is indeed a most beautiful bird) when Archie Clarke Kerr,* who had been, as usual, sunk in a kind of Taoist torpor, suddenly said "A fruit-eating bat", and immediately closed his eyes again. It sounded so perfectly apposite that we were momentarily silent, and Emerald was quick enough to guess the train of associations that was passing through our minds. The subject was dropped, and we all soon recovered.

To be one of Lady Cunard's regular guests was to have reached somewhere very near the top of unstuffy, new world society. At the very summit of this society was Sir Philip Sassoon. He was a kind of Haroun al Raschid, entertaining with oriental magnificence in three large houses, endlessly kind to his friends, witty, mercurial and ultimately mysterious. When I was appointed to the National Gallery he was Chairman of the Board, and he immediately invited us down to meet him. He was staying at a house he had built in Kent called Port Lympne, and we arrived in pouring rain; an inauspicious prologue to a meeting with the Sun King.

We were received by a small, dark, unprepossess-

---

* Archie Clarke Kerr, later Lord Inverchapel, had been British Ambassador in Moscow, and was later our Ambassador in the United States. I suppose none of us knew what the face of a fruit-eating bat was like, but were persuaded by the name. In fact it is the second largest of all flying mammals, and its face bears no resemblance at all to that of Lady Cunard.

ing lady, who gave her name as Hannah Gubbay, but did not explain her *raison d'être,* which remained mysterious to the end. Even on a wet day the view over Romney Marsh from the terrace of Port Lympne is breath-taking, and we admired it, Jane adding "It's so peaceful." "You won't find any peace in this house" said Mrs Gubbay in her sour, staccato, toneless voice. At this moment our host appeared, apologising for his absence by saying that he had been answering a telephone call from the Prince of Wales "who always talks for half an hour". He was dressed in a red shirt open at the neck and velvet slippers embroidered with PS in gold, and looked exotically out of place in the wet Kentish landscape. After a minimum of formalities, he offered to show us round the house. It had been built for him by the favorite architect of the Establishment, Herbert Baker, a polite and thoughtful man with a positive genius for errors of design; in his public buildings every proportion, every cornice, every piece of fenestration was (and unfortunately still is) an object lesson in how not to do it. Port Lympne was no exception, and Philip's taste for interior decoration had not improved matters. The chief sitting-room was hung in white lamé, the furniture was white and gold, the books bound in vellum. On the walls hung pictures by Sargent of white marble ruins, framed in off-white mouldings. One of them, representing Venice on a wet day, was a great relief. The dining-room was panelled in lapis lazuli, surmounted by a frieze of Negroes by Glyn Philpot. None of the windows looked over the view. Under ordinary circumstances I don't think we could have disguised our feelings, but in the first minute we had been won round by the charm of our host.

Philip, more than almost anyone I have known except for Maurice Bowra and Vivien Leigh, had an idiosyncratic and infectious *style.* He moved quickly and always seemed to be in profile, like an Egyptian relief. His mind moved equally quickly and, as his most unexpected comments were made without any change of inflection, they often took people by surprise. He saw the ridiculous side of Port Lympne. Going round the house we came on a particularly hideous bathroom, panelled in brown and black zig-zags of marble. Philip said, without altering his tone of voice "It takes you by the throat and shakes you."

The point of Port Lympne was the garden. Philip's extravagance, which was such an agreeable feature of his character, expressed itself in the deepest and long-est herbaceous borders, the most colossal beds of blue delphinium, the most imposing staircases of yew hedges. He told us with great satisfaction that he had heard a guide taking round a party of visitors and say-ing "All in the old-world style, but every bit of it sham." The layout had been planned by an architect of considerable talent named Philip Tilden, and el-derly ladies, known as 'great gardeners', who, in those days, moved from one country house to another, came down to give advice. But ultimately the garden at Port Lympne, and the almost equally dazzling gar-den at Trent, his home near London, were Philip's creations and the best expression of his taste. Once in the garden our enthusiasm was genuine, and as a re-sult our visit was a success. I do not remember the National Gallery being mentioned. A few days later Philip was heard to say that he was "crackers about the Clarks", and for the next six years we were whisked along in his train.

It was an intoxicating experience. I enjoy intoxica-tion as much as the next man, but its results are de-batable. In retrospect I see that I was in the wrong box. Our fellow visitors at Trent or Lympne were practically all politicians, and I do not remember a single artist or writer (except Mrs Belloc Lowndes), still less a scholar or member of my own chosen pro-fession. Of course these politicians were remarkably intelligent, much more so, I have no doubt, than most of my colleagues. There was the fun, eloquence and historic vision of Mr Winston Churchill, the quick and subtle mind of Lord Hugh Cecil, the harsh, prac-tical good sense of Philip Cunliffe Lister, and all this was kept in motion by Philip himself, who juggled with his distinguished guests like a conjuror. I remained silent, and I suppose that the other members of the party were unaware of my existence. Curiously enough practically no part was assigned to the ladies. I remember seeing a few old friends of Mr Churchill, like Venetia Montague, who were asked down to play bezique with him, a few heiresses like Barbara Hutton and the contemptuous young wives of viscounts. But none of them gave me a kind word or, indeed, spoke to me at all. The only exception was Philip's adorable sister, Sibyl Cholmondeley. She was, and has remained, beautiful, dauntless, intelligent, and a most loyal friend.

The politicians who accepted Philip's hospitality might be described as the unorthodox Tory fringe. The only exception was Anthony Eden, the darling of the gods. I doubt if Mr Baldwin ever crossed one of Philip's thresholds, but Mr Ramsay MacDonald did, and was made a fool of. He would go droning on, telling stories about his house in Hampstead, to which no one paid the least attention. It was evidently undergoing some repairs because at one point his voice could be heard saying "They're boring holes in ma sweetheart", and there was a hush, in hopes that something interesting would follow. But it soon became clear that the subject had not changed. "It's only the house again" said Philip briskly, and conversation was resumed. The thought that this vain old man, whose mind was only just turning over, was Prime Minister of a still great country, was rather distressing. But my acquaintances took it all for granted; politics were like that. And no doubt in the Cabinet room, if his position had been threatened, Mr MacDonald would have practised the art of self-defence with some of his old skill.

The only time I sat in the Cabinet room with him was at a meeting of the Chequers Trustees, of which the Director of the National Gallery was an honorary member. Mr MacDonald's mind was running on the molehills that disfigured his lawn, and every few minutes he would interrupt the trivial, necessary matters of administration by saying "What about the moles?" No doubt the Cabinet room was 'bugged' by the Germans, and I liked to think that they took this repeated question as a code name for some secret underground weapon.

He was kind to me. "Never let the Tories get ye, Kenneth" he would say, as Lady Londonderry offered him a Tranquillising pill; and I never have. He would tell me long stories of his youth in Lossiemouth, which had a flavour of Breughel as well as *A Cotter's Saturday Night*. I could not forget his early fight for the Labour movement, and his courage during the first war.

For seven years Philip played the same dominating part in my life that Maurice had played at Oxford. He was endlessly kind to us, having the whole family to stay at Trent for days on end, where the children were astonished by a platoon of footmen with red cummerbunds. He induced us to rent from him a charming house at Lympne, which stood opposite the gate of his drive, and invited us down to meals when he had guests of special interest, like T. E. Lawrence. As Bob Boothby and Nöel Coward lived nearby we did not lack entertaining neighbours. We enjoyed it all. But it was a different kind of education from that which had filled my life at Oxford or i Tatti, an education without books, without information and without ideas. I learnt adaptability and what is known in boxing as footwork. I had a front seat at Vanity Fair, but a back seat in Bartholomew Fair might have done me more good. However, that would have been incompatible with the position I had so unwisely accepted.

In the six months since my appointment I had learnt a little more about the state of affairs in the National Gallery, and I entered it, on the first of January, 1934, with rather less than my usual confidence. The door seemed very large, and at the end of the corridor leading to my room was the head of a

Mantegna cast in bronze, scowling contemptuously at those who were impudent enough to question authority. I did not know any of the staff and obviously my first duty was to present myself to my second in command, known as the Keeper. During the troubles before my appointment the Treasury had innocently appointed as Keeper someone from outside the museum world, an elderly inspector of education named Glasgow, who, in his youth, had published a book of drawings of Wadham College. I found him an affable and tolerant man, but when I asked him about his colleagues his face fell. The fact was, he said, that he had not met any of them. His room contained a book-case, and on one occasion the cleverest member of the staff named Ellis Waterhouse (who had left shortly before I arrived) entered it to look up a reference. The Keeper had advanced towards him with outstretched hand, saying "I'm Glasgow". Waterhouse, without turning round, had replied "I'd assumed that", and walked out. This was my initiation into the *moeurs* of museums and galleries, with which I was later to become painfully familiar. I commiserated with Mr Glasgow, but before I could say any more my first visitor had arrived. This was Sir Robert Witt, who came to tell me that anything I did must be attributed to the National Art Collections Fund; he was followed immediately by Sir Eric Maclagan, who came to tell me that, whatever I did, I must have nothing to do with the N.A.C.F. I was fully launched on my new career.

I knew nothing of administration, nothing of finance or fund raising, nothing of how to deal with Government departments. I was an aesthete and art historian, and my only thought was to buy some good pictures for the Gallery, and to re-hang certain rooms. We were very weak in fifteenth-century Sienese art, and I knew that seven of the eight scenes from the life of St Francis, by Sassetta, that once surrounded Mr Berenson's sublime effigy of the saint, and formed Sassetta's masterpiece, belonged to Mr Clarence Mackay. I had heard that he was in financial difficulties and thought that this might be an opportune moment to secure them.

This exercise naturally involved my Trustees, and I must now say something about them. In a sense the most eminent was the Prince of Wales, but he did not often come to Board meetings as he was not allowed to smoke. At my first meeting he asked me "What does a picture cost?" It sounds an absurd question, but in my subsequent experience I found that pictures did fall into three categories, £5,000, £10,000 and £20,000, to which at the present day must be added a nought or two. The senior trustee was a picturesque old scallywag named Viscount d'Abernon. I liked him because, when director of the Ottoman Bank, he had got into trouble and escaped over the tiles, like Casanova. Subsequently Lloyd George had made him our first Ambassador in Berlin after 1918. By the time I knew him he was a little deaf and suffered from almost total *extinction de voix*. "WHAT DO *YOU* THINK, EDGAR?" Philip Sassoon would bellow at him, to which he would reply in an almost inaudible whisper "offer half". He was an amateur dealer, and probably in the pay of Duveen. Duveen also had a considerable influence with Evan Charteris, the most elegant figure of his time, who for years had been at the summit of the literary *beau monde*. Having practised at the bar he could present a case very persuasively. He was a consummate liar, but always gave one a warning when he was going to tell a lie by delicately patting his moustache with a handkerchief. In contrast with these picturesque but disingenuous characters was Ormsby Gore, industrious, well-informed, combative and tactless. He was at this time Minister of Works, and it was through his efforts that the National Gallery first obtained artificial lighting. We gave a party to inaugurate the event (at which the Treasury 'in its wisdom' refused to allow us to engage a band, or give refreshments), and this led to a mammoth row between Ormsby Gore and Philip Sassoon as to who should receive the guests. I was the intermediary, and when I suggested that they should stand side by side, and it would be a matter of chance who had his hand shaken first, they both seemed quite content. Political differences are not always so easily settled.

Finally, Lord Duveen, who had been made a Trustee thanks to the influence of Arthur Lee and Lord d'Abernon, from both of whom he had bought pictures at inflated prices. Quite apart from these material benefits, he was irresistible. His bravura and impudence were infectious, and when he was present everyone behaved as if he had had a couple of drinks. He worked entirely by instinct and was incapable of writing a letter or making a coherent statement; and he had rightly seen that, whereas in America it paid him to be very grand, in England he could get further by bribing the upper classes and playing the fool.

His instinct usually told him exactly how far he could go, but in the case of the Sassettas it let him down. I had for some reason decided that the right sum to offer for the seven panels was £35,000. Mr Mackay was said to have paid double, but I saw no reason to behave charitably towards an injudicious millionaire. I persuaded my Trustees to make this offer (which was in line with Lord d'Abernon's 'offer half'), and a letter was sent to Mr Mackay. Weeks passed without an answer, and I was instructed to send a telegram. No answer. Another telegram. Still no answer. All this was reported at a Board meeting at which Lord Duveen was present. "Of course he hasn't answered," he said, with his most expansive smile "he never saw the letter". "Nor the telegrams?" "Of course not! I know Mr Mackay's butler." That a Trustee of the Gallery should have bribed a vendor's butler not to show him our offer was a bit thick, and even Philip could not suppress a note of surprise. Duveen's stipendiaries shifted uneasily in their seats. "Send another telegram", said Philip, "and see that it reaches Mr Mackay".

Duveen rang up Philip next morning. "That Board meeting—I was quite upset. When I got home Elsie said 'Joe, you are not looking *at all* yourself.' I took a sleeping pill. It did me no harm." His confidence thus restored, he asked me to go for a walk with him in Hyde Park. We talked of irrelevant matters, and I remember that Duveen paused at the perambulator of a sleeping baby and poked it with a large forefinger. Its nurse ran forward in a frenzy of indignation. "It's all right" said Duveen, with a disarming smile "he can sleep for the rest of his life; he'll only see Joe Duveen once."

Towards the end of the walk (followed by his Rolls) he came to the point. Mr Mackay had never paid for the Sassettas. They were entered in the firm's books at £70,000, but no money had passed. It would have been tactless to ask him how much he had paid M Chalondon for the pictures; clearly it was much less than our proffered £35,000. But his pride was at stake and he could not bear to rewrite the entry in his books. Finally we came to an arrangement by which the price of the Sassettas was £42,000, and it was stated in the press release that the purchase was made possible 'through the good services of Lord Duveen'.

Lord Duveen was genuinely a great giver. His generosity may have paid, but it was part of his whole expansive personality. How many successful English art dealers have presented pictures or whole galleries to the nation? Scarcely one. The reason is that they have made their fortunes by prudence, whereas Duveen made his by reckless ebullience. When his term as a Trustee came to an end Philip said "Now the meetings will be a bore: like a harlequinade without the clown."

I will not weary the reader by describing the purchases I made for the Gallery during my first few years. The Gallery grant was very small, never more than £7,000 a year, which was frequently cut to £5,000. The N.A.C.F. could give only limited help. Looking back from 1974, it seems a miracle that I was able to purchase such great masterpieces as Rubens's *Watering Place,* Rembrandt's *Saskia as Flora* and *Mrs.*

Tripp, Jerome Bosch's *Crowning with Thorns,* Ingres's
Madame Moitessier, Poussin's *Golden Calf,* Niccolo
dell'Abbate's *Rape of Proserpine* (for £315), the four
scenes from the *Life of St. John the Baptist* by Giovanni di Paolo, which, together with the Sassettas, represented the Sienese *quattrocento* by pictures of the
highest quality. At the same time, I was able to put
on exhibition a number of great paintings which
would have been much beyond our restricted means.

The story of how this was done introduces a new
character, Calouste Sarkis Gulbenkian. In the 1930's
he was the most awe-inspiring collector in Europe.
He was an Armenian who lived in Paris and kept his
collection in a large house in the Avenue de Jena
"built like a battleship, my friend". It was supposed
to be inaccessible, but we received a courteous invitation to visit him. We were ushered into a waiting
room containing some pictures by Fantin Latour and
Carpeaux's marble crouching figures, and spoke to
each other in tones of admiration considerably greater
than we felt, Jane having sensibly warned me that all
we said would be relayed to our host. After about ten
minutes he was evidently reassured and came down
the hall to greet us. He was short and dense like a
mole, but one did not think of him as either small or
fat, because one's eyes were concentrated on his magnificent head. It was bald, with a deeply cleft chin,
bushy eyebrows, and eyes as menacing as those of Mr
J. P. Morgan. He greeted us with Oriental ceremony,
and began the tour of his collection immediately. Owing to his high vitality it was painful for him to sit
still, and he could not walk. He trotted or, rather,
scuttled like a spider in pursuit of its prey. In spite
of the horrible spotlights which were *de rigueur* in
all millionaire collections of the 1930's, I could see
that he owned some magnificent pictures. Our admiration was sincere, but our real feelings were revealed only when we came to the top floor. Here Mr
Gulbenkian had been able to create a garden in the
Persian style, with quite large trees, golden pheasants
and a few hens. In his bedroom, containing the furni-

ture of Talma, Napoleon's favourite actor, was a silver gilt tazza designed by Percier, on which lay two beautiful brown eggs for his breakfast. This Persian *douceur de vivre* delighted me, and thenceforward I spoke to my host with added warmth. Nothing escaped him, and our friendship probably dated from that moment.

A few weeks later the telephone rang at about 10.30 p.m. I was asleep. A voice said "This is Mr Gulbenkian. Would you like to take some of my pictures on loan at the National Gallery?" "Yes, I would like it very much." "How many?" I rapidly calculated the capacity of the only available room. "Forty." "You do not ask your Trustees?" "No." "You do not ask what I send?" "I have perfect confidence that you will send us the best." "I will send them tomorrow." And he did send the best, except for a portrait of a lady ascribed to Ghirlandajo which, if not an actual fake, is so restored as to be the equivalent. It was one of the most popular works in the collection.

I used the word 'friendship'. It would be foolish of any man to say that he had been Mr Gulbenkian's friend, but I think I can claim that, during the next ten years, I came to know him as well as almost anyone outside his family circle. He was undoubtedly one of the most formidable human beings I have ever encountered. His will-power and energy go without saying; but in addition he had a most powerful mind. I have known very few men—perhaps only Bertrand Russell and Maynard Keynes—who could analyse a statement in concrete terms more rapidly and conclusively. When he was young his whole ambition was to go to Cambridge and become a senior wrangler. His father said to him "Calouste, do not look up; look down". "So I looked down and I found oil". Mr. Gulbenkian liked to speak in such quasi-biblical aphorisms; in fact he had taken a long course of geodetics in London University.

In spite of the rewarding redirection of his gaze, he continued to speak of himself as a dreamer. "Not an office man, Mr Clark"; and sure enough he had no

office. In summer he did his work in the park of St
Cloud. His secretaries were seated at folding card
tables situated in the boscage at intervals of about half
a mile. He would trot up and down between them,
with two detectives, heavily invisible, padding along
in the adjoining path. I sometimes accompanied him
in these walks, and his mind moved with such precision that by the time we reached the next card
table he was ready to dictate a detailed technical letter. In this way I came to learn quite a lot about the
oil industry, which I have long ago forgotten. Many
of these letters were to check, double check and
treble check promises or even binding agreements.
Mr Gulbenkian was intensely suspicious. "Check,
check, check" were the words most often on his lips.
I know that whenever he asked my advice about the
purchase of a work of art he double checked to make
sure that I was not being influenced by the vendor.
He took his meals at peculiar hours (luncheon at
3.15) so that he had the dining-room to himself, and
always sat in a corner table. If by some chance he
could not secure one he had an unobtrusive mirror
on the table beyond his plate, so that he could scut-
tle away from anyone who took him in the rear. The
first time we lunched with him in London was at the
Ritz Hotel, where the food was notoriously bad. I
commented on the excellence of our meal. "I bring
my own cook" said Mr Gulbenkian, "he is a Turk. I
can trust him." No doubt a lot of people wanted to
get rid of him, although whether they would have
gone so far as to poison him I cannot say. Later in
this book I shall describe how far they were prepared
to go.

After his pictures had hung for some months in the
Gallery, and Mr Gulbenkian had approved of their
installation, he broached the question of their ultimate
destination. He often referred to them as his children
(or his harem), and could not bear the thought of
their being entombed in some unvisited museum like
the Jacquemart André or the Cognac Jay. I therefore
proposed to him that he should build an annexe on

the vacant ground to the west of the National Gallery which would be accessible both from the outside (Whitcomb Street) and also through the Gallery. His pictures would be at Gallery level, the rest of his collection would be on the ground floor. In retrospect this does not seem to me a good idea. The National Gallery should remain itself, independent of those excrescences which so often destroy the character of American museums. But I must plead in mitigation that I foresaw a great rise in the cost of pictures which our tiny purchase grant would be entirely unable to meet. With Mr Gulbenkian's endowment we should have become the richest gallery in the world. No one could have foreseen the enormous sums of money that the Government now spends on works of art. In the 1930's, when the country was at least ten times as rich as it is today, the Treasury 'in its wisdom' twice found it necessary to cut off our annual purchase grant altogether.

Mr Gulbenkian accepted my proposal. I then had to get the consent of the Office of Works, the Treasury and the Prime Minister. To my astonishment, they all agreed. The Office of Works even agreed that Mr Gulbenkian could employ his own architect, and he commissioned William Delano, then the most accomplished of conservative American architects, to produce a model. This vast object may still be in the cellars of the National Gallery, as a tangible proof of how far we got.

Needless to say, all these activities had to be carried out in almost total secrecy. All Mr Gulbenkian's correspondence was kept in a special file in my room. He hated all publicity. "Quietly, steadily, my friend." But there remained an almost insuperable obstacle. Mr Gulbenkian was determined not to pay English estate duty on his bequest. To have achieved this would have meant an Act of Parliament. Worse still, he was a French resident, and if his Will were sent back to France to be proved (a process known as *le renvoi*), a third of his estate would have had to pass to his family, a thought that greatly distressed him. We talked for hours about this problem, and I came to know almost as much about the international laws of testamentary disposition as I did about the oil industry. Switzerland? One Canton seemed promising. Venezuela? Very helpful, but still that terrible *renvoi*. I rather doubt if we could ever have found a way round, and the Gulbenkian bequest would not have come to London, even if more dramatic incidents had not taken place.

Compared to my Trustees and my benefactor my fellow directors of museums and galleries were somewhat colourless. The ablest of them, Eric Maclagan, had already become a friend through Edith Wharton. He was the son of a bishop, whose Victorian upbringing had been polished by long residence in France—a sidesman in Sloane Street, whose heart was in Paris. As a result he was one of the most civilised men in London, and an excellent director of the Victoria and Albert Museum. The only one of my colleagues to whom the word colourless certainly did not apply was J. B. Manson, the director of the Tate, of which I was ex-officio a trustee. He was a painter in the manner of Spencer Gore and, as so often happens when painters are put in charge of galleries, he would not admit any picture which was not more or less in the style of himself and his friends. He refused to accept the Stoop bequest, although it contained a superb Degas, because it also included an early Picasso and two Matisses. He was a man of great charm, with a flushed face, white hair and a twinkle in his eye; and this twinkling eye got him out of scrapes that would have sunk a worthier man without a trace. He drank; and from time to time Evan Charteris, who was Chairman of the Tate, was rung up in the early hours of the morning. "Is that a Mr Charterice? It's the Walworth police 'ere; we've just brought in a man giving 'is name as Manson who wants you to come out and go bail for 'im." Evan would rise, put on his stays, his butterfly collar and his exquisite grey coat with a velvet collar, and by his legal powers of persuasion secure Manson's release.

Manson was so confident in his charm that he used to appear drunk at Board meetings, and I remember one occasion when he fell off his chair and had to be carried out wrapped in a blanket. His place was then taken by a much less charming, but almost equally drunken subordinate named Fincham, who had no interest in art, but had married Lord d'Abernon's niece.

Nothing in Manson's career became him like the leaving of it. The crucial episode took place on the 4th of March 1938, at a banquet given to inaugurate the British Exhibition in the Louvre. I had been the organiser of the Exhibition; Evan Charteris was the chairman. The banquet in the Hotel George V was a very grand affair, with a long high table, and about forty smaller tables below it. I was sitting at the high table, not very near the centre. Jane was sitting in a more exalted place next to the French Minister for Education, M Jean Zay. Quite early in the meal ominous farmyard noises came from one of the small tables where Manson was seated beside some embarrassed members of the British Council. By the second course these had been succeeded by remarkably life-like and penetrating 'cock-a-doodle-do's'. At this point Manson set out on his first peregrination. His aim was to complain to M Jean Zay that he was not getting enough drink. "Tell him to step on it" he repeated. M Zay who, like all French Ministers of Education, did not understand a word of English, turned to Jane for a translation. She replied "C'est un bon vieux peintre qui demande si M le Ministre va prononcer un discours", and then, turning to the unsteady Manson, who was leaning on her chair, she hissed "Go and talk to Mr Ormsby Gore". Such is the force of her personality that Manson obeyed, and Billy Gore got him back to his table. But not for long. After a few more cock crows he set off on a second expedition and, after several false starts, found his way back to the high table. He picked out a more docile victim, Lady Phipps, the wife of the British Ambassador, who was, I suppose, our hostess, and leaning over her chair said "You come and see me when next you are in London, my dear. I'll show you something that isn't in the Tate Gallery." Lady Phipps was a delicate, sensitive person, a devout Catholic, unaccustomed to manifestations of the Old Adam. She should have told him to go to hell. Instead she leant forward on the table, her hands clasped as in prayer, and turned to her husband. He immediately rose to his feet. We all rose and walked rather sheepishly out of the dining-room. In the crowded anteroom I found myself next to Evan Charteris. He said "I don't think they noticed that anything was wrong, do you?" As we had left before the coffee this was obviously untrue, and Evan mopped his moustache with a handkerchief. The dining-room was deserted, except for a few bewildered waiters, and Manson was having the time of his life, going round from table to table, drinking the wine that the guests had been forced to leave in their glasses. From time to time he emitted cock-a-doodle-do's, as loud but less precise than those that had preceded them: "Blow, bugle; answer, echoes, dying, dying, dying."

We went out of the hotel into the pale spring sunshine of the Avenue de Jena. I had managed to compose my face into the expression of slightly pained gravity that was being worn by my colleagues. Once out of sight I could release it. I began to laugh. I laughed so much that I had to lie down on a green park bench. I had not laughed so much since the Bing Boys. It is the only public banquet that I have ever really enjoyed. There was (for me) an agreeable sequel. The Paris newspapers reporting the episode attributed this splendid performance to the Director of the National Gallery. For a few weeks the image of a conceited, priggish young Director was somewhat modified, and decent people thought the better of me. For Manson things did not go so well, and, at the request of the Foreign Office, he was asked to resign on the grounds of ill health.

The year after my becoming Director of the National Gallery I made a serious mistake. This was not due to an error of judgement, but to lack of determination. Collins Baker, who had doubled the role of Keeper with that of surveyor of the King's Pictures, accepted a post in Pasadena, and the King's Pictures became vacant. Owen Morshead thought I would be a suitable successor, and mentioned my name to King George V, who had a great regard for him. I was summoned by the Lord Chamberlain, Lord Cromer, and asked if I would accept the post. I declined, for two reasons; first, that the Royal Collection was the size of a great public gallery and required the full time services of at least two men. It had been shamefully neglected in the past. Secondly, my appointment to the National Gallery had been premature, and to follow it in a year by another important post would arouse resentment and indignation amongst my colleagues, who had hitherto treated me with restraint.

Lord Cromer brushed the arguments aside, but I held my ground, and left him with relief. A complicating factor was that the ideal candidate for the post was disqualified. This was a Finnish art-historian named Tancred Borenius. He was a good scholar, a pleasant companion and a passionate upholder of the concept of monarchy. He would have made an ideal courtier. Unfortunately he was known to have followed the continental practice, described above, of taking payment for certificates of authenticity; and, what was worse, quite small payments (known as 'smackers under the table'); if he had taken large payments, like a few scholars on the continent, no one would have objected. This circumstance was reported to the Lord Chamberlain by everyone whom he consulted, and being, like all royal servants, terrified of a scandal, he would not accept Tancred as a member of the Household.

At this point the Great Clark Boom began to operate and, to my horror, George V sent word that he and Queen Mary would like to visit the National Gallery. No reigning monarch had visited it before. I thought that this breach of precedent might be avoided, because the King's heart was already giving him trouble, and there was no lift in the Gallery, only a hand-operated picture lift, which came up through the floor. It often stuck, and a vision of the King and Queen trapped on this unstable platform, with only their heads above floor level, went beyond even my love of the grotesque. However, the King's doctors were persuaded to let him mount the Gallery steps, and we duly made a tour of the collection. Such tours are exhausting, because royal personages are totally unselective and have to look at every item. All went well till we reached the nineteenth-century English room, where the King was much disturbed by the Turners. "I tell you what" he said "Turner was *mad*", giving the last word the full force of his naval officer voice. "My grandmother always said so." We then came to the real purpose of his visit. He stopped his routine progress, faced me and said "Why won't you come and work for me?" I replied "Because I wouldn't have time to do the job properly." He snorted with benevolent rage. "What is there to do?" "Well, sir, the pictures need looking after." "There's nothing wrong with them." "And people write letters asking for information about them." "Don't answer 'em." And then, with great emphasis "I want you to take the job." As he was accustomed to addressing reluctant Prime Ministers (if such exist), Viceroys and Governors-General, the force of his command could not be resisted.

The result of my appointment was exactly as I had predicted. My colleagues, even the friendliest of them, thought that I was a place-hunter; and I soon found that I was ill qualified for the kind of work expected of me. The English are not very fond of art but they are very fond of pedigrees. Going round a country house collection one passed from one dreary seventeenth-century portrait to another, while one's hostess described how the sitters fitted in to the family history. "That's the one that married the heiress. Do you think this one could be the second son . . . ?" When it came to the Royal Collection this condition was intensified. I should have spent my time reading the history of the Hanoverians and working in the National Portrait Gallery. But I was too obstinately committed to aesthetic values to give up my time to the second-rate limners of royalty. There was also an administrative problem. Royal servants in general are not a sympathetic body, and those who were responsible for the pictures in Hampton Court, Buckingham Palace and Windsor were, of course, perfectly ignorant, and bitterly resented the fragile authority of an outside expert. In spite of these drawbacks my employers treated me very kindly. No one would maintain that King George V was overburdened with intellect, but he had a warmth of heart and frankness that were most appealing. He genuinely thought of himself as the father of his people, and as one drove through the streets with him he would comment on the passers-by, shoppers or workmen, with a kind of simple affection. Next to his people, King George V loved postage stamps. Late in his life he asked me to come and see him. "You're a young man" he said "and I'm an old one—haven't long to live. I want you to make me a promise. Never allow them to make all those fancy issues of stamps like some ridiculous place like San Marino. We invented the postage stamp—all it had on was the sovereign's head and Postage and its value. That's all we want." There was something very touching in the earnestness of his tone, and I gave my promise. When Mr Anthony Wedgwood Benn was Postmaster General he asked me to come and see him. I was the chairman of the Postage Stamp Committee and he announced his intention of making frequent issues of illustrative stamps: he suggested a series of old cars. I told him that I could not agree with this and offered to resign, an offer that was most gladly accepted. I then told him the story of King George V: he thought I must be a little mad.

We lived in a house in Portland Place. We had bought it on the rebound, after various frustrations and disappointments, and it was far too big for us. The whole *piano nobile,* with beautiful 'Adam' rooms, marble chimney pieces and painted ceilings, was completely unnecessary. We furnished them sparingly, at enormous cost, and occasionally gave parties there. These have faded from my memory, all except one in which the candles in the regency chandeliers, which were being 'boosted' by some fancy system of electrical illumination, all melted and the burning wax fell on the bare shoulders of the ladies. There were loud screams, and in a panic I turned off the lights, which did not stop the wax from falling, but led to a wild rush for the door. It was a scene worthy of Rowlandson, or, perhaps, Gustave Doré. Fortunately Jane was downstairs in the large, comfortable library, where most of our entertaining was done. In general our parties were more successful. We had a first-class cook, provided excellent wine, and Jane was a born hostess. By her warmth and sympathy and by a naïve confidence that all intelligent people would get on together, she managed to make a harmonious mixture out of the most diverse ingredients. Her charming appearance was now enhanced by exquisite clothes. She loved clothes, not out of vanity (few women with her looks have been less vain), but as an artist loves his medium; and she found a fellow-artist, Elsa Schiaparelli, to interpret her desires. Descended from a long line of *savants* and art-historians, Schiaparelli could look at Jane with the same understanding as her great-uncle, the famous Egyptologist, had bestowed on Nerfertite. Men are not good at remembering women's clothes, but some of Jane's dresses remain in my mind as works of the most brilliant and perfectly appropriate fantasy and, although we never sought the company of fashion editors or shiny journalists, she was often referred to as the best dressed woman in London.

Luncheons, dinners, weekends: how did we fit it all in? And in addition to work and entertaining we travelled. We went to Madrid, we went to Vienna, where I was horribly persecuted by art-dealers: I remember early one morning sleepily walking across the hall of our suite to go to the bathroom, and finding three of them with pictures on their knees already sitting there. They rose simultaneously, said "Bitte, Herr Direktor" and held out their dubious wares. We went to Cracow to see the Leonardo; we went to Berlin and Munich; we went to Russia on a small steamer that chugged slowly up the Baltic, and, in spite of the interminable meals and the absence of hot water, we loved it. We went to Venice every year; and, since we shared a love of opera, we went every year to Milan to hear Toscanini conduct at the Scala. We went frequently to Paris, partly to see Mr Gulbenkian, partly to visit the dealers. I am a passionate admirer of Ingres, and was determined that he should be worthily represented in the National Gallery. I got in touch with Ingres's niece (it sounds incredible, but Ingres's second wife had been much younger than he was) who owned a grisaille of the *Grande Odalisque*. It was seductive, but after a few minutes began to look like a studio replica, and still does every time I see it in New York. However, it was nice to hear the proprietress refer casually to 'mon oncle', and to see various Ingres relics, including the jug held by the young lady in *La Source*. The portrait of Madame Moitessier standing, dressed in black, was for sale with Paul Rosenberg, and I was on the point of showing it to my Trustees when I heard that the Madame Moitessier seated in white might also be available. Much circuitous diplomacy, at which I am extremely bad, led me to a lawyer's office of the humblest kind, smelling terribly of cabbage, and there from behind a hideous wardrobe emerged the great image. I had her sent immediately to London, and even under a dirty yellow varnish she enchanted my Trustees. They bought her immediately, with one proviso, that I took her out of her original frame of 1857 and put her into a frame consonant with their own fine taste in furniture. I agreed, but kept the frame (it exactly fitted a Turner!) and she is now back in it again.

We continued to buy pictures for ourselves, and in 1933 we had a piece of luck. Between two trains we called on Paul Guillaume, the most intelligent dealer in Paris, who showed us a pile of about a hundred drawings and watercolours that the son of Paul Cézanne had brought in for sale. We just had time to go through them, selected fifty, many of them familiar from reproduction in Vollard's book, gave him a cheque for £250 and dashed to the station with our portfolio. Through Lionello Venturi, an Italian art historian who lived in Paris as a refugee from Fascism, we obtained the entrée to Vollard's establishment. By this time he had become a recluse. He had always taken a low view of collectors and could now afford to ignore them. Nor would most of the rich and wilful people who were beginning to collect twentieth-century painting have found a visit to Vollard very gratifying to their self-esteem. One entered by the back stairs, passed through the kitchen, where the cook loudly abused one for admitting a draught, and sat in a small square room, which was always being re-painted—on one occasion by the artist F. X. Roussel, who I suppose had fallen on hard times. After a long interval Vollard would shuffle in through another door. I need not describe him, for few men have been the subject of so many remarkable portraits, by Cézanne, by Renoir (three times), by Picasso, by Rouault, and many others. Of these, the best likeness is the Rouault. What these pictures do not show is that he was very tall; also that his craggy old face could sometimes dissolve into a sardonic but rather engaging grin. He had some Negro blood —he was called *un Laurent de Medici nègre*—and the only time I saw him ruffled was when I happened to visit him on the day after the Hoare-Laval pact. (Incidentally, I was staying in the Embassy at the time, and met the Signatories coming down the staircase. I have never seen men more pleased with themselves.) Vollard was extremely consistent in all his dealings. His prices went by the size of the canvases, whether they were by Cézanne, Rouault or anyone else: £1000 for the large standard size, £750 for the small size, etc. At that date his famous closet was still full of pictures, and he would shuffle in and out returning with a large or small Cézanne, three of which, on various visits, we bought. Then came the obligatory purchase of a book. He was extremely proud of his rôle as publisher, and, as I am very fond of books and his books were admirable, I was glad to indulge him. The book had to be paid for in cash, so one had to return next day with an attaché case full of notes. Vollard would grasp them and count them carefully, saying as he did so "C'est le meilleur livre". If he was in the mood he would take one to the Gallery downstairs. It was hung with magnificent unknown pastels by Dégas, all beautifully framed, but it was never opened. One year he said it was too cold and he must change the heating; next year that the new system smelt; I forget the subsequent excuses. Just before the war I paid a large deposit on the edition of Rouault's *Misérérés et Guerres,* but Vollard was killed in a car crash during the war, and his affairs were taken over by a bookie with whom his brother was financially involved, so needless to say I never got even one of those marvellous etchings.

Finally, in the catalogue of our travels, I must mention the U.S.A. Strangely enough, considering what a part America has subsequently played in my life, we did not go there till 1936, when I was invited to give a series of lectures at Yale University. My memories of Yale are dim, but New York made a deep impression on me. The vitality, the contrasts, even a certain ferocity, fascinated me and has continued to do so ever since. There are grim, suicidal days and days of unbelievable exhilaration. We had the good sense, on our first visit, not to live in a small, suitable hotel, but to take an apartment on the twenty-eighth floor of the Waldorf Tower. In the evening, looking over the expanse of twinkling lights, we seemed to be 2000 leagues under the sea, and would not have been surprised if a huge fish had bumped its nose against our window.

Such impressions, like fireworks, are exciting but ephemeral. To an aesthete the lasting experience of the U.S.A. in the '30's was provided by the marvellous collections of French painting from Cézanne to Matisse. I have already described how such pictures were excluded from the Tate Gallery; they were equally excluded from the Luxembourg, and the Jeu de Paume was not opened till after the war. There were some fine pictures by Dégas in the Cammondo Collection, almost inaccessible in an upper room of the Louvre. Otherwise our appetite for the dominating art of the last fifty years was fed only by dealers. In America four or five private collectors had been for a long time picking out the finest examples of the *Ecole de Paris* (although not quite as omnivorously as the great Russian collectors, Schukin and Morousoff) and visits to their houses were intoxicating. I use the word accurately because (with one exception) these collectors combined their love of painting with a love of Scotch whiskey, and after two hours with Chester Dale, what with the excitement and the outpouring of my national beverage, I had almost to be carried into the waiting taxi. The Lewisohns provided less whiskey and fewer pictures; but they were shown to more advantage. I will not attempt to describe the glorious higgledy-piggledy of the Chester Dale Collection, except to say that it proved, what I knew already, that the love of art is in no way related to culture or refinement of manners. And this leads me to say a word about the legendary figure of Dr Barnes. Knowing his dislike of museum officials, I had said in a telegram asking to see his collection that I was the Director of the National Gallery. We were invited to visit him the following week. It happened that we were staying the night before with his arch-enemy, Mr Joseph Widener, a collector in the old style, so courteous as to be practically indistinguishable from his butler. We took the precaution of leaving Mr Widener's car a quarter of a mile from Dr Barnes's Gallery. After careful scrutiny by a man who could properly be described as a roughneck (one could have struck a match on his neck) we were admitted, and found our host alone in his fabulous Gallery sitting on a kitchen chair, listening to a tape recording of his own speech of welcome to Vollard. We did not disturb him but ran rapidly round the other rooms, expecting at any moment to be chucked out by the roughneck. After about twenty minutes he confronted us, with beetling brows. He was dressed in St Tropez style, and Jane was inspired to say "What a beautiful shirt you have on, Dr Barnes". "Yes," he said "it's a good one. And I wear red pants on Sundays." This was the foundation for a friendship which became, in the next five years, almost embarrassingly warm. I put it like that because Dr Barnes was not at all an attractive character. His stories of how he had extracted Cézannes and Renoirs from penniless widows made one's blood run cold. But his passionate love of painting made him supportable. Ever since my time in Bath, Cézanne had been the nineteenth-century painter who meant most to me, and to see ninety-two in an hour was a stunning experience. When the light began to fade Dr Barnes used to dispense whiskey with great solemnity. "I'm a doctor, you know. This is a scientific high-ball" and he measured each tot in a test tube and weighed the cubes of ice. As usual with Dr Barnes there was an element of spoof, and the result was as intoxicating as the vulgar high-balls of Mr Chester Dale.

Our stay in New York was a highly organised affair, with literally scores of letters of introduction, of which we delivered a quarter. Lord Duveen was uneasy lest we should fall into the wrong hands (meaning, presumably, Knoedler), and provided us with one of his own secretaries, who answered every phone call and gave Lord Duveen a copy of every letter I wrote or received. As I was not interested in the internal struggles of the art-market this was money wasted. We visited him in his establishment—what Sam Behrman called the Ministry of the Marine, and which was in fact a reduced replica of Gabriel's two blocks in the Place de la Concorde. In the hall was a baroque figure of the Virgin and Child. When I entered the great man's office I spoke of it with admiration. "Rubbish", he said "rubbish. My poor old father bought it. I'll sell it to you for . . ." And he named a ridiculously small sum. I interpreted this as meaning that he had bought the piece as a Bernini, but could not get it authenticated; and although I recognised that this was a sort of bribe, I accepted, because he could never have sold it without a name. It is probably by a Flemish sculptor resident in Venice named Giusto Corte, a pupil of Bernini, who decorated the high altar of the Salute on Bernini's recommendation.

Duveen's show rooms were a triumph of architectural ingenuity. They consisted of six small rooms draped in different coloured velvet. The pictures were brought out from velvet cupboards and placed on velvet easels. One went from one room to another by a circuitous route, and when one returned to the first room the position of the easel had been changed, so that one didn't know that one was back at square one till one had gone the circuit several times. Duveen had not yet made his great sale to Mr Mellon, so he had a large stock of famous pictures, many from the Benson Collection, and each time one entered a 'new' room a different picture was on the easel. We were accompanied on our peregrination by a heavily built man called Bert Boggis, who had worked in the packing department and who had all the qualifications of a chucker out. Since he had for long accompanied Lord Duveen as a personal guard he had come to know the names of painters, which is more than Lord Duveen ever did. "There you are", Duveen would say, as we entered the room "it's a Blado, Baldo—what is it, Bert?" "Baldovinetti". "That's right, a Bladonetti. What do you think of it?" "Well, I'm afraid it's been a bit restored." (It was in fact a completely repainted work of a painter called the pseudo-Pier Francesco Fiorentino.) "Restored? Ridiculous. Bert, has it been restored?" Silence. "Ah!

247

he knows. Next, next." A profile head appeared. "It's a Polly, Polly—what is it, Bert?" "Pollajuolo." Silence all round. If the picture exhibited was one of his favourites, Lord Duveen would blow kisses at it. Occasionally his enthusiasm would make him giddy with excitement. Then Bert would say "Sit down, Joe, keep calm," and the great man would passively comply.

Duveen gave us a grand dinner in his house. It was large and pretentious, and on the walls were copies of English eighteenth-century full length portraits of the kind that had made his fortune, men in red coats, ladies in large hats. All his richest clients were present, the men with white ties and creaking shirts, the ladies so weighed down with jewellery that a few of them (no one will believe this, but it is true) brought pieces of jewellery in their hands and laid them down on the dinner table. This could have happened in the Middle Ages. We dined on a blue and gold Sèvres service made for the Empress Catherine of Russia. Since my boyhood I have had a mania for ceramics, and I expressed my delight to Lady Duveen. She replied "Yes; it is nice. And we don't get it out every day, I can tell you. The last time we used it was for Mr Ramsay MacDonald." After dinner I said to my host (whom one had to address in his own language) "Marvellous that Sèvres service. Privilege to eat off it." "Sèvres service", said Lord Duveen, "Sèvres service? Nothing. Eat off it every day." That was the real Duveen. After dinner we adjourned to the drawing room, also hung with copies of English portraits. A huge soprano from the Metropolitan Opera, swathed in pistachio-coloured satin, accompanied by a small orchestra, sang pieces of Puccini at the top of her voice. Nobody paid the slightest attention. Duveen was regal. In London he might be a clown; in New York he was a king.

And what, in this welter of worldliness, grandeur and official business, had happened to the scholar-aesthete whom I have tried to rediscover in earlier chapters? Well, he was not as much deformed as one might have expected. My early upbringing stood me in good stead. The display of wealth neither impressed nor depressed me. I took it for granted and maintained my independence. And during the same years that I was making friends among the rich, I was making far more lasting and rewarding friendships with artists. The reader may recall that up to the time of my winning a scholarship at Oxford I never had any doubt that I would become a painter. 'Work' meant for me 'drawing', and although my drawings became worse and worse, I always hoped that this was a passing phase, and that if I could get to know other artists the stimulus of their company would show me a way out. After four years at Oxford, and two in Italy, all this was behind me, and I have never touched a brush or pencil since, but I still craved for the company of artists, whose point of view was nearer to my own than that of academics. Fortunately I was in a position to buy the work of those whom I admired, and thus to make their acquaintance. Of course artists like to sell their works, but I do not think I am deceiving myself in thinking that this was the sole reason why several of them became my closest friends. They accepted me as one of themselves, who had wisely accepted an inability to paint like some physical accident, but who in other respects saw things as they did. This has not only enriched my life, but has had a determining influence on my work. If my blend of history and criticism has any value it is due to the fact that I have never lost sight of the actual works of art or forgotten the character of the men who created them; and I have learnt from personal experience how to relate one to the other—pictures, drawings, sculpture have never become pawns in a metaphysical game of chess, but the products of individuals with exceptional skills and powers of imagination.

The first of our artist friends were Duncan Grant and Vanessa Bell, whom we had known when still living in Richmond. Roger Fry and Clive Bell had long maintained that Duncan was the only living

English painter who could hold a candle to the French, and there is no doubt that as a young man he had shown, in addition to overwhelming charm, a remarkable talent for painting. But where precisely that talent lay was always in dispute. There were those who thought it lay in poetic fancy and decoration. There were those who felt he should try harder (as the schoolmasters say) and realise solid pieces of naturalistic painting. Roger, although he recognised the lyrical quality of Duncan's art, which seemed to come spontaneously from his happy character, could not help urging him to 'realise' in the same laborious manner that he, Roger, did himself; and when we first frequented his studio it contained groups of rustic pottery, gathering dust, and vases of mimosa which had long since lost all the colour of life. On these unappetising themes both Duncan and Vanessa concentrated their talents, and I must confess that our hearts sank at the sight of their brown and purple canvasses. Fortunately we discovered, and bought, some brilliant pastels by Duncan, where the medium had saved him from the virtuous application of Bloomsbury mud. We commissioned him to paint Jane's portrait. It took a long time and, as she came to know him better, she found under his bed some beautiful drawings and oil sketches. In an attempt to revive his interest in decorative art we asked him and Vanessa to paint us a dinner service. As usual with commissions it turned out differently to what we had expected. Instead of a gay cascade of decoration like the best Savona, Duncan and Vanessa conscientiously produced forty-eight plates each of which contained the portrait of a famous woman (Bloomsbury asserting its status as a matriarchy). These are in effect forty-eight unique paintings by Duncan and Vanessa, for which they made innumerable studies, and which will give posterity a good idea of their style in the '30s.

A more ambitious attempt to use Duncan's gifts as a decorator ended in a defeat. I had secured for him the commission to do three large decorative pictures in the main lounge of the *Queen Mary,* then under construction. How I managed to sell the idea I cannot remember, but of course I sold it to the architect in charge of the interior fittings, and not to the directors of the line. Duncan executed three huge panels for a very small sum, and they were duly installed. But sooner or later they were bound to be noticed by the Chairman of the Cunard Line, Sir Percy Bate. He was affronted; and his wife, who was very artistic, was even more shocked. "We must have little deer", she said. "You know, gazelles." And, although I put a lot of pressure on other directors of the line, Duncan's panels were removed, and disappeared. Almost forty years later they were bought by my son, and now hang in Saltwood Castle; so it wasn't a complete disaster, after all.

Duncan and Vanessa were the least worldly people one could imagine, and it is a tribute to their fairmindedness that they should not have rejected us as beyond redemption. Vanessa in particular was the embodiment of Cambridge integrity. She was not at all dogmatic, but she never relaxed her standards, and in a quiet, hesitant voice would expose false values and mixed motives. I was devoted to her, and when asked to do something questionable, I would think to myself "What would Vanessa say?" Although she dressed in the Bloomsbury uniform, long purple skirt and black shawl, she enjoyed looking at Jane's clothes, and on one memorable occasion—the evening party at the National Gallery to which I have already referred—she allowed Jane to dress her and make her up. She had fine features, and when they were enhanced by make-up, which she had never worn before, she looked dazzling. People at the party wondered who this new beauty could be.

During my first two years at the Gallery we continued to see a good deal of Roger Fry, and dinners in his dingy room, where food was brought out from under his bed, were amongst the happiest experiences of our lives. One might have supposed that Roger, who had been offered the directorship of the

National Gallery in 1906, and declined only because he had already accepted a job in the Metropolitan, would have been a help to me in my new position. But this turned out not to be the case, and I formed the strong opinion that Roger would have been a bad director of a great gallery. The only picture he persuaded me to buy, a small Corot portrait of a woman called *La Rose,* has spent thirty years in the 'reference' section and is never likely to rise to the surface. It is a private picture. Roger hated pictures that spoke in a loud voice, and he hated what he called 'finish', which he associated with slave labour. It was part of his Quaker background. But pictures in galleries cannot afford to be self-effacing. There will always be small pictures that give particular pleasure, but they must have a certain air of authority. The very word 'authority' was repulsive to Roger; he would probably have turned in horror from Ingres's *Madame Moitessier.* I must add in fairness that he was totally inconsistent—in other words that his natural responsiveness to art often outweighed his love of theory. Then he would suddenly apply all his marvellous powers of persuasion in the opposite direction, leaving his disciples breathless and bewildered.

One evening in September, 1934, we were dining with Bogey Harris, and waiting for Roger to arrive, when the telephone rang and Helen Anrep (who lived with him*) told us that he had slipped on the linoleum and seemed to have broken his leg. I ran round immediately and found him crumpled on the floor, saying "This is a nasty business." He had broken his hip. I rang for a doctor who (I think unwisely) had him moved to a hospital immediately. He died two days later. Jane and I were deeply miserable. For the first time in my life I realised acutely that good things can't last forever.

After having been turned down as Slade Professor by shameful academic intrigues, twice in Oxford

* Roger's wife had shown signs of madness in 1898 and was in a mental home from 1910 onwards. She outlived him.

(1904 and 1927) and once in Cambridge, Roger had at last been made Slade Professor in Cambridge in 1933. He was 66, but with dauntless optimism he had decided to give a series of lectures in which he could examine, more or less chronologically, the visual art of the whole world in the light of his aesthetic theories. They were written with his usual mixture of diffidence and dogmatism, and produced some strange results: Negro art came out at the top, Greek art at the bottom. The first two lectures had been carefully considered; the rest were written hastily, often on scraps of paper while waiting for trains. Nevertheless it was thought desirable after his death to print them, and I was asked to edit them with an introduction.* I filled in gaps and wrote an introductory note with love and admiration, but it did not please the members of his family, who have not spoken to me since.

This episode had one good result. In trying to identify the illustrations that Roger refers to I was helped by a young painter called Graham Bell. He was large, gentle and extremely intelligent. We became friends, and he came to live in an upper room in Portland Place. He was one of a group of young men whose patient, unemphatic realism had made them Roger's favourites. This group he, so to say, bequeathed to me. I had, in fact, already bought a picture by one of their number named Victor Pasmore; and I was shortly afterwards to meet the artist himself. I was in the English room in the National Gallery, trying a new frame on Turner's *Interior at Petworth*. It had always seemed to me crushed by its heavy gold moulding, and I had been conned into having a silvery frame specially made for it, which would 'show up' the red and yellow colours of the painting. It looked horrible. As I was contemplating my mistake a young man with bright black eyes came up to me and said "Hey, what's going on here?" I said that I was trying a new frame on the Turner.

* *Last Lectures* by Roger Fry, 1938.

"Well", said the young man "I don't know who you are, but whoever you are you've no taste." I agreed, and the frame was hastily removed. The young man was Victor Pasmore. I told him of my admiration for his work, and we formed a friendship which has lasted undiminished till this day. I have owned at least twenty of his pictures, but, as I wanted his work to be known, have given a number to public galleries, where the sight of them gives me a pang. He was not only the most gifted painter of the group, but, in my opinion, one of the two or three most talented English painters of this century.

Next to Duncan and Vanessa our closest friends were E. McKnight Kauffer and the lady who was, in effect, his second wife, Marion Dorn. Ted had been born in Montana and brought up in Indiana. At an early age he had run away with a theatrical touring company, and slept, traditionally, in a coil of rope behind the stage. He was both in character and appearance one of the most aristocratic men I have ever known. His appearance has been well described by Colin Anderson as 'like a slim russet eagle'. Paradoxically he applied his fastidiousness to the popular art of the poster; it suited him perfectly, because he was too perceptive to believe in himself as a painter and had the aristocratic love of economy which made the simplification of the poster agreeable to him. Moreover he was extraordinarily sensitive to what was coming to life in the art of his time, and saw how new pictorial ideas could be simplified to catch a rapid glance. Ted's workroom was a complete contrast to a Bloomsbury studio; everything scrupulously neat and tidy, every pencil sharpened to the finest point, drawing boards hinged on aluminium contraptions with nicely balanced springs, materials filed in shining drawers, and Ted himself exquisitely dressed. Marion Dorn, an admirable textile designer, was a large, handsome, warm-hearted Californian lady, who perfectly complemented the slight austerity of her companion. We spent a lot of time in their company, going every year to the circus at Olympia, where several of the clowns were old friends of Ted's from his Indiana days, and where Ted, who could use a gun like the hero of a Western, caused dismay in the shooting booths. I remember dining with them alone with Mr Eliot after the first night of his *Family Reunion.* I was so bumptious as to ask him if he had not been reading Kipling (then a forbidden name in highbrow society). Mr Eliot gave me a quick, amused glance, and said "How did you know?" I had, of course, been thinking of some late Kipling stories, like *In the Same Boat,* which had very much the same atmosphere as *Family Reunion.* Far from resenting my impudence, it was the formation of a friendship between us; and a few years later he published his selection of Kipling's verse. On another occasion a young woman of ravishing grace and beauty played on Marion's clavichord. As I have said earlier in this chapter, the ladies I met in Philip Sassoon's world gave me no more than a disdainful glance, and I had come to suppose that I had no charm for the opposite sex. But the young clavichord player gave me a glance of such sweetness that I changed my mind. A few months later I met her again staying with a friend in the country, and there could be no doubt about her feelings, or mine. The modern reader will assume that we became lovers, but this is incorrect. Neither of us is by nature monogamous and there was an abundance of love between us, but some instinct told us that, in order to preserve it, we should go no further; and we have preserved it till the present day.

When the invasion of England looked imminent all American residents were exhorted to return to their own country. With terrible heartburning Ted and Marion left. Marion set up as a designer in New York and had as much success as cruel competition would permit. Ted's spirit was entirely broken. He felt, quite illogically, that he had betrayed his friends and his adopted country. When I saw him in New York a few years later he was like a beautiful, empty shell, and nothing I could say would bring him to life again.

The 1930's was the golden age of the poster. This was in no way due to popular demand: on the contrary, as soon as 'artistic' posters were made the subject of market research it was proved that they were a positive deterrent. The excellent posters of the '30s were due to the patronage of two enlightened individuals, Frank Pick at London Passenger Transport and Jack Beddington at Shell Mex. They were the most opposite characters it is possible to imagine, Frank Pick a square-faced puritan, earnest, industrious, dogmatic, teetotal; Jack Beddington, known to his friends as 'Beddy-old-cock', looking like a Levantine pirate who had tactfully removed his ear-rings, accepting with enthusiasm a second or third cocktail. Lovers of art are not classifiable. In 1935 I opened in the Burlington Galleries an exhibition of Shell Mex posters, described by Tom Driberg as 'fifty yards behind the Royal Academy and fifty years ahead of it'. I am afraid these poster artists were not as 'advanced' as they seemed. Apart from Ted Kauffer, most of them were mediocre, their muted English academism thinly disguised by a few 'post-impressionist' simplifications. But one work stood out—a poster of the Great Globe at Swanage. It was by an artist whose name was unknown in Bloomsbury circles, although his etchings had already been bought for the British Museum by Campbell Dodgson: Graham Sutherland. I asked Beddy-old-cock to introduce us. In contrast to the gauche and somewhat bucolic products of the average English art school, he turned out to be a self-possessed, highly intelligent man of the world, with bright eyes which suggested, but in no way revealed, exceptional depths. A few days later he came to see us (accompanied by his wife, who was as pretty as a Geisha, although very different in other respects), carrying a few of his recent watercolours and one oil. Although they still owed something to the memory of Samuel Palmer, they were much more contemporary and original than the Great Globe or the early etchings. I bought them all immediately, with great excitement. Ever since Oxford I had been hoping to find an English painter of my own generation whose work I could admire without reserve. I respected the honourable intentions of Roger's young disciples and I liked them personally. But their work did not excite me, and I felt fairly certain that spatial construction and careful realisation were not the natural inheritance of English painting. Whereas the visionary intensity with which Graham Sutherland looked at small corners of the Welsh coast, and the colouristic freedom with which his skillful hand conveyed these visions to canvas, seemed to place him in the same tradition of lyrical art as Blake, Turner and Samuel Palmer. I have heard it said that I 'discovered' Graham Sutherland (often, alas, by young artists who wish me to 'discover' them). This is quite untrue. His gifts were already recognised by his friends and would soon have made him famous without my intervention. I had no influence on Graham, but he had considerable influence on me, by showing me a way out of the virtuous fog of Bloomsbury art. I cannot believe that Roger would have looked at Graham's painting with anything but distaste. He hated romanticism, was horrified by Turner and never mentions Palmer in his book on English art. The gifted group of English painters of the thirties, that included not only Graham Sutherland but Francis Bacon and John Piper, would surely have distressed him.

The Sutherlands did not recoil from smart society, and came frequently to our dinner parties, where they were much admired. I am not sure how much this is desirable for an artist, except, of course, for a professional portrait painter. Bébé Berard was one of the few painters I have known to have survived (and only just survived) the intoxicating speed of society chatter. The artist must go at his own speed. His whole life is a painful effort to turn himself inside out, and if he gives too much away at the shallow level of social intercourse he may lose the will to attempt a deeper excavation. Graham Sutherland was always able to retreat into the depths behind his eyes where he found those curious equivalents of *objets trouvés*—dead trees, thorn bushes, and imaginary, mutilated plants—that are the true inhabitants of his imagination, and for which a series of famous faces has not always been an adequate substitute.

John and Myfanwy Piper lived, and still live, in a plain, square farmhouse called Fawley Bottom. When I first knew them John's abstract pictures were dissolving into landscapes and architecture, and he had already discovered the charm, both decorative and symbolic, of some neglected aspects of English building—seaside terraces, Methodist chapels. It was a discovery similar to that of his friend, John Betjeman, when he found poetic material in the loves and beliefs of almost forgotten sections of society, the bouncing daughters of Metroland and the lonely celibates of north Oxford. To stay with the Pipers at Fawley Bottom, to poke the ashes of the dying open fire, while the children rammed one in the stomach, to sleep in a room full of dark brown books on Gothic churches, with a heavy heraldic banner on the bed; to enjoy Myfanwy's cooking, a bottle of wine and the conversation of two of the most completely humanised people I have ever known, was the perfect antidote to life in London, even though Jane did find a mouse drowned in the glass of icy water beside her bed.

Finally I must try to say a word about the man who, with Maurice Bowra, has been our dearest friend, Henry Moore. From the first minute I saw his work in an exhibition at the Warren Galleries in 1928 I had recognised that something extraordinary and completely unexpected had happened in English art. I was not alone in this—Eric Maclagen, Jacob Epstein, Eric Gill all bought work in this exhibition. I have two of the pieces still, and, although vitalised pebbles give no indication of the magnificent construction to come, they still look like works of genius. We must have met Henry soon after we went to live at Lympne. At that time he lived in Kent, first in a cottage almost touching the little church of Barfreston, which contains some of the finest Romanesque carving in England, later at Kingston, both within forty minutes' drive from Lympne. He was bursting with creative energy. Every time we went to Kingston there was a new crop of sculptural ideas, carvings, lead figures, which we saw cast with great excitement, after the lead had been melted in Mrs Moore's saucepan over a primus stove; finally a large wooden reclining figure which I tried to get the Museum of Modern Art to buy for £300: I can't think why I didn't buy it myself, except that I had nowhere to put it, and at the time no museum in England would have exhibited it. Henry was always himself, gay, confident, strong in the head and with a disposition to look on the best side of everything and everybody. The deep, disturbing well from which emerged his finest drawings and sculpture was never referred to, and no one meeting him could have guessed at its existence. Henry never reads the profound things said about him; it is part of an instinct for self-preservation that has saved him from the fate of Rodin. This stalwart friend, who happens also to be a great genius, has been a support and joy to us both for almost forty years.

I see that I have said nothing about our children. To see one's children one needs a garden and a large, accessible nursery, both of which we had in Oxford. At Portland Place they were hidden away at the top of the house and brought down to be exhibited as *objets d'art* to our friends. When they entered the room, the twins dressed identically in white fur coats and bonnets, the ladies of the party would emit sounds half way between a whoop and a moan, and dash over to embrace these exquisite little creatures, pushing aside the wretched Alan, whose stunning good looks had not yet become apparent. By all the rules in the text books, this should have poisoned his relations with his brother and sister, but in fact there can seldom have been a more united family. In those days small children did not go to school, and were looked after at home by governesses, usually (not always) foreign bodies introduced into the texture of family life, and some of the aversion one felt for the governess may have kept one away from the children. Things went better on the lawns of our pretty house at Lympne. Philip Sassoon used to jump the wall, and invite the children to various improbable treats, including flights in his private 'plane, when they swooped down to frighten Jane and me when we were playing golf at Littlestone. In 1935 'planes were in fact rather alarming forms of transport, especially with Philip (then Under-Secretary of State for Air), who would instruct his pilot to land in any field that was near a famous garden which he wanted to visit. By 1938 Alan had passed the *rebarbatif* stage, and become the warmhearted, intelligent companion he has been ever since. The twins looked enchanting, and were beginning to develop their strongly contrasting personalities. All three have been, and continue to be, the joy of my life, and of the many pieces of good fortune that have been poured out on me I count this as the greatest.

I had another escape from society and public business: writing. I have never ceased to think of myself primarily as a writer, and even during the most distracted period of my life have had a book on hand, several articles overdue, and two or three promised lectures looming up before me, still unwritten. They have always been delivered on time. Unlike Roger, I am no improvisor. I have to write every word in longhand, frequently altering the structure of a sentence and covering my manuscript with balloons. I had learnt from Logan not to disdain an occasional burst of 'fine writing', and tried to master the technique of introducing it into my text in such a way that the unwary reader did not realise when the temperature had changed. I will confess that the few passages—there are some in *The Nude, Piero della Francesca* and even in *Rembrandt and the Italian Renaissance*—in which I feel I have been lifted off my feet, are the things which (except for my family) have given me the most pleasure in my life.

The Catalogue of Leonardo's drawings at Windsor, which was well received, gave me the illusion that I was a scholar, and so, on finishing it, my first thought was to produce another work of scholarship, a study of that great *uomo universale* who preceded Leonardo, Leon Battista Alberti. It is a daunting subject, partly because Alberti, in spite of his multifarious talents and splendid profile, turns out, when one gets to know him (and one gets to know him very well), to be a slightly unsympathetic character. No one has written a satisfactory book on him yet. I slaved away at Alberti for over two years, spent months on his obscure, but fascinating, autobiography, his boring dialogues on society and morals, compared his book on architecture with Vitruvius, and of course studied and measured all his buildings. Nothing came of all this except several volumes of notes and a lecture on his book on the theory of painting, which is amateurish by modern standards, although it is, I believe, the first time that his influence on Leonardo's *Treatise on Painting* is firmly established. But the years spent on Alberti were not entirely lost, as they enabled me to enter more fully into the period of art in which I have always felt most at home, the first fifty years of the *quattrocento* in Florence.

At the same time I was attempting something which turned out to be more my *métier* than scholarship, a short, readable book on Leonardo. This occupied most of my spare time at the National Gallery and was not finished till 1938, which proves, alas, how little time I could give to writing: only the odd week-end, and our annual spring visit to Edith Wharton at her dotty, comfortable, converted convent in Hyères. In the end the book was too short but, as a paperback, it slipped easily into a pocket or handbag, and until *Civilisation* it remained the most widely read of all my books.

While at the National Gallery I wrote a few 'learned' articles and lectures. Looking through them I am

agreeably surprised to see how bad they are. The
intervening years have not been entirely lost. The
only pieces that give an indication of how things
might go are the introduction and notes to a book
called *One Hundred Details from the National Gallery*. I believe it was my friend Yukio Yashiro who,
for the first time, in his book on Botticelli, used
photographic details to increase an understanding of
pictures. It seems incredible that no one had thought
of this before, but the best critics of the time were
dwelling on composition, spatial construction and
other large virtues, and thought that to look at details in a Ruskinian manner might lead them into that
most damnable error, a literary approach. At the Gallery I had always taken pride in our publications
department, and had encouraged our excellent photographers (then, I believe, the best in the world) to
take photographs of details, ostensibly for scientific
purposes, but actually because they gave me pleasure.
I arranged these details in contrasting or complemen-
tary pairs; some of the notes were descriptive, some
analytical or historical. I wrote in an informal and
quasi-conversational style, which I now see has the
kind of immediacy that I was later to attempt on
television. The book is out of print and forgotten,
but, re-reading it, I recognise for the first time the
sound of my own voice.

In the end the antidote that saved me from the
poison of success in the world was the same that had
saved me from the effects of failure at school: an unabated and insatiable joy in the contemplation of
works of art. If trouble arose in the offices of the
National Gallery, I had only to go upstairs. If the
pressure of society became intolerable I had only to
go to the Prado, the Louvre or the Mauritshuis, or
return to Florence to sit in S Lorenzo or potter about
Santa Croce or stand spellbound in front of the
Masaccios in the Carmine. Then I knew that I was
back on course. A visit to a new gallery excited me
so much that it disturbed my normally tolerant di-
gestion, so that I have become an authority on the

lavatory accommodations of various galleries: Tretya-
kov bottom, National Gallery of Washington top. We
visited Chartres every year, Rome every year, and
the Acropolis three years running. It was an extension
of the discipline that I had willingly adopted at Oxford. In all these expeditions Jane was the ideal companion, eager, perceptive, thirsty (more thirsty than
I was) for information. These were the times when
we were happiest together.

VII

Rain on the Lawn

I HAD REALIZED from the first that the Great Clark
Boom was bound to end badly. The envy it aroused
could not have been contained even by the most
circumspect behaviour, and I am afraid that my behaviour was sometimes rather off hand. With my
natural optimism I had not counted on the forces
that were piling up against me. To begin with there
was the hostility of my staff—I do not mean the
warder staff, who were helpful and even fatherly,
nor the photographic staff, who were adorable, but
what I suppose must be called the academic staff.
Two of them were heirs of the old conflict between
staff and Trustees, and they quite correctly came to
look at me as the ally of the Trustees. Before Trustees' meetings we lunched on gold plate at Philip
Sassoon's house in Park Lane, and arrived at the meetings looking offensively prosperous and well fed. I
would have been wise not to have attended these
luncheons. I would also have been wise to have dele-
gated more of the work of the Gallery. But I couldn't
delegate purchasing, and I love hanging pictures so
much that it would have been agony for me to have
handed over the re-hanging of galleries to someone
else who, I believed, would have been less good at
it than I am. My Keeper, who succeeded the unfortunate Mr Glasgow, was a mediocrity, but a good
union man, who was supposed to be an expert on

Spanish painting. It was traditionally the Keeper's duty to be concerned with the housekeeping of the Gallery and, as I have never learnt to read a balance sheet, I left this side of the work to him. One evening, on the way home, I saw on a poster the surprising announcement *National Gallery, Grave Scandal.* I had no idea what this could mean, but discovered that the accountant had been pinching the till, and fudging the accounts, which the Keeper had failed to check. Next morning he triumphantly informed me that I was technically accounting officer (a fact that had not been disclosed to me before), and was therefore responsible. I went to see the accountant, who was seated at his desk with a glassy stare. As I entered he pulled open his drawer and took out a large, archaic pistol. After a few minutes' persuasion he put it down, so I never discovered whether it was intended for him or for me. I called for our invaluable head attendant, who had several times carried out importunate visitors, and asked him to take the accountant to a doctor. The Keeper was nowhere to be seen.

The staff ended by locking me out of the Library and refusing to attend conferences. This was inconvenient, and had to be reported to the Chairman, then David Balniel, and to the Treasury. The leader of the rebellion was a man whom I admired as a scholar and respected as an individual. Davis questioned him sympathetically, and asked for concrete examples of things I had done wrong. Situations of this kind arise from a long series of incidents so trivial and so evanescent that they are impossible to describe. The only concrete fact that my colleague could think of was that he objected to my neckties. It is true that I am fond of neckties, and when depressed will buy one to cheer myself up, just as ladies used to buy hats, a source of comfort of which they have been temporarily deprived. Neckties, albeit to a less degree than hats, are symbolic and almost the last things that link us to the display rituals of birds (since I have never worn one, I see that I have forgotten American shirts). So my frustrated colleague's answer was quite justifiable by Warburgian standards. The Treasury took a less philosophical view of the matter, and intervened to restore order, for which I was extremely grateful.

One thing to which even my colleagues had been unable to object was my purchases. But when things were at their worst I made a mistake. I had been shown in Vienna, in the apartment of an entertaining but equivocal expert on Venetian sculpture named Planiscig, four small pictures illustrating episodes in a pastoral poem. They had obviously been decorations on a piece of furniture, perhaps the doors of a cupboard, and were executed with becoming simplicity; but they exhaled the bewitching poetry of Venetian painting in the first decade of the sixteenth century, that poetry which we associate with the name of Giorgione. I fell in love with them, began to dream about them, and, when they appeared in London for sale, could not resist showing them to the Trustees. I was careful to explain that they were not necessarily, or even probably, the work of Giorgione, but added that they were about as near as we were likely to come to the sound of Giorgione's music. Rather to my embarrassment, my Trustees were as much bewitched by them as I was, and determined to buy them. They were not expensive by modern standards, but cost more than the Gallery could afford (it was during a period when our grant was cut), and Sir Robert Witt, the forceful chairman of the National Art-Collections Fund, said that the Fund would present them. The Board accepted his offer. He then said that there was a condition: that the pictures should be labelled 'Giorgione', not 'school of' or 'manner of', but 'Giorgione'. In a moment of unforgivable weakness I agreed.

I had plenty of time to repent of my mistake. A massive attack was mounted and organised by my old friend Tancred Borenius. It was directed not so much against the charming little pictures, as against me, and was intended to force my resignation. Tancred would give a summary of my shortcomings, and end by saying "Think of all that and scales will fall from your eyes." He was indefatigable, persuading the most unlikely people to write letters of indignation to the *Daily Telegraph*. In addition I received dozens of letters of abuse from people who had hitherto shown themselves friendly or obsequious. Politicians must be hardened to episodes of this kind, although I am told that even they grow a trifle uneasy after a time; but for a fortunate young swimmer on the tide of success it was an unnerving experience. I learnt to sympathise with those who, like Rousseau, have suffered from persecution mania. There was nothing I could reply, and the situation was made even worse by the discovery that the panels were almost certainly early works by a second-rate painter named Previtali, by whom we had five pictures in the Gallery already. *Il ne manquait que cela.*

The controversy went on for months, and became the sole topic of conversation in the kind of society that forms the periphery of the arts. In so far as it was designed to force my resignation it was a failure. In the U.S.A. I should have been sacked, but the great American sport of sacking museum directors had not then been developed. My Trustees affirmed that they were delighted with the purchase. The Prime Minister, Mr Neville Chamberlain, came to look at the pictures, and loved them almost as much as I did. He took my article on them down to Chequers, read it carefully and told me not to worry. The little pictures themselves have not been exhibited since 1939, but can be found, close to the floor, in the so-called reference section of the Gallery and the few people who see them may wonder why I fell so deeply in love with them.

During the same unhappy period (the winter of 1937–1938) I was involved in troubles of an opposite kind. Lord Duveen, whose term of office as Trustee had expired in 1936, was once more eligible for re-appointment and his friends on the Board supported him persuasively. There were a number of good reasons why he should not be re-appointed. He saw all the pictures sent in to the Gallery for us to consider. If they came from rival dealers he was naturally hostile to them, and in consequence dealers were unwilling to submit them, and several very famous pictures were lost to us. If they came from private collectors his professional interests were aroused. A man of greater detachment and integrity would have seen the difficulties of the position, but Duveen was controlled solely by instinct and appetite, and was confident that his charm and generosity would get him out of any troubles.

The majority of the Board was against his reappointment, including my then Chairman, Samuel Courtauld. This quiet, modest man had formed a superb collection of French nineteenth-century painting, and had lent us three of his pictures, Cézanne's *Mont S. Victoire*, Renoir's *La Loge* and Manet's *Bar aux Folies Bergères,* as a sort of earnest that the greater part would follow on his death.* Sam Courtauld was a man of principle, if ever there was one, but he was not an intriguer, and could not counter the political cunning of Duveen's supporters. I was aware of this, and, since I felt strongly that Duveen's re-appointment would be a disaster (I am now inclined to think that this was a piece of priggish nonsense) I moved up my heavy piece, Mr Gulbenkian. He was very much opposed to Duveen: no doubt he had seen his operations from close quarters and was better able to judge them than most people. He told me that he would not make his bequest to the National Gallery if Duveen were a Trustee. This would have involved a loss to the Gallery far greater

* These pictures are now in the Courtauld Galleries, and, although they are well displayed, I cannot help thinking that if they had been in the National Gallery they would have achieved more fully Mr Courtauld's express wish that the art of the period should be widely appreciated. He changed his mind under pressure from Lord Lee, who wanted his own collection to be kept together in a private gallery and rightly believed that it would not be accepted unless it could be made part of a package deal with the Courtauld pictures.

than any benefaction that Duveen could make, and I therefore felt bound to put the matter to the Prime Minister, Mr Neville Chamberlain. The interview took place alone in the Cabinet Room. We sat on either side of the long table, covered in green baize. Mr Chamberlain said in his snappiest voice "Make your point." I made it. At the end of about six minutes he said "You've convinced me. The trouble is that I wrote to Duveen yesterday re-appointing him. I'll ring up New York immediately." Much has been written in denigration of Mr Chamberlain, but this episode shows the qualities that close observers, like Sir Alexander Cadogan, admired in him.

The effect of my action on those Trustees who were Duveen's friends may be imagined. Philip Sassoon nearly broke the telephone in his rage, and did not speak to me again for three months. Evan Charteris maintained a dignified silence, saying only "You do not know what harm you have done." Needless to say I never saw Lord Duveen again. I had not known at the time that he was already suffering from cancer. The rebuff added to his miseries, and not long afterwards he died. I suppose the moral is 'Never act on principle' or, in Mr Andrew Mellon's immortal phrase, "No good deed goes unpunished."

Although it might seem that by the spring of 1938 the picnic was over, an old diary of Jane's (the only one that either of us ever kept consistently) shows me that the Clark Boom continued, and actually spread to Paris. We spent about six weeks preparing the British Exhibition in the Louvre, and the diary describes us in the top drawer of Parisian society moving from one compartment to another. All this has faded from my mind, except for the proud, wilful, generous character of the Comtesse de Béhague, who formed a close friendship with Jane. My most vivid memory is of the team of workmen who helped me hang the exhibition. I learnt more about the French from them than from any book. One would have expected them to be hostile to a young Englishman put in charge of them, but on the contrary they treated me as an equal and a friend, actually referring to me as *un copain*. I shook hands with all eight of them six times a day—on entering in the morning, at the coffee break, on return from the coffee break, on going to lunch ("*à la soupe, mes enfants*"), on return from lunch, and on parting in the evening. They were all communists of the good old French school, that is to say they simply wanted to take away money from the rich and have it themselves. They used to discuss how they would split up the director's apartment. (I thought of them in 1968 when, during *les événements,* the idealistic students so unwisely invited the Renault workers to join them in the Odéon theatre.) They worked very quickly and were inconceivably reckless. Full length portraits in heavy frames with glass, which in the National Gallery we used to move with ceremony fastened to enormous turrets on wheels, were dumped on to a little scooter (known as *le chariot*), which looked like the wheel on which the goddess Fortuna is sometimes depicted in Italian painting, and shot about the galleries at a great speed by two men. I am by nature careless and irresponsible, and I found the risks taken with these National Treasures rather exhilarating. Thank God none of my colleagues were present. The exhibition was hung a day ahead of schedule, and the press were cheated out of the stories of last-minute scrambles, all-night working, etc. by which they had hoped to give some interest to an otherwise boring subject. To console them I made my *équipe* take down some of the heaviest pictures and pretend to be re-hanging them with frenzied haste, in front of a battery of photographers. They thoroughly enjoyed the joke. Thirty-five years later I still get winks and handshakes from very old attendants in the Louvre.

While we were enjoying our swimgloat in Paris, the news came through that Anthony Eden had resigned. We had, so to say, grown up together in Philip Sassoon's entourage, and I had heard him talk about his predicament. I was not at all surprised by his resignation, and wished only that it had come earlier. But in France it made a painful impression. The French had not realised that a complete conflict of views existed in England as to how the aggressive authoritarian countries should be treated. They had only one opinion about Hitler; *il est le maître*.

So much has been written about the years before the war that it may seem presumptuous of me to add my own trivial observations. I do so remembering the plea made equally by Stendhal, Flaubert and Henry James: "More detail, more detail". Since we had no political affiliations the leading figures on both sides of the conflict talked to us unguardedly, both of them assuming that we must be on their side.

I was in fact unequivocally on the side of Mr Churchill. I had lived in a German family, and listened to endless diatribes against the Jews. Before going to Germany I had read Heine's famous description of the ferocious, warlike spirit of the German people, which would one day turn itself on our Western civilisation and annihilate it. This seemed to me nonsense then, but my lonely life in Dresden had given me time to listen and observe, and I saw that the industry and docility of this marvellous people was already directed to a destructive end. Why didn't everyone recognise it? The intellectuals were obsessed by the Spanish civil war, and continued to be so even after many of their young men had returned disillusioned, and had seen their comrades shot in the back by members of the Republican Army. The establishment was obsessed by the Prince of Wales and Mrs Simpson and the moves leading up to the abdication. It was a wonderful subject of conversation and a chance for Mr Baldwin to use his art of sincere double-talk. The rich—and most members of the government were rich—closed their eyes to Hitler because they, mistakenly, supposed that the Nazis were less likely to take away their money than the Bolshies.

We were staying at Trent with several pro-Nazi cabinet ministers among the guests, when the news of the Roehm murders appeared in the evening papers. It was a complete surprise to them. "What do

271

you think of your playmates now?" said Mr Churchill. But this, and the subsequent horrors, seemed to make no impression at all on these rich, respectable men.*

The queen of this circle was a hostess whom I hesitated to describe in the preceding chapter (enough of hostesses!), Mrs Ronnie Greville, known to her old friends as Maggie. She was immensely rich and the only hostess who had any political power, not simply on account of her wealth, but because she was a shrewd and forceful personality. Her father had been the head of McEwen's Breweries; her mother had been his cook; as she often said "That's why I always understand the people so well." The directors of McEwen's had to come down to her house, called Polesden Lacey, for their board meetings, and one took place when we were staying there. Mrs Breville was in bed, and I remember seeing the directors leaving her room after the meeting in a very chastened frame of mind, some actually trembling. It is rare, and a great source of strength, for anyone to be totally consistent. Mrs Greville was totally material. She allowed herself the slight fantasy of cultivating royalty. She told me one day that during the morning three kings had been sitting on her bed, but, in general, she thought solely in terms of material gain. I see from an old engagement book that we visited her once a week: I can't think why as her dinner parties were the dullest I can remember, stuffy members of the government and their mem sahib wives, ambassadors and royalty. Perhaps the reason why we kept such bad company was that Bogey Harris loved her. He used to say, with his deep Jewish melancholy, "one can live without everyone, really; everyone but Maggie; she's like dram drinking".

I remember one lunch with pleasure. Mrs. Greville had two butlers, named Boles and Bacon. Boles looked and behaved like a butler, and fell heir to a large part of her fortune. Bacon claimed (and no wonder)

---

* I must record, as an exception, Philip Cunliffe Lister, later Lord Swinton, to whom, in retrospect, we may very likely owe our survival as an independent nation.

to be a communist. He was a short, stout, red-faced man who obviously put away all the drink left over by the guests. Mrs Greville's admirable cuisine was famous for one specialty, baby tongues. They were produced only for royalty. At the lunch in question I was sitting at the very end of the table, so could see round the screen that hid the serving hatch. When the baby tongues came up I saw Bacon looking at them with insuperable longing; he swayed backwards and forwards in his desire. Finally he could contain himself no longer. He stretched out his hands and began cramming the baby tongues into his mouth. The sauce ran down his shirt front, his jaws worked furiously. During the hiatus Mrs Greville said "Boles, what's become of the baby tongues?" "There were none to be had in the market this morning, Madam." I expect she guessed. Bacon, his face purple with gratified desire, put a napkin over his shirt, and carried in the next course.

The conversation at these parties was not even about money: mere generalities. But afterwards Mrs Greville would draw aside Sir John Simon, Sir Sam Hoare or some others of her regulars, and talk to them seriously. She sat back in a large chair, like a Phoenician goddess, while the cabinet minister or ambassador leant forward attentively. I have no doubt that she had considerable influence.

But of course the determining factor in our attitude to Nazi Germany was Mr Neville Chamberlain. I have already indicated that I had a certain sympathy with him. He was not thinking about money, but about peace. He thought with some justification that if we entered into a war with Germany we should be beaten. In contrast to his predecessor, whom he called The Great Illusion, he was a man of facts. He said to me "S.B. is always talking about his love of nature and the English countryside, and all that. He couldn't recognise five common English birds or English trees." I love information for its own sake and a walk with Mr Chamberlain through the grounds of Chequers was a pleasure to me. But when does an event or a condition become a classifiable fact? Were not Hitler's speeches and the horrors of Nazidom facts? Mr Chamberlain closed his mind to them. "All propaganda", he said, when I ventured to mention them to him. At about this time Jane was reading *Mein Kampf* aloud to me as I shaved, and told a friend in the government what a horrible and terrifying impression it was making on us. He asked to borrow the book, which she had marked, and was startled. He lent it to his colleagues. It turned out that in 1938 no one in the government had read, or had even contemplated reading, *Mein Kampf*.

Mr Chamberlain was not an imaginative man and was singularly devoid of 'antennae'. Decisions involving these qualities were made for him by an extraordinary character called Sir Horace Wilson. He sat in a small office outside the Prime Minister's room in Downing Street, and everyone with an appointment had to pass through this office and have a few minutes' conversation with Sir Horace. He was a fascinating contrast to his chief, very feminine, with a supple and what used to be called Jesuitical turn of mind. He used to sit with his long thin fingers pressed together, and held at the side of his face. I enjoyed my occasional conversations with him, and said so to Mr Chamberlain. His eyes lit up, he turned to look at me and said "He is the most remarkable man in England. I couldn't live a day without him."

There was a disastrous *fond* of naïvety in Mr Chamberlain's character. I remember lunching at Downing Street after Munich, and the butler offered me Hock. Being wary of government entertainment wines I had begun to decline when I saw Jane at the other end of the table making violent signs of assent. It was the best Hock I have ever drunk. Mr Chamberlain, who had observed our pantomime, was delighted. "It was given me", he said, "by the wine growers of Germany for having saved the peace of the world." After lunch he led us to a small showcase containing various trinkets and charms. "All these," he said, "were sent me in gratitude for the Munich Agreement."

I was educated as an historian, and so have a certain prejudice in favour of those who can think historically. Mr Chamberlain, although he had a fund of information on unimportant matters (he occupied a whole luncheon at Chequers in 1938 by giving Jane the history of every famous gem), had no conception of what Gibbon called 'The vicissitudes of fortune, which spares neither man nor the proudest of his works, which buries empires and cities in a common grave.' This sweep of historical imagination was one of the supreme gifts of Mr Churchill.

We met him many times at Lympne and Trent, and I did not suppose that he had been aware of my existence. But after a time we became friends, he invited us down to Chartwell and behaved to us with a great kindness. He was particularly fond of Jane. I remember him sitting next to her at lunch at Lympne and never speaking a word—one of the famous 'black dog' days. Lady Desborough, for whom good manners were a religion, ran up to her and began to console her. Jane said "Don't worry. It was exactly like K's father." That evening Mr Churchill made her an apology so touching and humble that I cannot bring myself to record it. We stayed several times at Westerham and I spent a good deal of time in Mr Churchill's painting room. His enormous appetite for life included an appetite for visual sensations and he put down what excited him with more gusto (in the modern sense of the word) than discipline. He had undergone several influences; that of Lady Lavery, that of Paul Maze whose character as a painter was all too like his own, and that of William Nicholson whose fine discrimination and sense of tone were exactly the qualities that Mr Churchill lacked. On one of our visits Nicholson, always referred to as the *cher maître,* was there and spent the weekend teaching me to throw a boomerang. The *cher maître* had no sense of time and would sit for an hour or two in my room in the National Gallery gossiping about figures of his youth, whom he assumed that I had known. "Do you remember that night when Phil came home with the eel?" A promising beginning but, as Phil May had died before I was born, I could not do it justice.

Mr Churchill would emerge about lunch time and waddle down to his heated swimming pool, of which he was very proud. He had been up till two or three in the morning dictating one of his histories. Once or twice I had a room over his study and, waking in the night, heard the peculiar rise and fall of his voice droning on as he dictated to some wretched secretary. When he writes in a Gibbonian manner I do not admire his prose, but his conversation was not at all like that because, however high the balloon of his historical imagination might rise, he was always ready to puncture it. Next to his warmth of heart, this vein of schoolboy naughtiness was the most endearing thing about him. The best idea of his conversation is not to be gained from his histories, but from certain pages in *My Early Life and Adventures,* which he wrote as a kind of diversion in 1930. I cannot help boasting that the most brilliant display of Mr Churchill's conversational powers I ever heard took place in our house. They were stimulated by the greatest listener of the age, Walter Lippmann. For three hours Mr Churchill described the rôle that the United States must play in the world when the hordes of Nazidom had passed and the British Empire become no more than a shadow. Harold Nicolson has described in his diaries this great burst of talk, but could not resist shampooing it; Jane also put an account of it into her diary, written with less art, but substantially true. The historian who uses 'original documents' must have a built-in lie-detector.

At about 1.30 a.m. Mr Churchill rose to leave us. He went out into a deserted Portland Place, the pavement glistening with heavy rain, so that it looked like a canal. Mr Churchill's car was waiting, and he told the chauffeur to take him to Westerham. "Good heavens" said Jane "you're not going all that way." "Yes, my dear, I only come to London to sock the Government or to dine with you."

By 1938 it did not require Mr Churchill's eloquence, nor the muddled, hysterical support of the left for Czechoslovakia, to arouse in the minds of ordinary men and women a sense of shame and foreboding. We realised at last that the pandering of successive governments to the peace-loving inclinations of the country in which, for once, materialism and idealism were united, had left us impotent. No one, not even Mr Churchill, knew exactly how weak we were. This feeling of frustration led to expressions of unnatural violence. I remember Bob Boothby, who was our neighbour at Lympne, asking if he could bring a friend to dinner. Bob's tolerance is without limit, and his friend turned out to be an indoctrinated Nazi, named Eckersley. Maurice Bowra was staying with us; fortunately Jane was in bed with a chill. Halfway through the meal Mr Eckersley began to show his guns, and very powerful guns they were, well aimed at the pleasures of bourgeois society that we were all enjoying so freely. A communist could not have done better. Bob chuckled, Maurice grew purple in the face, and suddenly let out a stream of abuse in sergeant-major language. "Very interesting", said Mr Eckersley icily, "I see that I have made my point." There was about half a minute's silence, during which Maurice looked at him balefully. Then he said, "I look forward to using your skull as an inkpot." I told Mr Eckersley that he would know the meaning of the word *hausrecht,* and I was going to exercise mine now. They both left, Bob still chuckling, but not with much conviction. As a pendant, I remember on the night of Duff-Cooper's resignation, Lady Willingdon, an ex-Vice-reine, saying to me, "I should like to crush his head to a jelly." It showed how rapidly civilised modes of thought and behaviour can vanish under the pressure of a bad conscience and the threat of danger.

Fortunately for me I was fully occupied during this miserable period. Philip Sassoon had persuaded

Lord Duveen to pay for redecorating the staterooms at Hampton Court, and I had the glorious opportunity of rehanging the pictures. They have remained in more or less the same places till today. But I must confess that, in spite of my early admiration of the Bolognese, I failed to recognise some famous Carracis and Guidos. They were consigned to back passages. I do not like to think that I have many blind spots where painting is concerned, but Annibale Carraci is one of them: I prefer Ludovico, and am thus put down to the bottom of the class by all right thinking art-historians.

In the National Gallery my chief occupation was to see that the pictures could be removed to safety the moment a war became imminent. This meant cutting all the frames of the larger pictures so that the glasses and the pictures in their 'slips' could be pulled out from the front, a depressing and wearisome business. I then had to discover 'places of safety' to which the pictures could be consigned, and plan for their transport. Here I had a stroke of luck. Some years earlier I had established, out of profits from the sale of postcards, a scientific department in the Gallery, and appointed as director a Cambridge scientist named F. I. G. Rawlins, who had specialised in radiology. He was a kind, good man, but one of the most relentless bores I have ever encountered, who fussed to me interminably over the most trivial details. I am no friend for a fusspot, and I am afraid I sometimes treated him brusquely. My good luck lay in the fact that he was a railway-train addict. His idea of a holiday was to visit Willesden or Crewe, and he read Bradshaw every night. So when we came to plan the removal of the pictures to large, empty country houses in what we took to be safe areas, he could tell exactly what lines were available and what hours were free for a special train. He could also find the right vans and have them lined with sorbo rubber.

We had a dress rehearsal for the big move at the time of Munich. I could not believe that Mr Chamberlain and Lord Halifax would let themselves be cheated into an agreement, and I therefore decided that I ought to close the Gallery section by section so that the pictures could be taken down and packed. To close the National Gallery would be a political act, and (since the Gallery reports directly to the Treasury) I had to get permission from the Chancellor of the Exchequer, Sir John Simon. He placed one hand on my shoulder, shook my hand with the other and said "My dear Kenneth, what can I do for you?" I began to explain my mission. A far away look came into his eyes, as it so often does with cabinet ministers when one is asking them to take a decision. "My dear Kenneth", he repeated, "in your great winter exhibitions, when you pay, as is most justly due, homage to the art of the past, and in your great summer exhibitions when, without fear or favour, you show all that is best in the art of present day . . ." I realised that he thought I was President of the Royal Academy. "Well, can I do it, then?" "Yes, of course, my dear fellow, do what you think right."

We closed the Gallery in sections and took the pictures to a 'bomb-proof' basement. The agonising discussions at Berchtesgaden lasted longer than I had anticipated, and before they came to an end a number of vans containing medium-sized pictures had arrived in Bangor. Then, as we were emptying the last room, came the news of the Munich agreement. I suppose that a sense of relief was inevitable, but very few people I talked to, except for hard line appeasers, were deceived.

The next year is a blank in my mind. Our too big house in Portland Place had become a nuisance to us, and we tried to sell the lease, being finally swindled out of it for a laughably small sum. We spent most of our time at Lympne, and, in London, moved impulsively to top floor 'chambers' in Grays Inn, which had taken our fancy owing to the views over the gardens and the original panelling. This contradiction and return to our earlier way of life was a great relief. The days of conspicuous waste were over. Things went better in the Gallery. It was in this period that we bought the Ingres of Madame Moitessier and one good thing came out of the threat of war. Looking for places in the cellars which could be made into air raid shelters I found, in a small and remote vault, some twenty rolls of canvas, thick with grime, which I took to be old tarpaulins. I was just about to tell the head attendant to throw them away when curiosity prompted me to ask him to bring them upstairs and unroll one of them on the stone floor of the office entrance. It disclosed what seemed to be a layer of soot-smothered paint. I sent for soap, a brush and a bucket of water and, to the general amusement, went down on my knees to scrub the filthy surface. Out came an unquestionable Turner. I had just enough strength of mind to stop scrubbing, and have the grimy rolls taken to the restoration department. They are now among the most admired Turners in the Tate Gallery.

In the late summer of 1939 Philip fell ill with a 'flu cold. He had long ago ceased to be a Haroun al Raschid figure to us and had become a true friend; and, when we went to say goodbye to him before going to America, we were sad to find him so depressed. Jane said "You'll be better long before we are back." "No", he replied "I shall never get better." On our return from America, when the tender came out to meet us in Southampton Water, we heard that he had died the day before. The picnic really was over.

Of the weeks before the declaration of war I remember only the turmoil and fatigue of evacuation. Our house at Lympne looked over Romney Marsh, which Napoleon had considered the only practicable place for an invasion of England, and I had surmised (correctly, as it turned out) that Hitler would think the same. We therefore decided to leave East Kent, and rented a house in Gloucestershire. Poor Jane had to organise the move of children, governess, cook and large Dalmatian dog, while I spent my time in the relatively easy task of evacuating the National Gallery pictures. Thanks to my railway addict everything went on time, and the last container rumbled away to Aberystwyth on the afternoon before war was declared. The reader may remember that we had been told to expect a devastating air raid within a few hours, so when our work was over I suggested that we should take a couple of taxis and go to St Paul's. We entered the Cathedral, and were met by a posse of vergers carrying their rods of office. "All out", they shouted, "all out." I suggested to one of them that we were virtually at war, and that this was a time when many people might wish to visit the Cathedral for prayer and solemn meditation. In a few hours the Cathedral might be destroyed. "All out", he said, "all out." He was not acting from panic, but because it was the official closing time. It would have been different in the Middle Ages.

We had not yet installed sleeping quarters in the air raid shelter of the National Gallery, so I had taken a room in an old-fashioned hotel round the corner to be on hand when the bombs fell. It was called The Stafford and had a distinguished Regency façade, behind which there were a very few uncomfortable bedrooms. An uneven corridor led to a large drawing-room, opposite the stage door of the Haymarket Theatre. Its walls were hung with canvas back-drops from some pre-1914 musical comedy and represented rose gardens and herbaceous borders in the style of Phil and Joseph Harker.

I heard Mr Chamberlain's tired old voice announcing the declaration of war in a café in the Charing Cross Road. At last he had acknowledged the reality of evil which had been dumbly recognised by his countrymen for the last two or three years. I walked aimlessly through the dark, empty streets and found myself standing in Waterloo Place. I looked past the Athenaeum Club towards the park, and then up Regent Street. Piccadilly Circus, without its vulgar illumination, achieved a kind of pathos. The large, dull, office buildings took on a grandeur and fatefulness that I had never felt before. The banal thought passed through my mind that even if they were not destroyed by bombs that night they would before long be deserted and crumble to the ground. It gave me a curious feeling of elation. The social system of which these featureless blocks were an emanation was a worn-out monster founded on exploitation, bewildered by a bad conscience. It would be better to start afresh. At this point the figure of an air raid warden materialised beside me and flashed a tiny torch to see if I was carrying the regulation gas mask. "O.K." and he vanished into the night. The gas mask, of course, was never used, and not a pane of glass was broken in the buildings that had been the object of my philosophic reflections. I made my way slowly back to my Floradora drawing-room in the Stafford Hotel.

Index

Aitken, Charles, director of Tate Gallery, 78

Alberti, Leon Battista, 261

Alexander, Sir George, 27

Altham, H. S., Winchester master, 84

Anderson, Colin, 254

Andrea da Firenze, 139

Anrep, Helen, 252

Antonello da Messina, *Condottière*, 48

Aris, Herbert, Winchester master, 38-39, 82

Art nouveau, 109

Ashmolean Museum, C. F. Bell as Keeper of Fine Arts, 105-8, 200; German engravings, 107, 202; English watercoulors, 108; department of antiquities, 108-9; the author succeeds Bell, 173, 200-2

Ashton, (Sir) Leigh, 116-8, 120, 121, 169

Bacon, Francis, 203 n, 208

Baker, Collins, 238

Baker, Herbert, Port Lympne, 224

Baldwin, Stanley, Earl, 225, 273

Balniel, David, 187, 265

Bancroft, Sir Squire, 27

Barker, Granville, 215-6

Barnes, Dr, 245-6

Bastianini, forger of *quattrocento* portraits, 57

Bate, Sir Percy and Lady, H. S., 251

Bath, 68-71, 87

Beardsley, Aubrey, 49, 50, 66-7, 180; *Yellow Book*, 73

Beddington, Jack, Shell Mex posters, 256

Beecham, Sir Thomas, and Lady Cunard, 219-20

Beerbohm, Sir Max, 214, 215

Béhague, Comtesse de, 269

Bell, Charles F., Keeper of Fine Arts at Ashmolean, 105-8, 200; friendship with author, 109-11, 171, 203; in Italy with him, 125-34; and BB, 129, 130

Bell, Clive, 66, 84, 100; *Art*, 76, 163; *Potboiler*, 76, 82

Bell, Graham, 253

Bell, Vanessa, 112, 249-51

Bellini, Giovanni, 62, 153, 186; *St. Jerome in the Wilderness*, 164

Bentinck, Mrs Cavendish, 183

Berard, Bébé, 257

Berenson, Bernard (BB), 63, 103 n, 117, 125; at Villa i Tatti, 129-30, 135, 141, 145-46, 148, 155, 157-60, 166; and the author, 130-31, 134-35, 145 ff; character and career, 135-45, 152, 159, 162-3; 'ideated sensations', 139-40; certificates of authenticity, 140-45, 147, 151, 164; in London, 193-95; *Central Italian Painters*, 76, 139; *Florentine Drawings*, 76, 107, 131, 143-4, 144 n; *Florentine Painters*, 77, 139; *North Italian Painters*, 144 n; *One Year's Reading for Fun*, 157; *Self-Portrait*, 136, 137, 138, 143, 158; *Venetian Painters*, 140

Berenson, Mrs (née Pearsall Smith, formerly Mary Costelloe), 130, 138, 142, 157; family background, 146; and her husband, 151, 162-63; and the author, 152, 154, 160, 161-2, 166-7, 169; clock tower for i Tatti, 165-6; in London, 193-5

Berlin, (Sir) Isaiah, 193-5

Bernini, Gian Lorenzo, 10, 247

Betjeman, (Sir) John, 102, 258

Birrell, Augustine, 194

Blaker, Hugh, 71, 79

Blakiston, Dr, 205

Blanche, Jacques Emile, 147

Bloomsbury, 107, 112, 115, 146, 193, 217, 250, 254

Böcklin, Arnold, *Meeresidylle*, 101

Bone, Muirhead, 59, 60 n

Boothby, Lord, 226, 277

Borenius, Tancred, 156, 186, 238; attacks the author, 266-7

Botticelli, 62, 139, 185; *Birth of Venus*, 184; *Primavera*, 132; S Spirito altarpiece,

209; Villa Lemmi frescoes, 48

Bough, Sam, 46

Bowra, (Sir) Maurice, 115, 191, 223, 277; scholarship, 101-2; influence on author, 101-3; in America, 103; at i Tatti, 171; and Yeats, 199

Bracken, Brendan, 62

Breszka, Gaudier, 54

Bridges, Robert, *Testament of Beauty*, 175

Buckley-Jones, Mrs, stepmother of 'Peter Warlock', 53

Burckhardt, Jacob, 115; *Cicerone*, 125

Burlington House, exhibition of Italian art, 179-80, 184-87; catalogue, 187-8

Burne-Jones, Sir Edward, 180, 193

Butler, Samuel, *Erewhon*, 83

Butterfield, William, 176; Moberly Library, 60; Thorburn's Chantry, 61 n

Carlyle, Thomas, 84; at Kinaird House, 4; *Past and Present*, 95

Carraci, Annibale and Ludovico, 278

Cecil, Lord Hugh, 224

Cézanne, Paul, 51, 58, 71, 111, 136, 203; 'one-man' show, 78; drawings and watercolours, 243; in Dr Barnes's Gallery, 246

Chamberlain, Lady (Austen), 179

Chamberlain, Neville, 213, 267, 269, 273-5

Charteris, Evan, 228, 229, 235-7, 269

Chinese literature, 82 and n; art, 144

Cholmondeley, Sibyl, Marchioness of, 225

Churchill, (Sir) Winston, 14, 208, 213, 217, 224, 271-2, 275-7; *My Early Life and Adventures*, 276

Claire, Ina, *The Girl from Utah*, 28

Clark, (Sir) George N., 105 and n

Clark, Jane, Lady (née Martin), 65, 241, 251, 263; meets the author, 123; engagement, 124; marriage, 167, 169; BB and, 170; children, 175-6, 204, 259; painted by Steer, 189-90

Clark, Kenneth, Lord, birth and parentage, 1-4, 12; early reading, 6-8; solitary childhood, 13-4, 25, 101; attitude to sports, 18-9, 20-1, 31-2, 90-1; and his father, 27-31; education, 33-6, 37-40, 84-6, 95-8, 120, 122; liking for feminine society, 37, 48, 73-4, 255; birth of aesthetic consciousness, 45-9, 82; appreciation of natural beauty, 58; novel reading, 68; poetry, 80; suffers from hypochondria, 93-4, 95, 122; social conscience, 113-4; on judgement of authenticity, 153-4; lecturing career, 185-6, 261; as a collector, 195-8; *Civilisation*, 62, 90, 116, 163, 261; *Gothic Revival*, 122, 174, 176, 203, 206; *The Nude*, 192, 260; *One Hundred Details from the National Gallery*, 262; *Leonardo da Vinci*, 177, 261; *Drawings at Windsor Castle*, 177-8, 200, 261; *Piero della Francesca*, 260; *Rembrandt*, 260; *Ruskin Today*, 176

Clark, Kenneth Mackenzie, f. of above, 11-2, 41-2, 50, 124; youth and early manhood, 1-3; in S France, 21-4, 86; appearance and character, 24-5, 27, 29, 32, 101-2; in Bournemouth, 87-9; Dolgarrog disaster, 88-9; death, 205-6

Clark, Alice (née Macarthur), w. of above, character, 3, 12, 29, 75, 101; and her son, 13-4, 71, 124, 169, 200; in old age, 94; and her husband's death, 204-5

Lorrain, Claude, *Ascanius and the Stag*, 202

Colefax, Sir Arthur, 103, 215

Colefax, Sibyl, Lady, 185 n; and the author, 171, 185, 216; social hostess, 214-8

Connolly, Cyril, 84, 148, 171; at Oxford, 99; *Enemies of Promise*, 98; *The Unquiet Grave*, 99

Constable, W. G., 180, 184, 211

Corot, Jean Baptiste, *Le Vallon*, 48; *La Rose*, 252

Correggio, Antonio, *Giorno*, 163; *Marriage of S Catherine*, 48; *SS Placida and Flavia*, 163

Courtauld, Samuel, 210, 211, 268 and n

Coward, Sir Nöel, 217, 226

Cunard, Lady (née Maud

Burke) Emerald, 51-2, 204, 218-21

Cunard, Nancy, 219

Cunliffe, Lord, 40-1

Cunliffe Lister, Philip (later Lord Swinton), 224-5, 272 n

d'Abernon, Viscount, 229, 236

Daniel, Augustus, 212

Dawson, Bertrand (Lord), 68, 73

Dégas, Edgar, 46, 51, 235, 244

Delacroix, Eugene, on Chopin, 71

Delano, William, 234

Dewar, Thomas R., 93; *A Ramble Round the Globe*, 15 and n

Diaghilev, Sergei, 72, 160

Dodgson, Campbell, 202, 256

Donatello, Donato di Niccolo, 164

Dorn, Marion, 254

Douglas, Langton, 'discovery' of Sassetta, 145 n

Driberg, Tom, 256

du Maurier, Gerald, 49

Duveen, Lord, 147, 159, 164, 228-30, 278; Trustee of Nat. Gallery, 229-30, 267-69; N.Y. showrooms, 247; death, 269

Eden, Sir Anthony (later Lord Avon), 225, 270

Edward VIII, 216-7; as Prince of Wales, 228, 271

Eliot, T. S., 69; *Family Reunion*, 255; *Waste Land*, 113

Encyclopaedia Britannica (11th ed.), 68, 113

Eugénie, Empress, 25

Evans, Sir Arthur, 108

Farquharson, Joseph, 50

Fleming, Peter, Ian and Michael, 90

Fra Angelico, 62

France, Anatole, 83, 86

Fry, Roger, 62, 66; art criticism, 67, 76, 250; as a lecturer, 111-2; as an artist, 111; Bloomsbury, 112, 180; enmity with BB, 156, 183; friendship with the author, 203-4, 251-2; death, 253; *Last Lectures*, 253 and n; *Vision and Design*, 111

Gauguin, Paul, 51, 78, 203 and n

George V, 17; official portrait (Sims), 52; and the King's Pictures, 238-40

Germany, engravers, 107, 202; art historians, 115, 202; visited by author, 115-6, 271

Gielgud, Sir John, 215-6

Giorgione, controversy over, 266-7; *Concert Champêtre*, 49; *Tempesta*, 184-5

Giotto di Bondone, 139, 162, 163, 186

Goes, Hugo van der, 71

Goethe, Johann Wolfgang von, 102, 139, 141-2

Goodwin, Albert, 59

Gosse, Sir Edmund, 147

Gothic Revival, 110

Grant, Duncan, 112, 250-1

Gregory, Maundy, sale of honours, 27 and n

Greuze, Jean Baptiste, *Cruche Casée*, 47

Greville, Mrs Ronnie, 272-3

Gulbenkian, Calouste Sarkis, 160, 232-34, 268

Hals, Frans, *Gipsy Girl*, 48

Hammond, J. L. and B., *Town Labourer; Village Labourer*, 113

Hampton Court, redecoration, 278

Hand, Judge Learned, 142

Harris, Henry (Bogey), 182-3, 252, 272

Hartley, Brig.-Gen. Sir Harold, 200-1

Hawtrey, Charles, 27-8

Herriot, Mme, buys *Katoomba III*, 21-2

Heseltine, Philip ('Peter Warlock'), 53; ed. *The Sackbut*, 53-4; suicide, 54

Hind, C. L., *Turner's Golden Vision*, 66

Holbein, Hans, *Erasmus*, 48

Holland, 120-1

Hope-Johnstone, John, 119

Horne, Herbert, 62, 183

Houghton, Edmund, 173-4

Huxley, Aldous, 105 n, 219; *Antic Hay*, 53, 54

Ingres, Jean Auguste, 55; *Grande Odalisque*, 242; *Madame Moitessier*, 242, 252, 280; *La Source*, 48, 242

Italy, 122, 124 ff.; Bologna, 125-6, 164-5; Florence, 126, 131-3, 165, 171-2, 175; Milan, 160-1; Rome, 168, 191-2; Padua, 164, 171; Venice, 171

'Jacker', the, Winchester master, 39

James, William, 136, 139

Japanese art, White City exhibition, 43-4; Chishaku temple, Kyoto, 44-5; collections of original drawings, 49-50, 56

John, Augustus, 54, 119, 189

Johnson, Samuel, 93, 102, 135; at Iona, 91

Kauffer, E. McKnight, 254-5

Keene, Charles, 49

Kerr, Archie Clarke (later Lord Inverchapel), 222 and n

Keswick, Tony, 39 and n

Kilroy, Dame Alix, 104 and n

Klemperer, Otto, 101

Knowles, David, 100

Lamont, Miss (Lam), 14; and the author, 23, 30, 33, 42, 43

Larionov, 72, 78

Lauder, (Sir) Harry, 15-16

Lavery, Sir John, paints the author, 28-29

Leader, B. W., 46

Lee, Vernon, (Violet Paget), 170

Lee of Fareham, Lord, 180, 206; career and character, 208-9; and Warburg Library, 210-1; and Nat. Gallery, 211-2, 229, 268 n

Leicester Galleries, 78, 79

Leigh, Vivien, 216, 223

Leighton, Frederick, Lord, *Iphigenia*, 47

Leonardo da Vinci, 40, 177; books on, 177-78; *Annunciation*, 177; Capella Paolina frescoes, 191; *Ginevra dei Benci*, 177; *Treatise on*

Painting, 261; Virgin and Child with Cat, 178

Lewis, Wyndham, 147; *Howitzer*, 77 and n; *Time and Western Man*, 220

Lippmann, Walter, 213, 217, 276

Llewellyn, Sir William, 184-5

Lloyd George, David, Earl, 160, 208, 210, 228; sale of honours, 27 n

Loeser, Charles, 136-7

Longden, Bobby, 85, 98, 120

Lotto, Lorenzo, 137, 138, 161

Louvre, descriptive text, 48; British Exhibition, 1938, 236-7, 269-70; Cammondo Collection, 245

Lunt, Lynn and Alfred, 217

Lutyens, Sir Edwin, 204

Macarthur, Mrs (née Flintoff), gm. of author, 69; at Castle House, 19, 49

MacCarthy, Sir Desmond, 46, 147, 172; ed. *Life and Letters*, 177

Maclagan, Sir Eric, 227, 258; director of V. and A., 235

MacColl, D. S., 180

Macdonald, Mr, art master at Winchester, 56, 72, 82

MacDonald, Ramsay, 212, 225-6

Mackay, Clarence, 227, 229-30

Makins, Roger (later Lord Sherfield), 85 and n

Mallett, Downey and Snookey, 74

Manet, Edouard, 71

Manson, James, director, Tate Gallery, 78, 235-7

Mariano, Nicky, and the Berensons, 149-50, 152, 154, 159, 160, 166

Marx, Karl, 113, 114

Masaccio, 164

Matisse, Henri, 78, 203, 235; *L'Atelier*, 197

May, Phil, 49, 276

Mein Kampf, 274

Memlinc, Hans, 48

Mentone, 21-3, 26, 42, 190

Meryon, Charles, 40, 59 and n

Michelangelo, 100, 106-7, 172

Michelet, Jules, history of France, 95

Millais, Sir John, *Murthley Moss*, 47

Modigliani, Amedeo, 79

Modigliani, Ettore, 184

Mondrian, Piet, 120

Monet, Claude, 71

Moore, George, and Lady Cunard, 219; *Esther Waters*, 219

Moore, Henry, 59, 79 and n

Morelli, Giovanni, art critic, 137, 147, 153

Morgan, Pierpont, 21

Morra, Umberto, 160, 170, 193

Morrell, Lady Ottoline, at Garsington, 112

Morshead, Owen, 177, 206, 238

Murray, David, 50, 185

National Gallery, 47, 93, 180, 209, 252; rows of 1932/3, 211, 264; the author as Director, 211, 212, 222, 227 ff., 261-2, 264-5; Trustees, 228-30, 264; purchases, 230-1, 242-3, 266-7, 279-80; and World War II, 278-80

Nichol, Erskine, 46
Nicholson, William, 275
Nicolson, Harold, 217, 276
Norton, Charles Eliot, 136

Ogilvie, (Sir) Frederick, 105 and n
Oppenheimer, Henry, 196
Orchardson, Sir W. Q., *The Last Dance*, 46
Orford, Suffolk, 4; Castle House, 19-20; Church, 58
Origo, Marchesa, 193 and n
Ormsby-Gore, David (William) (later Lord Harlech), 212 n; and Nat. Gallery, 211-2, 228, 236
Ouida, *Friends*, 127, 128
Oxford University, homosexuality, 74; the author at Trinity College, 85-6, 95-9, 100-9, 114; last year, 122-3

Palmer, Samuel, 59, 257
Papafava, Countess, 164
Pasmore, Victor, 253
Pavlova, Mme Anna, 28
Perrins, Dyson, 110
Pettie, John, 46
Philpot, Glyn, 223
Phipps, Lady, 236-7
Picabia, Francis, 100
Picasso, Pablo, 72, 100, 156
Pierce, Maresco, 193
Piero di Cosimo, *Forest Fire*, 201-2
Piero della Francesca, 36, 133, 139; Baptism, 133; Urbino diptych, 133
Pinsent, Cecil, at Villa i Tatti, 129, 157, 157-8, 165
Piot, René, i Tatti frescoes, 157-8
Piper, John, 257, 258

Pisanello, 62
Pissarro, Camille, 49, 78
Plato, 84
Pollen, Arthur Hungerford, 178-9
Popham, A. E., 184, 195
Popp, Anny, 191
Poster art, 254, 256-7
Post-impressionists, 203; exclusion from Tate Gallery, 78, 245
Potter, Beatrix, 7-8
Poussin, Nicolas, 111
Punch, 48, 49

Quennell, Peter, 97, 221

Rackham, Arthur, 8
Raphael, 106-7, 197
Rawlins, F. I. G., 278
Reading Without Tears, 6
Rembrandt, 100; etchings, 108; *Hendricke Stoffels*, 48
Rendall, Montague John, headmaster of Winchester, 61-5; Shrogus, 63-4
Reni, Guido, 126, 164
Reynolds, Sir Joshua, 76; *Discourses*, 125-6
Ricketts, Charles, 181-2, 184; and BB, 181, 183
Riegl, Alois, 115, 186; *Spät-Romische Kunst-Industrie*, 109
Roberts, William, *Gas Attack*, 77 and n
Robey, George, 28
Romain, Jules, *Dr Knock*, 93
Ross, Mrs, Villa Poggio Gherardo, 125, 126-9, 131, 133, 166-7, 170
Rouault, Georges, 243; *Misérérés et Guerres*, 244
Royal Academy, 50; Sims'

George V, 52; hostility to Old Masters, 185

Rubens, Sir Peter Paul, *Helena Fourment*, 48

Rubinstein, Arthur, 216-7

Ruskin, John, 56, 76, 99, 121, 136, 171; influence on the author, 113, 114, 176; *Praeterita*, 59; *Unto This Last*, 113

Russell, Alys (née Pearsall Smith), 146, 150

Russian Ballet, 72, 74

Ruysdael, Salomon van, 58

Sackville-West, Edward, 113; 'Gothick novels', 115

Sadler, Sir Michael, 203 and n

Salisbury, Frank O., 47

Salles, Georges, 117-8, 118 n

Saltwood Castle, 14; Grant murals, 251

Sargent, John S., Woodrow Wilson portrait, 178

Sassetta, Stefano, legend of St Francis, 227, 229-30

Sassoon, Sir Philip, 212; and the author, 222-4, 260; at Port Lympne, 224-6; Trustee Nat. Gallery, 228, 264, 269, 277-8; death, 280

Scotland, Poolewe, 30-3, 40; Ardnamurchan property (Sheilbridge), 89-90, 94-5, 175, 204-5; stalking, 90-1; Iona, 92

Scott, Sir George Gilbert, 176, 212 n

Sebastiano del Piombo, 172

Segonzac, Dunoyer de, 203

Settignano, Chiostro di San Martino, 169-71, 175

Shakespeare, William, 215-6; *King Lear*, 63-5

Shannon, Charles H., 181-2

Shaw, George Bernard, 3, 83; *Man and Superman*, 215

Simon, Sir John, 273, 279

Sims, Charles, paints the author, 50-1; Keeper of the RA, 51; suicide, 52, 55; *George V*, 52; *Lady Rocksavage*, 51; *Mischief*, 50, 52-3, 52 n

Smith, Logan Pearsall, 146, 147-9, 175, 194; *follie circulaire*, 149; *The Golden Urn*, 148; *Trivia*, 148

Spanish Civil War, 271

Sparrow, John, at Winchester, 81; Warden of All Souls, 81, 200; at i Tatti, 171

Spender, Stephen, 115

Steer, Wilson, 79; paints Jane's portrait, 189

Stoclet collection, Brussels, 118

Stoop, Mr and Mrs, art patrons, 118-9, 235

Strachey, Lytton, 112, 168, 176

Strygowski, Josef, 144, 156

Sudbourne Hall, architecture, 4-5, 9; Suffolk Punches, 11; shooting parties, 14-9, 20-1; sold to a speculator, 41-2; paintings, 46

Sutherland, Graham, 59; Great Globe poster, 256; and the author, 257-8

Tate Gallery, 78, 235

Tawney, R. H., *Religion and the Rise of Capitalism*, 113

Taylor, Myron, 221-2

Thompson, G. L., art master at Winchester, 54-5

Tintoretto, Jacopo, 197-8

Titian, 154, 161, 185; *Entombment*, 48

Tonks, Professor, 189

Toscanini, Arturo, 160

Trevelyan, R. C., 170

Turner, J. M. W., 66, 108, 280; *Interior at Petworth*, 253

United States, French paintings, 245; Chester Dale collection, 245; Dr Barnes's Gallery, 246

Upton, Florence and Bertha, Golliwogg books, 7, 20

Urquhart, F. F. (Sligger), 96-7, 121, 123; Swiss chalet, 99

Utamaro, Kitagawa, 56; *Pearl Fishers, Water Carriers*, 56

Van Gogh, Vincent, 51, 78, 120

Velasquez, Diego Rodríguez, *The Water Carrier*, 118 n

Venturi, Adolfo, 143

Venturi, Lionello, 243

Verdi, Giuseppe, 116

Vermeer, Jan, *Lacemaker*, 48

Veronese, Paolo, 116, 125

Victoria and Albert Museum (V. and A.), 117, 235

Vollard, Ambroise, 243-4, 246

Vorticism, 78

Wagner, Richard, *The Ring*, 116

Waley, Arthur, 168; translations from the Chinese, 81

Walker, Frederick, *Bathers*, 47

Warburg, Aby, and Renaissance art, 191; Library, transferred to London University, 191, 210-1

Warlock, Peter, *see* Heseltine, Philip

Warren Gallery, 79 n

Watson, G. L., yacht architect, 22

Watteau, Jean-Antoine, *Cythera*, 48

Watts, Sir Philip, 42

Waugh, Evelyn, *Decline and Fall*, 36

Wedgwood, Benn, Anthony, PMG, 240

Wharton, Edith, 93, 156, 212, 235, 261; character, 206-8; works, 206-7

Whistler, James McNeill, 66, 171; *The Convalescent*, 66; *Gentle Art of Making Enemies*, 55; *Ten O'Clock Lecture*, 55

Whitman, Walt, 194, 207

Widener, Joseph, 245

Wilde, Oscar, 182 and n

Williams, A. T. P., master at Winchester, 86

Wilson, Edmund, 103

Wilson, Sir Horace, 274

Winchester Cathedral, 58, 59-60, 61 n

Winchester College, 34; the author and, 37-40, 55-6, 74-82, 84-6; drawing school, 57-8; architecture, 59-60; Shrogus, 63; homosexuality, 73-4; physical conditions, 74, 75

Witt, Sir Robert, 180, 227, 266

Wixenford preparatory school, 34-7, 55

Wölfflin, 115, 186

Woolf, Virginia, 112, 160, 218

World War I, 38, 40, 71; Canadian War Artists' Exhibition, 77 and n

World War II, 271-7; and

Nat. Gallery, 278-80

Yashiro, Yukio, 45, 170, 262

Yeats, W. B., 101, 102, 151, 199

Zay, Jean, 236

These books? Fiction.
Keep telling yourself that as you read.

☐ **SOMETHING HAPPENED, Joseph Heller**   24575 2.25
The number-one best seller by the author of *Catch-22* is about ambition, greed, love, lust, hate and fear, marriage and adultery. It is about the life we all lead today —and you will never be able to look at that life in the same way again. "Brilliant."—Saturday Review/World

☐ **DOG SOLDIERS, Robert Stone**   24558 1.95
A landscape of violence. A world of drugs. A man and a woman's shattering odyssey. Co-winner of the 1975 National Book Award.

☐ **A HALL OF MIRRORS, Robert Stone**   24524 1.95
Three young drifters swept into the rootless world of New Orleans during Mardi Gras . . . caught in a maelstrom of corruption and violence that turned their love to death and the American experience to a nightmare.

☐ **THE HAIR OF HAROLD ROUX, Thomas Williams**   25300 1.95
The nostalgia of *Summer of 42*—the power, passion, and frankness of today. Co-winner of the 1975 National Book Award.

☐ **ONE MAN, HURT, Albert Martin**   24956 1.75
After 18 years of marriage, and four children, Al Martin's wife asked him for a divorce. This journal reveals the emotional trauma and upheaval he suffered.

☐ **NATURAL ENEMIES, Julius Horwitz**   24973 1.75
An hourly account of a successful publisher's killing of his family and himself. "Reminiscent of Joseph Heller's *Something Happened* . . . it will not be easily forgotten."
—Chicago Sun Times

Available at your bookstore or use this coupon.

BB   **Ballantine Mail Sales**
Dept. LE, 201 E. 50th Street
New York, New York 10022

Please send me the books I have checked above. I am enclosing
$.................. (please add 50¢ to cover postage and handling).
Send check or money order—no cash or C.O.D.'s please.

Name_____

Address_____

City_____State_____Zip_____
Please allow 4 weeks for delivery.

L-1-76